AF251916

Encountering the Other

Encountering the Other

The Artwork and the Problem of Difference in Blanchot and Levinas

Alain P. Toumayan

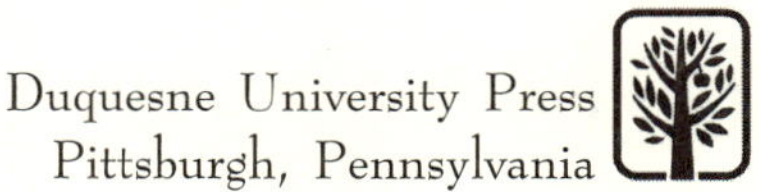

Duquesne University Press
Pittsburgh, Pennsylvania

Published in the United States of America by:
DUQUESNE UNIVERSITY PRESS
600 Forbes Avenue
Pittsburgh, Pennsylvania 15282

Library of Congress Cataloging-in-Publication Data
Toumayan, Alain.
    Encountering the other: the artwork and the problem of difference in Blanchot
and Levinas/Alain Toumayan.
        p. cm.
Includes bibliographical references.
    ISBN 0-8207-0347-8 (cloth: alk paper)—ISBN 0-8207-0348-6 (pbk.: alk. paper)
    1. Lévinas, Emmanuel.   2. Blanchot, Maurice.   3. Arts—Philosophy.
4. Difference (Philosophy)   I. Title.
    B2430.L484T488 2003
    194—dc22   2003017618

Contents

List of Abbreviations

In order to avoid an unwieldy system of references, I have adopted the following system of abbreviations to indicate the works of Blanchot and Levinas. When possible, I have quoted their texts in available English translations, with page references to English editions followed by page references to French editions. Where I did not have access to English translations, I translated the texts and provided page references to the original text. I followed this practice with secondary sources as well. Where particular points of language are at issue, the original French text is included in brackets in the translated passage. Since some of the works of Levinas and of Blanchot are available in compilations of essays, I have included several of these compilations among the sources to which I shall refer.

Works by Emmanuel Levinas

Autrement qu'être	AE
Otherwise Than Being	OB
De Dieu qui vient à l'idée	DDVI
De l'existence à l'existant	DEE
Existence and Existants	EE
Difficile liberté: Essais sur le judaïsme	DL
Difficult Freedom: Essays on Judaism	DF
En découvrant l'existence avec Husserl et Heidegger	EDE
Discovering Existence with Husserl	DE

"The Trace of the Other" in *Deconstruction in Context*	DC
Entre nous: Essais sur le penser-à-l'autre	EN
Entre Nous: On Thinking-of-the-Other	en
Ethique et infini	EI
Ethics and Infinity	ei
Humanisme de l'autre homme	HAH
L'intrigue de l'infini	II
Noms propres	NP
"La réalité et son ombre"	RO
The Levinas Reader	LR
Collected Philosophical Papers	CPP
Sur Maurice Blanchot	SMB
Le temps et l'autre	TA
Time and the Other	TO
Totalité et infini	TI
Totality and Infinity	Ti

Works by Maurice Blanchot

L'arrêt de mort	AM
Death Sentence	DS
L'attente l'oubli	AO
Awaiting Oblivion	ao
Au moment voulu	AMV
The Station Hill Blanchot Reader	BR
L'écriture du désastre	ED
The Writing of the Disaster	WD
L'entretien infini	EnI
The Infinite Conversation	IC
L'espace littéraire	EL
The Space of Literature	SL
Faux pas	FP

Le livre à venir	LV
The Sirens' Song	TSS
"Notre compagne clandestine" in Laurelle, ed., *Textes pour Emmanuel Levinas*	NCC
"Our Clandestine Companion" in Cohen, ed., *Face to Face with Levinas*	OCC
La part du feu	PF
The Work of Fire	WF
The Gaze of Orpheus	GO
Thomas l'obscur	TO
Thomas the Obscure	TtO
Le très haut	TH
The Most High	MH

Works by G. W. F. Hegel

The Phenomenology of Spirit	PS
La phénoménologie de l'esprit, vols. 1 and 2	PEI, PEII

Works by Jacques Derrida

Margins of Philosophy	mp
Marges de la philosophie	MP

Introduction

Emmanuel Levinas (1906–1995) and Maurice Blanchot (1907–2003) are two of the most creative and compelling thinkers of the second half of the twentieth century. Their works, usually in the form of analytic essays complemented in the case of Blanchot by a substantial corpus of literary narratives, are strikingly original, intricate, and subtle. Together, they present a rich and provocative encounter of literature and criticism and modern continental philosophy.

The purpose of this book is to study Blanchot and Levinas at points in their work representative of each thinker's broader work and that demonstrate particularly significant intersections in either the structure or the content of their thinking. My focus will be on the question of the work of art, and, in relation to the artwork, the problem of death and the complication in Being and nothingness which Levinas designates in his concept of *il y a*. For Blanchot and for Levinas, the artwork and the very fact or existence of art attest a basic involvement of the human subject with a foreignness, an otherness, an alterity. This study will examine particular moments of this involvement and describe its broader consequences as drawn by Levinas and Blanchot.

This purpose requires careful consideration of necessarily limited sectors of their works with attention to, as Heidegger puts it, "the path of thought as well as its content." Therefore, beyond the necessary minimum required to provide an adequate and clear context for their works, I will eschew a comprehensive, panoptic presentation of Blanchot's or Levinas's writings and will generally avoid the broad brush strokes which, in any case, have been wielded with considerable mastery and virtuosity by such readers of Blanchot as Gerald Bruns and Leslie Hill and by such readers of Levinas as Alphonso Lingis, Adriaan Peperzak, Edith Wyschogrod, Colin Davis, and Robert Bernasconi.[1] Instead, I will attend to the intricate arguments and thought patterns in Blanchot and Levinas.

However, the somewhat narrow focus adopted here reflects an assumption that the pertinence and usefulness of the problems under consideration surpass the limited scope of the chapters that follow. The subjects of this study were therefore chosen based upon three criteria: first, how representative they are of each thinker's work; second, the degree to which a particular question illustrates the mutual influence of Blanchot's and Levinas's work; finally, the importance of the concept of difference in the individual analyses.

The subjects of the chapters that follow focus on well-known analyses and subjects that have been recognized by Blanchot, Levinas, and their principal commentators as centrally important to each writer. Thus, the *il y a*, for example, is the central concern of *Existence and Existents* for Levinas; its importance is acknowledged by Blanchot in relation to Levinas's work in general, and it has been adapted by Blanchot in numerous and creative ways. Furthermore, as I shall note in chapter 4, Levinas initially thematizes the *il y a* in, among other contexts, that of the artwork. The structure of substitution, which I will consider in the first chapter, is the core argument of *Otherwise Than Being*; it provides a particularly salient and clear illustration of Levinas's use of the concept of difference in his ethical definitions and represents one of Levinas's most original and provocative contributions to the analysis of modern ethical subjectivity. Blanchot's analysis of the myth of Orpheus, which will be considered in chapter 3, is for Blanchot the point to which tend the various arguments in *The Space of Literature*. Similarly, the general problem of death and the first chapter of *Thomas the Obscure* have been recognized by Blanchot's principal commentators as being of central, exemplary, or inaugural significance in relation to his work in general; these issues will be examined in chapters 1, 2 and 4.

The second criterion guiding this analysis is those questions that manifest proximities, intersections, and spheres of mutual influence, exchange, and creative appropriation in Blanchot's and Levinas's works. The *il y a*, for example, may be the site of the richest continual encounter of the thought of Levinas and Blanchot, an encounter acknowledged by each writer in such works as *Existence and Existents* and in "Literature and the Right to Death." Consideration of the role of the *il y a* will figure prominently in chapters 2, 4 and 5. This criterion also explains in part the prominence accorded in this study to the problem of art, a problem which Levinas will eventually deem somewhat obsolete. In general terms, many commentators of Blanchot and Levinas have observed that it is often difficult and somewhat futile to trace univocal lines of influence in the thought of Blanchot and Levinas.[2] On the other hand, even cursory scrutiny of their writings will confirm what Levinas and Blanchot both recognized about their friendship and their intellectual affinities and differences, and what Marie-Anne Lescourret, Levinas's biographer, notes very succinctly: it was Levinas who introduced Blanchot to German philosophy, particularly phenomenology; it was Blanchot who introduced Levinas to French literary texts, particularly those of Proust and Valéry, and thus to a distinctly modern reflection on literature and, more generally, on the work of art.[3] In many of the analyses that follow I observe Blanchot gleaning particular philosophical concepts, terms, or positions from Levinas and fitting them to his purposes, often adapting and modifying them in subtle and markedly creative ways in a manner that could be characterized as Blanchot's aestheticizing Levinas's texts, a stance which Bruns formulates as Blanchot's "refusal of philosophy."[4]

It is possible by this distinction to characterize some deeper proximities and differences in the thought of Blanchot and Levinas. Levinas's ethical thought, his analyses of the relation to the other, originally borrow the form of the aesthetic relation. Levinas, however, eventually abandons this model. On the other hand, while increasingly drawn to the ramifications of the ethical problems that interest Levinas, including the problem of the Holocaust, Blanchot rejects any formulations which appeal to God, or to an "ordination" which has a divine character.[5] More generally, when Levinas's attention turns from the concept of a totality or an identity disrupted by the enigma of alterity to a positive structure of identity which derives from varying forms of relation to the other (for example, a relation of responsibility), and thus to a structure of identity no longer based on totality, Blanchot does not follow. His readings of Levinas show that his interest and analyses tend to remain focused on the first problem, the disruptive enigma of the other. Because Levinas's later work manifests a clear and quite explicit departure from problems to which Blanchot remains fundamentally committed, this study emphasizes the problems of the *il y a*, death, and the artwork and gives more limited consideration to later works of both thinkers and especially to Blanchot's later commentaries on Levinas. While the friendship of Levinas and Blanchot and the pattern of mutual commentaries extends well beyond the texts and problems under consideration here, the degree of influence is less pronounced and less significant.[6]

The third criterion governing my choice of subjects and determining my approach to them is based on attentiveness to the logical procedures and principles, the forms of argument, and the movement as well as the development of the analyses of Blanchot and Levinas. This is particularly important in the case of Blanchot for, as review of critical commentaries of Blanchot will sometimes reveal, the particular logic of many of Blanchot's analyses, and the back-and-forth conceptual movement that this logic dictates, make it difficult and occasionally misleading to evaluate a given proposition in isolation from the context in which it has been elaborated.[7] It is thus awkward to attempt to distill or encapsulate many of Blanchot's positions; the process and procedures of their elaboration are often instrinsic to the positions themselves. At issue in Blanchot's analyses is not only a particular subject, theme, or problem, but the manner of approaching, evaluating, and thinking the subject. In fact, many of the subjects that tend to interest Levinas and Blanchot involve attention to and consideration of the very manner in which we think. This, in part, accounts for the prominent place of the theme of death in their work and in the present consideration of it.

In this context, I will organize and further delimit my investigation of Blanchot and Levinas by attending to the concept of difference in the analytic methods of both thinkers. Several commentators of Blanchot and Levinas have considered this concept, particularly Libertson, who tends to express it using such terms as proximity or proximal, communication or communicational.[8] In chapter 1, I will explore systematically and track various articulations of the problem of difference in Heidegger and Derrida, and I will seek to demonstrate the pertinence of difference to the texts of Blanchot and Levinas. The perplexing concept of a relation that precedes relata, things related, will yield two distinct formulas which recur in the works of Blanchot and Levinas: first, a logical challenge to totalization, and second, a concept of identity in terms other than those of totalization. Both of these formulas tend, since the notions of identity and totality are put into question, to generate contradictory, paradoxical, or aporetic expressions. Where one is not attentive to the particular logic which governs these expressions, it seems that interpretive options are limited to three possibilities: first, evaluating these statements as poetical or metaphorical formulas; second, assuming erroneously that the logic that underlies these expressions must be dialectical; or finally, concluding an aporetic impasse and hence a theoretical impenetrability of these texts.[9] Many commentaries of both Blanchot and Levinas reflect these interpretations. It is my view that the concept of difference avoids these interpretive extremes and errors and affords a cogent and coherent manner of formulating many of these problems. This is why I begin this study with sustained attention to the problem of difference.

In a well-known quote from his story *The Crack-up*, F. Scott Fitzgerald advances what he deems a "general observation": "the test of a first-rate intelligence is the ability to hold two opposed ideas in the mind at the same time, and still retain the ability to function" (69). In a vastly different context, Laclos observes that "often paradox is the beginning of a truth,"[10] an indication of truth rather than the evidence of logical fallacy and of analytic impasse. The writings of Blanchot and Levinas in general, and the particular configurations of difference in their work both correspond to the spirit of these two quotations and afford an opportunity to weigh the second.

A guiding metaphor in my consideration of Blanchot and Levinas is the theme of the encounter. This metaphor suggests the richness of the encounter of literature and philosophy in the writings of Blanchot and Levinas, as well as the numerous productive encounters of their thoughts. But the encounter also designates a common theme examined with some consistency by both writers.[11] It involves an event which occurs beyond the willful plans and purposes of a subject and which disrupts the subject's foundation of selfhood, the subject's fundamental spatial and temporal coordinates, and generally, the subject's conceptual resources. Blanchot's analyses and narratives often examine in intricate, almost clinical, detail the disarming nature of such encounters, and he underscores those elements in them that are threatening and terrifying. Levinas observes this as well; as I note in chapter 5, the image that dominates Levinas's thematization of the *il y a* is that of horror. However, Levinas subsequently identifies two other characteristics of this theme, both of which differentiate his later thinking from that of Blanchot. First, adopting a perspective that Blanchot refuses, he observes that this disruption is also a form of our relation to the divine.[12] Second, he notes that such an experience always assumes an initial position of relative safety and security. But where priority is accorded to an involvement with the other that itself confers on the subject the terms, fabric, and foundation of selfhood—thereby determining the position occupied by the subject—the drama of the encounter becomes less threatening though still radically perplexing. The prospect of an unlimited, absolute responsibility is a far more dramatic predicament than threats to individual security since this responsibility is now understood to extend beyond the subject's power, even beyond the subject's own death.[13] Despite these differences, the encounter provides a useful theme and image to unite a set of representative problems and central texts in the study of Blanchot and Levinas. This unifying thematic is expressed in the general title of this study as well as in the individual titles of its five chapters.

ONE

Identity and Difference

The problem of difference can be stated simply as a relation which is prior to and more fundamental than the related terms or elements. The straightforwardness of such a formulation, or one equally simple such as Saussure's "differences without positive terms," is somewhat deceptive, however. It appears inconsistent with common sense as well as with Descartes's third methodological principle that something abstract and complex should supersede something unitary, basic, elementary, tangible, or concrete. Unity, totality, autonomy, or completeness does not describe an identity that is secondary to and a function of relationality.

These problems have been elaborated and mapped out theoretically in two short essays, Heidegger's "The Principle of Identity" (in *Identity and Difference*) and Derrida's "La Différance." A brief consideration of both works will supply a broad conceptual outline of the concept of difference as well as a schematic framework and background for more detailed consideration of how this concept informs the writing of Blanchot and Levinas. The specific problems of conferring identity through prior relationality, and the revision of the fundamental characteristics of identity will then be located and examined in specific texts by Blanchot and Levinas: in Blanchot's *Thomas the Obscure*, which enacts, in a fictional context, the problem of thinking subjectivity through difference, and in Levinas's *Otherwise Than Being*, in which the priority of the ethical relation in the constitution of subjectivity is established.

"La Différance"

Derrida's examination of the problem of difference in his essay "La Différance" is framed by Saussure. A detour in his exposition of the linguistic unit leads Saussure to formally investigate the problem of identity. In the phrase "differences without positive terms," Saussure demonstrates an awareness of the counterintuitive and strange nature of identity through difference.

As the title of Derrida's collection of philosophical essays *Margins of Philosophy* suggests, he is less interested in difference as such than in the "place" that such a "concept" might occupy within the tradition of Western thought. However, as a meditation on other expressions of difference, as an attempt to adjust the concept, to explore some of its consequences, and to generalize its purview, and, finally, as an analytic instrument that Derrida derives from Saussure and applies to Levinas,[1] this essay deserves a short comment.[2]

Sausssure extends the principle of difference from the phoneme to the signifier and finally, to the level of the signified concept (thus basing meaning on difference). This has predictably important consequences since difference supplies a mechanism potentially capable of accounting for any concept and for any conceptual opposition. To paraphrase Saussure, fundamental to the structure of any language and to any conceptual system generally, is the principle of difference which then becomes the basis of both language and of the conceptual edifice of civilization. Derrida reminds his reader that according to Saussure the principle of difference affects the "*totality* of the sign, that is the sign as both signified and signifier." Derrida then observes that what he calls "différance," that is the abstract principle of the "systematic play [*jeu*] of differences," to which he has now added a temporal dimension suggested by the polysemy of the French verb "différer," "is thus no longer simply a concept, but rather the possibility of conceptuality, or a conceptual process and system in general" (mp, 11/MP, 11). In consequence, Saussure's thought suggests an extended comparison with the broad outlines of Darwin's argument in *Origin of Species*. Both texts elaborate the mechanisms that account both for states and for the forces that, over time, have produced these states. In both cases, the mechanisms involve the articulation of a dynamic of arbitrariness or random variability with the forces of outside pressures which tend to fix and preserve certain elements or characteristics. And just as Darwin has displaced the principle of independent (or divine) origins of complex animal or natural forms, Saussure — and here Derrida — potentially displace the principle of independent origins of complex cultural forms.

Derrida's analysis is primarily focused on difference as a principle of meaning which cannot itself be properly accounted for, thematized, or formulated within the systems of meaning for which it nevertheless accounts. Hence lies its essential "marginality" although, as Derrida emphasizes, these margins are also to be found within the text of Western metaphysical thought. Still, in his examination of the consequences of Saussure describing identity as secondary to the principle of difference, Derrida articulates quite clearly two distinct characteristics of any such identity. Both involve thinking about identity in terms other than totality and unity, or unicity: first, the tendency of any "element" both to "overflow" itself and to be subject to the "overflowing" pressure of surrounding elements; thus, in the temporal sequence of this particular example: "keeping within itself the mark of the past element, and already letting itself be vitiated [se laissant déjà creuser] by the mark of its relation to the future element" (mp, 13/MP, 13); second, that any identity or entity, when considered as such, fails to meet the standards of a unit and will, instead, appear as non-self-coincident, mediated, divided into component parts, and referring elsewhere.[3] The unit *qua* unit is necessarily already riven, divided, and constituted as a relation. Identity is thus formulated in terms of heteronomy, not autonomy.[4] In the following passage, Derrida applies the principle of difference to "an element appearing on the scene of presence" and succinctly outlines the two characteristics of an identity deriving from a relation of difference.

> It is because of "différance" that the movement of signification is possible only if each so-called "present" element, each element appearing on the scene of presence, is related to something other than itself, thereby keeping within itself the mark of the past element, and already letting itself be vitiated by the mark of its relation to the future element, this trace being related no less to what is called the future than to what is called the past, and constituting what is called the present by means of this very relation to what it is not: what it absolutely is not, not even a past or a future as a modified present. An interval must separate the present from what it is not in order for the present to be itself, but this interval that constitutes it as present must, by the same token divide the present in and of itself, thereby also dividing, along with the present, everything that is thought on the basis of the present, that is, in our metaphysical language, every being, and singularly substance or the subject. (mp, 13/MP, 13–14)

The above example involves an analysis of difference and identity applied specifically to the thematization of presence. This particular example is strategic and important for Derrida for several reasons: first, because of the temporal dimension that he has introduced to difference itself; second, because of his general critical investigation (or deconstruction) of the status of presence as the fundamental value in the philosophical currency of Western thought; third, because the specific opposition of presence and the present is investigated by Heidegger in his attempt to characterize the ontico-ontological difference, and one of Derrida's aims, in "La Différance" is to situate "différance" with respect to Heidegger's thinking of Being and the ontological difference.[5] Still, this example documents with unusual clarity the manner in which difference reconfigures the problem of identity in a particularly complex way.

Derrida ends his essay with an assertion as bold and as provocative as Saussure's assertion that "in language there are only differences . . . *without positive terms*." In fact, Derrida's proposition can be expressed as a generalization of Saussure's: in Western thought, there are only differences — whose principle is "différance" — without positive terms. Neither Being nor God is a fundamental founding name; prior to the Word, was difference.

> This unnameable ["différance"] is not an ineffable Being which no name could approach: God, for example. This unnameable is the play which makes possible nominal effects, the relatively unitary and atomic structures that are called names, the chains of substitutions of names in which, for example, the nominal effect *différance* is itself *enmeshed*, carried off, reinscribed, just as a false entry or a false exit is still part of the game, a function of the system. What we know, or what we would know if it were simply a question here of something to know, is that there has never been, never will be, a unique word, a master-name. . . . There will be no unique name, even if it were the name of Being. (mp, 26–27/MP, 28–29)[6]

While less interested than Derrida in examining the particular location of difference within the Western philosophical tradition, and while not explicitly deriving it as Saussure has done, Blanchot and Levinas make frequent use of the concept of difference in a broad spectrum of texts and contexts, and this study will examine a number of them. Indeed, the dual characterization of identity through difference observed above, will be invoked frequently in the readings that this study comprises, both in its broadest outlines and in the particular example at hand. The analysis of the present through difference correlates very precisely with some of the most striking and creative examinations of temporality and difference in the texts of both Blanchot and Levinas. Moreover, Derrida's assertion that such problems as subjectivity, which are traditionally thematized on the basis of presence, need to be rethought in terms of difference, or "différance" essentially defines the problems in the next two sections of this chapter, the examination of Blanchot's *Thomas the Obscure* and Levinas's ethical subject. Both Blanchot and Levinas, although principally the former, explicitly examine the manner in which difference exists side by side with other oppositional figures such as dialectic, and both thematize explicitly the tendency to take one for the other.

The Principle and Leap of Identity in Heidegger

In "The Principle of Identity," the first section of *Identity and Difference*, Heidegger investigates the problem of identity and gives a characteristically succinct, rigorous, and elegant elaboration of difference.[7] While undertaken independently of Saussure's linguistic analysis, Heidegger's analysis presents certain notable similarities with it, in particular in the movement from a consideration of identity to the problematic idea of a relation that precedes and supersedes identity.

After briefly distinguishing equality from identity, and thus indicating the inadequacy of the traditional expression of identity in the form of A = A, Heidegger analyzes the problem of identity through a close reading of two quotes: the first, from Plato in "The Sophist," the second from Parmenides. In the first quote, the context of which is the figure of the Stranger in "The Sophist," demonstrating to Theaetetus the complexity involved in describing rest and motion in terms of difference and sameness, the Stranger twice uses the expression "same as itself" (254d, 256). Such a formulation suggests that identity is both unity and unification. In the dative form, identity implies a relation, the relation of "with," "for," or, in the translation cited here, "as." Identity, writes Heidegger, implies mediation and connection (*eine Vermittelung, eine Verbindung*). Revising the formulation of identity to express its true meaning, which would be sameness rather than equivalence, Heidegger proposes "A is A." This formulation presupposes, as Heidegger puts it, that identity is a characteristic of Being, that it has to do with the manner of Being of a being: "The principle of identity speaks of the Being of beings. As a law of thought, the principle is valid only insofar as it is a principle of Being that reads: To every being as such there belongs identity, the unity with itself" (26).

Because identity thus construed is a fundamental characteristic of Being, Heidegger next turns his attention to Parmenides, who, he asserts, first and "most authentically" in Western thought made the ontico-ontological difference or the distinction of the Being of beings. In one of his best-known fragments, Parmenides associates thinking and Being in a relation of sameness. In paraphrasing Parmenides, Heidegger notes that the relation of sameness in this case means a relation of belonging together (*Zusammengehörigkeit*). Yet this, he argues, reverses the order or the priority that was observed in the case of Plato's "Sophist." In Parmenides, instead of identity being viewed as a characteristic of Being, the reverse is the case: "Being is determined by an identity as a characteristic of that identity" (28). In other words, instead of identity construed as a characteristic of the manner in which beings are, Being now is understood as in a relation of identity, and determined by a relation of identity (Kockelmans, *On the Truth of Being*, 91). Thus Heidegger writes: "The Sameness of thinking and Being that speaks in Parmenides's fragment stems from further back than the kind of identity defined by metaphysics in terms of Being as a characteristic of Being" (28). A general problem can be anticipated at this juncture: how is one to think something that has priority over Being and, for that matter, over thought itself? This is, in simplified form, the task that Heidegger sets for himself in his analysis of Parmenides' fragment.

In order to examine the relation of sameness or identity expressed by Parmenides, Heidegger investigates the meaning of the expression "belonging together" (*Zusammengehören*). He distinguishes two possibilities which he differentiates by alternately underlining the verbal (*gehören*) and the adverbial (*zusammen*) elements of the expression. The first, or "customary way" determines the belonging by the notion of "together." This is the simple, intuitive relation that is represented in philosophy as "*nexus* and *connexio*, the necessary connection of the one with the other." A relation of synthesis or unity is established between prior elements or among basic units. A second possibility reverses this priority: "belonging together can also be thought of as *belonging* together. This means the 'together' is now determined by the belonging" (*Identity and Difference*, 29). Instead of clarifying this relation, Heidegger suggests it as the correct interpretation of the relation expressed by Parmenides in the fragment concerning thought and Being and he attempts to interpret the fragment in this light. As he does so, he dramatizes several errors made as the attempt to analyze the relation is repeatedly initiated by one or the other of its terms. No matter how carefully and rigorously one approaches the problem, the attempt to think man and Being in terms of Zusammen*gehören* always turns out to be *Zusammen*gehören. In attempting to think relationality, we always and without realizing it insert or presuppose terms. Something structural appears to be preventing thinking the relation as such.[8] Categories, it turns out, are always categories of terms; mediations are always mediations of units which are assumed. According to Heidegger, one can not avoid construing the relation as *nexus, connexio,* coordination, or intertwining: "We stubbornly misunderstand this prevailing belonging together of man and Being as long as we represent everything only in categories and mediations, be it with or without dialectic. Then we find only connections that are established either in terms of Being or in terms of man, and that present the belonging together of man and Being as an intertwining" (32).

This structural impediment is no less than the "attitude of representational thinking," or "the horizon of metaphysical thinking" which considers Being as the "ground in which every being as such is grounded." This is, then, the problem referred to earlier:

how is one to think something that has priority over Being? An abrupt exit from this horizon must be effected; hence a spring or leap (*Satz*) is required (Kockelmans, *The Truth of Being*, 90). Lest that spring lead only to an abyss, it must itself be represented outside of the horizon of representational thought; in other words, the spring must be away from the conception of Being as the ground of beings to the notion of Being as something that *belongs* essentially, quintessentially, to man. In Heidegger's words, "for only with us can Being be present as Being, that is, become present" (*Identity and Difference*, 33).

Heidegger's use of the two meanings of *Satz* at this particular juncture is clever and is another example of the many clues and cues that he is wont to find in language and in linguistic structures.[9] Just as Derrida finds in the French verb "différer" distinct meanings which determine "différance," Heidegger's title "Der Satz der Identität" clearly indicates both metaphysics (principle or proposition) and the requisite exit from metaphysics (leap or spring): it suggests therefore a question posed in metaphysical terms requiring an exit from metaphysics to a region prior to metaphysics. Through the relation of the two different meanings, the pun then indicates both relatedness prior to opposition, and difference prior to sameness. Both will be pertinent to Heidegger's subsequent analysis.

How does the spring or leap out of metaphysical thinking help our understanding of the *belonging* together, the Zusammen*gehören* of man and Being? The answer involves a series of metaphors, an empirical, historical analysis of the relation of man and Being, and finally, a series of logical instruments designed to afford a nonrepresentational thematization of this relation.

Initially, Heidegger uses a series of metaphors to suggest how man and Being reach each other in the deepest, most intimate recesses of their defining essences. He speaks in terms of "mutual appropriation," of an interpenetration of each one's "active nature," of a giving over of each to the other: "The spring is the abrupt entry into the realm from which man and Being have already reached each other in their active nature, since both are mutually appropriated, extended as a gift, one to the other" (*Identity and Difference*, 33). No doubt realizing that even these images still assume entities entering a configuration of mutuality, Heidegger effects an abrupt transition to an empirical example which demonstrates this mutual *belonging*. The modern age, with its emphasis on planning, calculation, and technology, particularly by the trajectory toward atomic energy, has made it uniquely possible for man to understand his "constellation" with Being. But this relation has been overlooked because technology is always envisaged either in terms of man, or in terms of the beings that are the domain and the objects of technology and calculation. The particular manner in which Being now addresses and claims man through technology has not heretofore been noted. Thus when the focus on atomic energy remains on its "peaceful use," a limitation is imposed which results in atomic energy being calculated, not thought, and atomic energy remains at the level of a technical challenge. The more authentic question, the question of Being, remains unposed.

Heidegger now introduces two logical instruments, one static, one dynamic, for expressing in nonrepresentational terms the *belonging* of man and Being for which the previous argument has provided evidence. Both the "frame" or "framework" (*Ge-Stell*) and the "event of appropriation" (*Ereignis*) express the mutual "challenge," mutual "concern," mutual "confrontation," the delivering over, the "strange ownership," and "strange appropriation" of man and Being.[10] Metaphors of sound and energy, particularly of vibration, express this appropriation whose basis is found in language. And here, Heidegger recalls the polysemy of the word *Satz* in his title. In this polysemy, language itself indicates the transformation that thinking must undergo in order to think identity as prior to Being. "On its way from the principle as a statement about identity to the principle as a spring into the essential origin of identity, thinking has undergone a transformation. Thus looking toward the present, beyond the situation of man, thinking sees the constellation

of Being and man in terms of that which joins the two — by virtue
of the event of appropriation" (*Identity and Difference*, 39–40).
Though Heidegger does not say that in language "there are only
differences," he does identify difference as a principle of language
since he identifies language as the basis of the appropriation. The
metaphor that he uses at this juncture is unusual. Speaking of the
appropriation, Heidegger refers to a "self-suspended structure" (*in
sich schwebenden Bau*) in language "Thinking receives the tools
for this self-suspended structure from language. For language is
the most delicate and thus the most susceptible vibration holding
everything within the suspended structure of the appropriation"
(38). The image of self-suspension, or of a suspension without, or
prior to, an anchor expresses ingeniously and almost concretely a
relation which is prior to the related elements. Language, "which
at one time was called the house of Being" (39), contains the means
for thought to apprehend the self-suspension of the appropriation,
its principle of difference: the relation that supersedes the things
within the relation.

Like Saussure, Heidegger derives the principle of difference by
investigating the concept of identity.[11] At the conclusion of his analysis, Heidegger's attention returns to the *Ereignis* rather than to the
complex set of steps and the unusual logic that he has followed in
order to formulate it. The thinking of difference then makes possible the expression of the unique configuration of man and Being
which appears in the *Ereignis*: "This being-called-and-looked-at
constitutes the true specificity of humanity in relation to animality:
man no longer needs to comprehend Being in a transcendental way;
he is now needed by *Ereignis* for the propriation of beings (Dastur
in Sallis, ed., *Reading Heidegger*, 364).

The relation of Heidegger to Blanchot and Levinas is extremely
complex and involves both deep intellectual affinities and influence
and, in the case of Levinas, an increasingly marked desire to distance
himself from Heidegger, from ontology, and from Heideggerian

aesthetic analyses. Levinas repeatedly voices his admiration for *Being and Time*, attributes to it and to Heidegger his own discovery of the "verbality" of Being, and professes less interest in or knowledge of the "later" Heidegger of *Identity and Difference*.[12] On the other hand, Blanchot, in *The Writing of the Disaster*, terms the *Ereignis* the "'ultimate' word of thought" (WD, 104/ED, 162).[13]

Levinas emphasizes that his alienation from Heidegger is not limited to his profound repugnance for Heidegger's political involvement with National Socialism. Yet, many of Heidegger's basic ideas implicitly or explicitly inform much of Levinas's thought and many of his analyses, even if Levinas's procedures can be described as reversing the polarities of or otherwise revising the Heideggerian formulas (Manning, *Interpreting Otherwise Than Heidegger*, 7–8). Thus, whether the subject's trajectory "out of Being," the questioning of the "fundamental" status of ontology, the horror of the *il y a* opposed to the generosity and abundance of the *es gibt*, or the thematization of the artwork as effecting an event of obscuring, dislocation, and "wresting" from the world, Heidegger's concepts often provide the raw material for many of Levinas's most provocative and most creative analyses. It is difficult to evaluate how much Heidegger's understanding of difference, as shall be noted subsequently in this chapter and in other parts of this study, also informs some of Levinas's most original analyses.[14]

Entering the Element: Blanchot's Thomas the Obscure

One of the ways in which difference is formulated by both Blanchot and Levinas is through the Levinasian concept of the *il y a*. While this concept is defined by Levinas, Levinas's references to Blanchot — in particular, to Blanchot's story *Thomas the Obscure* — demonstrate mutual inspiration. The asymmetrical disruption and reconfiguration of identity through the approach of an elemental space of formless indeterminacy, the use of metaphors of submergence and emergence, and the figuration of death in terms of ambiguity or indeterminacy are among the common features of their reflections on the *il y a*.[15]

The first chapter of Blanchot's narrative dramatically illustrates a complex and unusual configuration of subjectivity metaphorically "ungrounded," in accordance with the principle of difference. A reading of the story not attentive to difference as a principle of identity will quickly reach a logical impasse and simply articulate a series of contradictions and paradoxes.[16]

Several critics have observed that many of Blanchot's narratives tend to reproduce the Orphic scenario that is so central to his theoretical reflections.[17] This is true of the entire thematic movement of *Thomas the Obscure*. The first chapter of the story records the entrance of the protagonist into a foreign element, the central episode of the story chronicles the entrance of the character Anne into the space of death where Anne is compared to Eurydice (this chapter anticipates *Death Sentence*, especially the first part of that story). The last chapter of *Thomas the Obscure* presents the return of Thomas to the world of the "day," to linear time, and notes the gradual onset of the forgetting ("oubli") that is one of the conditions of that return. The present focus on only the first chapter recognizes the inaugural, even emblematic character of this chapter with respect not just to this story, but to Blanchot's fictional work in general that has been noted by Jean Starobinski in a sustained, phenomenologically informed analysis of this chapter.[18]

Since Heraclitus's famous fragment which states that one cannot enter the same river twice, the aquatic element has been a privileged metaphor of flux and change to the point that the questioning of identity and the figuration of time in aquatic terms have become literary and philosophical clichés. The well-known literary works exploiting this metaphoric association have been inventoried by Bachelard in his phenomenological analysis of aquatic imagery in literature, *L'Eau et les rêves* (1942). Both the Heraclitean fragment and Bachelard's analysis of swimming are pertinent to the first chapter of Blanchot's story. The thematization of subjectivity and relation is established at the outset of the story. The first sentence of the novel, "Thomas sat down and looked at the sea" (TtO, 7/TO, 9) establishes two relations: first, a conventional relation of a subject capable of voluntary, transitive actions over himself ("s'assit") and second, the relation of a subject in a transitive phenomenal posture with respect to an object ("looked at the sea").[19] Having established these two relations, the first chapter records immediately a modification of the transitivity of the phenomenal relation to the sea. The object of his gaze, the sea, approaches Thomas, crosses the intentional interval, and reaches him. Thus, prompted by the sea, Thomas enters the water to go swimming: "Then, when a more powerful wave reached him, he went down onto the sloping sand and slipped among the currents, which quickly immersed him" (TtO, 7/TO, 9).

Initially, the text then appears to record Thomas entering and apparently losing himself in the very object of his intentional gaze. But this episode involves more than a reversal of a conventional relation in which a subject appropriates the object of his intentional gaze. As Levinas frequently notes, such a reversal would preserve the basic symmetry of the relation by reversing its terms. If here the water is initially the object of Thomas's gaze, once he has entered it, it becomes instead the interval of empty space that on solid ground would guarantee Thomas's access to and apprehension of an object. In other words, within the space of the water Thomas's immediate relation is no longer to things or objects but to the medium or the element of relation as such. That entering the water has "asymmetrically" modified the principles of subject and object relations is confirmed when once in the water, Thomas can no longer simply reverse his initial intentional relation and, for instance, look at the shoreline from the perspective of the water. As soon as he enters the water, the shore and even the waterline can no longer be distinguished because of fog: "The fog hid the shore. A cloud had come down upon the sea and the surface was lost in a glow which seemed the only truly real thing" (TtO, 7/TO, 9). Blanchot's story *When the Time Comes* [*Au moment voulu*] records a comparable relation in the form initially of fog, then snow, then dust: "The flakes had been followed by powder [poussière], and the powder by an attractive, radiant outdoors [dehors], something too manifest, an insistent appearance, almost an apparition — why that? Was the day trying to show itself?" (BR, 229/AMV, 80–81). This sequence, the insidious transition or "glissement" (Blanchot uses the verb "glisser" to describe Thomas's entrance into the water), suggests that in entering the water, what Thomas enters, metaphorically speaking, is difference itself, or, more concretely, the space of differential relation. In other words, difference as interval, which by virtue of its very invisibility normally guarantees the appearance of the physical, concrete world, becomes visible. The space of separation, put simply, "appears" — though not in the form of disclosure and though Thomas himself does not perceive it, at least not in the same manner in which he perceived the sea in the initial sentence of the novel.

This initial "appearance" of difference as space, as the interval of relation, and as the medium or element of correlation (in the form, for example, of subject and object) is followed by a further displacement as the relation itself acquires logical priority over the terms in the relation. The priority of relation over things in that relation manifests itself in this scene in the problematic experience of subjectivity that occurs while Thomas is in the water. For Bachelard, the act of swimming is representative of the archetypical struggle of man with nature; in the act of swimming, man measures his power and the efficacy of his technique against the power of the foreign, natural element: "Already, in his reverie, he addresses himself to the ocean: 'Once again, I will swim against you, I will fight, proud of my newfound powers, in full awareness of my overabundant strength [mes forces surabondantes] against your numberless waves.' This exploit imagined by the will, is the experience celebrated by poets of stormy waters. It is less a product of memory than of expectation. Stormy water is a schema of personal courage" (*L'Eau et les rêves*, 226).

This is very much the manner in which Starobinski considers the swimming episode. He notes: "Thomas's contact with the water occurs in its elementary mode of an adversary [sa forme élémentaire d'adversité]" ("Thomas l'obscur," 502). And he concludes: "Thomas, enriched by the experience of loss of selfhood [riche de tout ce qui l'a dépersonnalisé], has acquired a power that he did not possess at the outset" (512), thus implying that Thomas's trajectory is comparable to the journey of Ulysses.[20]

In fact, Blanchot's Thomas substantially revises this scenario which posits a constituted subject in a relation of which the ultimate horizon, and bottom line, so to speak, is power, and in which the relation with the exterior so enhances or enriches the subject in his interiority. For Thomas, the act of swimming is more extreme and more fundamental. It is, first of all, a problematic experience of the self. Steven Ungar suggests, plausibly but inadequately, since necessarily metaphorically, that Thomas may actually drown in this scene. This interpretation is made possible since the act of swimming is represented metaphorically as drowning: "when this ideal sea which he was becoming ever more intimately had in turn become the real sea, in which he was virtually drowned" (TtO, 8/TO, 11).[21] What can be more positively asserted is that entering the water and swimming, an act which, at an initial level of understanding, should induce an immediate awareness of the self as an interiority separate and distinct from the exterior by confirming the limits of the self due to the pressure of the outside on the body, does in fact quite the reverse in that now it is the self's openness to the outside, its communication with the exterior that is affirmed. In this scene, Thomas enters into what Levinas, in various contexts, will call, using the ethnological language of Lucien Lévy-Bruhl, a relationship of "participation."[22] First, Thomas begins to confuse himself with the water: "whether from fatigue or for an unknown reason, his limbs gave him the same sense of foreignness as the water in which they were tossed" (TtO, 8/TO, 11). Then, as the water enters Thomas, as "Thomas sought to free himself from the insipid flood which was invading him," he himself begins to overflow the boundaries of the self: "As he swam, he pursued a sort of revery in which he confused himself with the sea. The intoxication of leaving himself, of slipping into the void, of dispersing himself in the thought of water, made him forget every discomfort" (TtO, 8/TO, 11).

An initial consequence of the self's constitution in terms of difference is the self's essential openness or permeability to the outside. This does not, however, mean loss, destruction or dispersal of the self. Among the critics of Blanchot, Joseph Libertson, following Levinas, has demonstrated with the most insistence and clarity that the mystical dispersal or loss of self in the exterior is simply the negative — symmetrical and reciprocal — correlate of the self's fundamental closure, identity, and solidity; it respects, by reproducing it in negative terms, the logic of the self's autonomy and totalization.[23] Blanchot's Thomas presents an alternative configuration of the self; the self is preserved but it is "grounded" in heteronomy or difference, reconfigured such that relation to the exterior has logical priority over its unicity. The story now represents some of the multiple configurations of the self in difference.

Among the various possible forms of the subject in this context is the self in a relation of non-self-coincidence. Hence, the self will manifest both a spatial dislocation and/or a temporal lag or delay in relation to itself. Thus, Thomas seems, for example, to precede himself in space, or to enter a space already occupied by himself. "[I]t was like an imaginary hollow which he entered because, before he was there, his imprint was there already" (TtO, 9/TO, 12). Another configuration, in a more pronounced spatial and temporal dislocation, is in the apprehension of the self as other. Having exited the water, Thomas seeks to survey the area where he was swimming and will, at that point, again through the fog apprehend one who appears to be his double in the water. "Peering out, he discovered a man who was swimming far off, nearly lost below the horizon. At such a distance, the swimmer was always escaping him. He would see him, then lose sight of him, though he had the feeling that he was following his every move: not only perceiving him clearly all the time, but being brought near him in a completely intimate way, such that no other sort of contact could have brought him closer" (TtO, 9/TO, 13). This configuration of Thomas and his double valorizes both the etymology of the name Thomas and the Biblical referent of the name (*didyme*) since both signify "twin."[24] The thematic possibility that Thomas will exit the water and apprehend his obscure twin (or remain in the water to be apprehended by his twin, who has exited the water prior to him), then be accompanied by this double or twin is consistent with the thematic movement of the episode as well as with the subsequent development of the story.[25] In a subsequent chapter, the character Anne refers to this complex spatial configuration of the subject Thomas when she expresses the desire to see him alone, though the text makes no mention of another character at that particular juncture (TtO, 55/TO, 57).

Thomas's exiting of the water appears problematic and paradoxical since he exits the water at a point of particular depth, a point used by other swimmers for diving: "At last he had to come back. He found his way easily and his feet touched bottom at a place which some of the swimmers used for diving" (TtO, 9/TO, 12). This detail, among others in this episode, suggests Levinas's analyses of the "element" in *Totality and Infinity*, an element often described by Levinas in terms of aquatic imagery and for which the verb "baigner" is frequently used. Levinas says that the element reverses (asymmetrically) the parameters of space; this remark enables us to coherently interpret Thomas's exit from the water: "To tell the truth the element has no side at all. One does not approach it. The relation adequate to its essence discovers it precisely as a medium [un milieu]: one is steeped in it [on y baigne] . . . the adequate relation with the element is precisely bathing. . . . To bathe in the element is to be in an inside-out world, [monde à l'envers] and here the reverse is not equivalent to the obverse [l'envers ne vaut pas l'endroit]" (Ti 131–132/TI, 138–139).

The theme of the element indicates the relevance of the first chapter to other sequences in the story, particularly those that concern language: first, because swimming will be the subject of conversation of various characters (on two occasions, for example, characters will ask each other if they have been swimming [TtO, 19, 79/TO, 22, 87]); second, and more important, because the theme of silence as the element of speech will appear in episodes of the story which examine the intersubjective relation.[26]

To the extent that in entering the water Thomas enters the element or the space of difference, it becomes clear why the assertion that Thomas drowns is not adequate. First, since the relation of Thomas and the sea has acquired priority over their separateness (a separateness established in the initial sequence of the story), the possibility of Thomas's drowning would involve his drowning, at least partially, within himself. Punning on the words "mer" and "amèrement," the narrator writes: "What escape was there? To struggle in order not to be carried away by the wave which was his arm? To go under? To drown bitterly in himself [Se noyer amèrement en soi]?" (TtO, 8/TO, 11–12). Second, because difference will also now describe the relation of life and death, the relation of these concepts must be understood to be prior to and more fundamental than their separateness or distinctness. Thus, while Thomas does not die in this scene and in this element, cannot logically die, when he emerges from the water he will emerge in an intimate relation with death. In subsequent chapters, particularly chapters 2 and 5, Thomas will enter the space of a tomb (TtO, 13, 35–36/TO, 15, 38–39). Within the space of difference, and in his relation with death, what Thomas will experience is again the impossibility of self-coincidence: "This grave which was exactly his size, his shape, his thickness, was like his own corpse, and every time he tried to bury himself in it, he was like a ridiculous dead person trying to bury his body in his body . . . there was another dead person who was there first, and who, identical with himself, drove the ambiguity of Thomas's life and death to the extreme limit" (TtO, 35–36/TO, 38–39).[27] This, of course, reproduces the movement of the first chapter and the dislocation of the self in the experience of swimming. Many of the relations into which Thomas will enter in the story — the relations with the night, with language, with a book, and intersubjective relations — will tend to be described in terms of aquatic imagery.[28] Thomas's relation with death, referred to in the above quote as "extrême ambiguïté" culminates in the image of Thomas as a paradoxically authentic Lazarus in whose person death itself is resuscitated. The impossibility of death, which mirrors that discovered by Phaedra in Levinas's analysis of the *il y a* (EE, 62/DEE, 102; Ronchi, "La Realtà," 77–86) effects a joining of the attributes of life and death in a relation which is prior to their distinctness. Blanchot describes Thomas's "strange horror" as "passing the last barriers, he appeared at the narrow gate of his sepulcher, not risen but dead, and with the certainty of being snatched [arraché] at once from death and from life. He walked, a painted mummy; he looked at the sun which was making an effort to put a smiling, lively expression on [his absent] face [sur sa figure absente]. He walked, the only true Lazarus, whose very death was resurrected" (TtO, 37–38/TO, 42).[29]

The Heraclitean fragment states that one cannot enter the same river twice. Normally this is understood in temporal terms; by the time one is able to reenter the river, it is no longer the same river.[30] Considered in the spirit of the later Zeno and his paradoxes which strikingly contradict intuitive perceptions,[31] the fragment could suggest the recognition that what accounts for the identity of the river is not the material of which it is formed but difference. Blanchot's Thomas also proposes that the same person does not emerge from the river. Leaving the *terra firma* of material or substantial identity and entering the much less stable dimension of logically prior relation implies a dramatic revision of subjectivity. The end of the first chapter specifies that the laws of solid ground have been irrevocably modified; this is manifested by Thomas's experience of an excessive freedom: "There was in this contemplation [Thomas's apprehension of his double] something painful which resembled the manifestation of an excessive freedom, a freedom obtained by breaking every bond" (TtO, 9/TO, 13). This shift in emphasis from the problem of identity as the aquatic element expresses it to the problem of identity as it pertains to the question of subjectivity mirrors Levinas's references to Heraclitus in *Time and the Other* and *Totality and Infinity*. Indeed, Levinas prefers, as he puts it, the version of Heraclitus's fragment expressed in Plato's "Cratylus"; according to Levinas, a river which one cannot enter even once. In *Time and the Other*, Levinas uses this image to describe some of the characteristics of the *il y a*: "But if it were necessary to compare the notion of the *there is* with a great theme of classical philosophy, I would think of Heraclitus. Not to the myth of the river in which one cannot bathe twice, but to Cratylus' version of the river in which one cannot bathe even once; where the very fixity of unity, the form of every existent, cannot be constituted; the river wherein the last element of fixity, in relation to which becoming is understood, disappears."[32]

Starobinski is quite correct to emphasize the inaugural, even emblematic character of this chapter of Blanchot's novel. The displacements and dislocations that the chapter chronicles are indeed representative of other displacements and dislocations, particularly of identity, that occur in Blanchot's fiction and which are analyzed in his literary and critical writings. And Starobinski has correctly noted that the first chapter recounts a radical transformation of the self, a metamorphosis, a becoming other [un être-autre] ("Thomas l'obscur," 507). Yet Starobinski's insistence on predicates of power and his restoration of the concept of the self, "enriched" (512) by his becoming-other and which thus undergoes, in his view, only a temporary alienation,[33] belies the phenomenological assumptions of his approach, an approach no doubt informed by Bachelard. Such principles, which assume stable entities entering into a relation of mutuality, are precisely those that Thomas leaves as he enters the aquatic element. In the metaphoric terms of Blanchot's aquatic imagery, the story effects an ungrounding of subjectivity. What Thomas leaves is the *terra firma* of subject-object relations in which the former transitively appropriates the latter in a stable relation of power secured through a negative interval.

This ungrounding involves two distinct steps. Initially, the space of relation or interval appears; the element becomes visible or palpable very much in the manner described by Levinas in *Totality and Infinity*. Second, the interval, as the space of relation, as separation or opposition, acquires priority over the related entities. Thomas and the sea are related in such a way that their relation has priority over their distinctness and separateness. Thus, Blanchot's Thomas provides a striking fictional example of the concept of difference applied to the problem of subjectivity; Levinas's ethical relation will provide another example. In an interesting thematic coincidence, the image of the ocean is employed by Zosima in Dostoevsky's *Brothers Karamazov* to describe the ethical engagement of a heteronomous subjectivity able to transcend the "fearful isolation" of "self-contained individuals" (387, 366).

Levinas: Difference and the Ethical Relation

The first chapter of Blanchot's *Thomas the Obscure* dramatizes configurations of the subject in the context of difference, described theoretically by Derrida in his essay "La Différance": the "doubling" thematically suggested by the protagonist's name and the tendency to overflow himself, to spill over his boundaries, and to be intimately subject to the overflowing of an outside with which he turns out to be related. In the case of Levinas's ethical subjectivity, a comparable, though distinct, problem is involved: the consequences of the relation's priority over identity. It should be recalled that the priority of this relation is both logical and chronological. This means, among other things, that any unit, when apprehended or examined, will fail to meet the requirements of sameness. It will present itself as riven, already related or influenced, already committed elsewhere. This section will highlight specific instances of how Levinas's definitions of ethics, his description of ethics as "first philosophy," and his concomitant subordination of ontology to ethics can be related to the concept of difference in so far as difference subordinates identity and unicity to relation (Ciaramelli, in Bernasconi and Critchley, *Re-Reading Levinas*, 85). Indeed, many of Levinas's texts translate various facets of this problem and seek ways of expressing concretely the counterintuitive character of this relation.

The particular difficulties of Levinas's texts and his pronouncements on the subject of analytic method require and justify the method that has generally been adopted for this study: to follow the organic development of arguments, to observe the form and evolution of thought as well as its content, to focus principally on texts and to attempt to elucidate particular thought patterns and specific demonstrations. Levinas's method of exposition requires an attentiveness to what Heidegger calls "the path of thought not just its content." Furthermore, Levinas's themes, his concepts, and his terms undergo continual revision and rewriting. He revisits previous texts, expands his arguments incrementally, modifies his terminology, and displaces subtly the emphasis of previous arguments. His thought is therefore very difficult to characterize broadly and superficially as this introduction to Levinas must do.[34] Moreover, the present study's attempt to bring together a series of Levinas's arguments and demonstrations into a unifying, coherent principle or concept is an approach generally rejected by Levinas. According to the logic of many of his critiques of Western thought, such an approach reproduces the perennially intellectualizing reductiveness of totalization and accords pride of place to a conceptual enterprise whose persistent strategy is to thematize in terms of the Same. Both of these risks must be run here for the sake of simplicity and brevity. The focus of the present chapter is, indeed, on a concept and its role and function in Levinas's thought. Subsequent commentaries will, however, privilege the method of analytic reading outlined above and in the introduction of this study.

Some of Levinas's early studies appeal to a model of subjectivity, derived from the ethnographic writings of Lucien Lévy-Bruhl, which challenges the subject's autonomy, identity to self, self-possession, and unicity. This model, called "participation," describes an animistic, prerational involvement with the exterior, a passive affectation by the exterior, an overflowing of the self's boundaries, or rather, a primitive, incomplete, "permeable" form of the self which is anterior to these boundaries.[35] In this model of subjectivity, Levinas's thought perhaps approaches Bataille's most closely through the common inspiration of Durkheim.[36] The concept of "participation" is employed sporadically in Levinas's writings: it allows him to thematize concretely, for example, the involvement with the *il y a* (EE, 60, 61/DEE, 98, 99, 100), it provides a model of the aesthetic experience which contrasts with the conceptual grasping or appropriating in "Reality and Its Shadow" (LR, 132–33/CPP, 4/RO, 774–76), and it offers an example of the pre-originary anarchy and violence which the idea of the Same, in Western philosophy, has sought to tame (EDE, 166/CPP, 48). In *Totality and Infinity*, however, Levinas suggests that participation, like Heidegger's *Zusammen*gehören, is not an adequate concept because it presupposes the identity of the terms it relates. "Participation presupposes the fundamental relations of the logic of objects, and even in Lévy-Bruhl it is treated as a psychological curiosity" (Ti, 276/TI, 309). Thus, in *Otherwise Than Being*, participation is replaced by models of subjectivity which use difference more explicitly and thus lend themselves more readily to the ethical interpretation of subjectivity's basis.

The derivation of identity or unicity through a relation which is prior to it is a persistent structural feature in many of Levinas's texts. This can be observed first in the manner in which subjectivity as an identity and a unicity is constituted through relation, and second, in the manner in which a subjectivity so constituted apprehends itself in terms of a relation that is imperious (since it is constitutive of the subject), anarchic (since it precedes the subject), and transcendant (since the subject is unable to make sense of this to the extent that it precedes consciousness, reason, freedom, and willpower). In the examples that follow, the logical priority of relation over identity will determine such terms as responsibility, diacony, obsession, nonindifference, hostage, substitution, assignation, ordination, and accusation. The chronological priority of this relation will determine such concepts as anarchy, anachrony, immemoriality, "pre-originarity" [le "pré-originaire"], recurrence, indebtedness prior to contract, obedience prior to order, and obligation prior to consciousness.[37] All of these terms occur in *Otherwise Than Being* and in texts related to it with the insistence and frequency of waves striking a beach, to borrow Derrida's apt metaphor regarding *Totality and Infinity*. Through the repetitiveness of these formulations, Levinas appears to be "trying out" various formulas, inserting different elements into parts of a single equation. In any case, given this repetitiveness, the references that follow will aim for representativeness rather than exhaustiveness. Generally speaking, the fourth and fifth chapters of *Otherwise Than Being* formulate these theses; the former is indicated by Levinas as the "centerpiece" of the work (OB, xli/AE, 10).[38]

Perhaps the clearest and most ingenious of Levinas's demonstrations of the logic of difference is the articulation of an identity, a unicity and uniqueness of the subject which derive from responsibility. Although Levinas generally wishes to subordinate the subject to the other, a simple subordination will not suffice in his view since it involves only a reversal of the traditional position of the subject in Western thought. The subordination of the subject to the other must be asymmetrical, nonreciprocable. Levinas initially formulates this notion in *Totality and Infinity* in terms of the other's superiority or "hauteur" vis-à-vis the subject.[39] This position evolves in subsequent texts, particularly in *Otherwise Than Being*; what

Levinas proposes now is the constitution of the subject as an identity, as an irreducible uniqueness and unicity not through the other as such, but through the relation to the other which is cast in terms of a nonreversible relation of responsibility.

Many of Levinas's commentators have analyzed the difference in the theses, methods, and procedures between his two principal studies *Totality and Infinity* and *Otherwise Than Being*.[40] From the perspective of the problem of difference, this distinction can be characterized as follows. *Totality and Infinity* and the studies which precede it, principally *Time and the Other* and *Existence and Existents*, chronicle — in terms that Levinas eventually deems excessively ontological[41] — the emergence of the subject out of the formless anonymity of the *il y a* and record various stages of its positioning with respect to different forms of otherness. This mode of analysis obviously privileges and focuses on the subject as term or unit that emerges, positions itself, and establishes relations which, as in the case of the face, will ultimately call it into question. In this context, *Otherwise Than Being* appears to work backwards. While retaining the basic structure of the hypostasis of the subject out of the *il y a*, the emphasis shifts to the subject as constituted by and through a relation of responsibility which antedates the subject. In other words, instead of proceeding from the term to the relation, *Otherwise Than Being* proceeds from the relation to the term although by this reversal the relation becomes highly problematic. Hence, his reasoning suggests another example of "differences without positive terms" or of Zusammen*gehören*. Thus, broadly speaking, the methods of *Totality and Infinity* and of *Otherwise Than Being* can be distinguished on the basis of the function of difference in their arguments: rather than characterizing that which potentially or actually *disrupts* the subject — the *il y a*, the time of the other, the mediation within the present — difference now serves to *define* the subject as a unity whose density and substantiality derive from a prior relation.

Thus, as Levinas will show, the subject's unicity or identity can neither be established nor justified on its own terms through a logic of autonomy (OB, 106/AE, 168); rather it is established by way of a relation, through heteronomy (OB, 148/AE, 232; en, 111/EN, 121). This occurs because the subject is unique and irreplaceable in his obligation, his duty, his absolute responsibility for the other and for the other's welfare. "Here the identity of the subject comes from the impossibility of escaping responsibility, from [the impossibility of avoiding] the taking charge of the other [L'identité du sujet tient ici en effet à l'impossibilité de se dérober à la responsabilité, à la prise en charge de l'autre]" (OB, 14/AE, 29). Or again: "Here uniqueness [unicité] means the impossibility of slipping away and being replaced, in which the very recurrence of the I is effected" (OB, 56/AE, 95). Calling this relation variously election, assignation, accusation, ordination, diacony, inspiration, obsession, persecution, and the state of being hostage and in a position of substitutability with respect to the other, among other names, Levinas notes that

> The singularity of the subject is not the uniqueness of an *hapax*. For it is not due to some distinctive quality, like fingerprints, that would make of it an incomparable *unicum*, and, as a principle of individuation, make this unity deserve a proper noun, and hence a place in discourse. The identity of the oneself is not the inertia of a quiddity individuated by an ultimate specific difference inherent in the body or in character, or by the uniqueness of a natural or historical conjuncture. It is in the uniqueness of someone summoned [l'unicité de l'assigné]. (OB, 194, n. 9/AE, 166, n. 1)

In *Entre nous*, Levinas gives a particularly succinct formulation of this relation: "Unicity derives its meaning from the relation of impermutability which belongs or returns to the I in the concreteness of a responsibility for others" (en, 227/EN, 239). Again, in *L'Humanisme de l'autre homme*, Levinas formulates this principle: "Hence to be an I, signifies to be unable to avoid one's responsibility, as if the entire edifice of creation rested on one's shoulders. But this responsibility which empties the I of its imperialism and of its egoism, — be it even an egoism of salvation — does not transform the I into a moment of the universal, [instead] it confirms the unicity of the I. The I's unicity is in the fact that no one can answer [or answer for the other] in my place" (HAH, 53–54).[42]

Under the names previously evoked as well as others, Levinas explores and articulates various facets of this configuration of the subject. Since to be a subject is to be constituted by a relation to the other, and thus in a position of irreducible secondarity, subjectivity is a subjection (OB, 116, 127/AE, 183, 202; Peperzak, *To the Other*, 223), a submission (OB, 118/AE, 187; Malka, *Lire Levinas*, 23). A subject's position is to be "de-positioned," "de-posed" (OB, 127/AE, 202), or "de-nuclear" (OB, 141/AE, 221). In this sense, the subject's condition can be compared to that of being held "hostage" by the other (Lingis, Introduction to OB, xiv); it can be called an "assignation" by the other, and as something prior to consciousness and reason, it can assume the form of an "obsession" with the other, an ordering which is also an "ordination" (OB, 11/AE, 26) by the other, an expression which suggests both passivity and transcendence, and thus nonreciprocity in the relation. ("The word 'ordonné' in French means both having received orders and having been consecrated" [en, 111/EN, 121]). It also implies that in order to call himself present, the subject must be responding to the call of his responsibility for the other. Hence, Levinas describes a subject who does not announce himself in the subjective case, the nominative, but in the objective case: "An identity which is established at the outset in the accusative case of the expression '*me voici.*'"[43] Levinas finds models for this in both *Exodus* and *Isaiah*, emphasizing once again the transcendent character of the "calling" to which the response is the subject's very subjectivity. When God calls to Moses on the mountain, the latter responds: "me voici!" (Exod. 3:4). Isaiah announces himself in the same manner, as a servant (diakonos): "me voici, envoie-moi" (Isa. 6:8; AE, 228, n. 1/OB, 199, n. 11). Heidegger noted the concept of mediated identity linguistically in the dative form (*Identity and Difference*, 24).

Levinas expresses the idea of a relation prior to subjectivity and to nomination through an accusative logically prior to the nominative: "The hypostasis is exposed as oneself in the accusative form, before appearing in the said proper to knowing as the bearer of a name. . . . The uniqueness [l'unicité] of the self is the very fact of bearing the fault of another. In responsibility for another subjectivity is only this unlimited passivity of an accusative which does not issue out of a declension it would have undergone starting with the nominative" (OB, 106, 112/AE, 167, 177; see also OB, 11/AE, 26). Playing on the meanings of "accuser" as both accusation and revelation or indication and inserting the verb "s'accuse" in the place of the verb "se nomme" Levinas writes: "In the accusative — not the modification of any [prior] nominative — in which I approach the neighbor [le prochain] for whom, without having wished or desired it, I must still answer, the irreplaceable is announced [or revealed] [s'accuse l'irremplaçable]" (OB, 124/AE, 197, passim).[44] Playing also on the two meanings of the word "nom" as noun and name, Levinas expresses this relation as the priority of pronominality over proper nominality (AE, 95, 168, 169, 284/OB, 56, 106, 107, 185). Another formulation of this position of the subject in terms of difference is "non-indifference"; relatedness prior to unicity is also an involvement, a concern, an impossibility of turning away (HAH, 108–9; AE, 217, 218, 221, 258, 265, 273, passim/ OB, 138, 139, 141, 166, 171, 178, passim; Libertson, *Proximity*, 297–310).

The term "substitution" then expresses the properly ethical dimension of this relation: my unicity, the uniqueness of my identity derives from my impermutable responsibility for the other. This responsibility is absolute and limitless, going as far as the offering of myself in the place of the other, the total assumption of his suffering and his burdens: "The non-interchangeable par excellence, the I, the unique one substitutes itself for others. . . . But this desire for the non-desirable, this responsibility for the neighbor, this substitution as a hostage, is the subjectivity and uniqueness of the subject"

(OB, 117, 123/AE, 184, 196). This arrangement is radically asymmetrical and nonreciprocal. While no one can replace me in my duty to the other, I must be prepared to assume a responsibility for the other that goes as far as replacing him, substituting myself for him; this arrangement, however, is not a loss of self, but the very basis of my unicity.[45]

After Libertson, many commentators have, with varying degrees of explicitness, formulated the logic of difference that structures Levinas's definitions of the subject in *Otherwise Than Being* (Libertson, *Proximity*, 310–18). Ciaramelli is perhaps the most explicit: "The relation, characterized by a radical non-reciprocity, is prior to the relata — before the 'I am' — and I cannot escape its orientation" (in Bernasconi and Critchley, *Re-Reading Levinas*, 88; see also 83, 86). The principle of difference is implicit in Lingis's formulation of the self: "Less than identical with itself, in deficit with regard to itself, unable to catch up with itself, unable to achieve presence and self-presence, the self cannot be conceived as an entity. . . . On the other hand, this incomparable unicity and singularity is paradoxically enough, what is universally substitutable" (Introduction to OB, xxxi; also xix). Without explaining it, Malka notes the "strangeness" of this relation (*Lire Levinas*, 23). At the other extreme, Haar and Ricoeur, not alert to the problem of difference in Levinas's analysis, are unable to resolve the apparent paradox to which Lingis refers above and which Peperzak formulates as follows: "But does there not follow an existential contradiction [une contradiction existentielle (ou même existentiale)], if it is the case that the I is constituted in the form of a dual belonging [double adhérence]: both the active identification of an independent self and a servant belonging to others?"[46] In a structural error now observed in several contexts, Haar construes Levinas's various formulations as modes of relation of prior subjects and thus is forced to ascertain a basic contradiction in Levinas's argument: "But is it not contradictory to assert that the Other constitutes the Self and is, at the same time, radically foreign to it?" (526) His analysis culminates in a series of questions, some quite emphatic, which are answerable only by attentiveness to the manner in which difference informs Levinas's definitions.[47] Ricoeur's assessment of Levinas's argument in terms of paradox demonstrates the same error.[48]

Finally, Blanchot appears to amalgamate the logic of *Totality and Infinity* (whereby the other disrupts the subject's identity) with that of *Otherwise Than Being*, in which the relation of responsibility is the very principle of the subject's unicity. In a sense that appears contrary to the logic of *Otherwise Than Being* (or at least to its use of the logic of difference as observed above), Blanchot wants to preserve, in the context of the other's singularization of the subject, the other's disruption of the subject. "It is through the other that I am the same, through the other that I am myself: it is through the other who has always withdrawn me from myself. The Other, if he calls upon me, calls upon someone who is not I: the first come or the least of men; by no means the unique being I would like to be" (WD, 18/ED, 35).[49]

*   *   *

The logical priority of relation over identity, unicity, and subjectivity is also a chronological one, an anteriority. This presents a problem comparable to the one faced by Heidegger in his essay on identity. In that context, Heidegger considers how to approach something which has priority over Being, to wit, the relation of thought and Being. Here, Levinas must consider how subjectivity approaches or experiences a relation which is anterior to the subject's constitution as such while implicated in that very constitution. This means that prior to the subject's subjectivity, before its assumption of its attributes of consciousness and knowledge, memory, freedom, power, and spontaneity, the subject is involved in a complicated intrigue and yet deprived of the means to evaluate, understand, or formulate that involvement. The subject has prior commitments which it did not make, prior obligations of which it cannot even be fully conscious, debts which it has not contracted. Since these debts, obligations, and commitments precede the subject and thus cannot be correlated to words, deeds, or actions that might be recalled, the subject finds itself in a curious and uncomfortable position with regard to time.[50]

Before examining expressions of this problem in *Otherwise Than Being* and texts generally contemporary with it, it is useful to recall various ways Levinas has articulated the problem of time with the other. In general terms, Levinas tends to characterize the alterity of the other by associating the other with a temporal experience which cannot be thought of in terms of presence or the present. Thus, the other will be associated with a past which does not correlate with any present or with a future wholly incompatible with an anticipated present.

In *Time and the Other*, which provides a rough outline of the theses which will be developed in *Totality and Infinity*, Levinas relates the otherness of death and the otherness of futurity ("our relationship with death, which is a unique relationship with the future" [TO, 71/TA, 59]). Both are beyond grasping, beyond light, both are beyond possibility, both deprive the subject of its initiative and power. The relation with a future which is not an anticipated present but wholly other with regard to the present provides one model of the relation to the other; hence, Levinas argues, "The other is the future. The very relationship with the other is the relationship with the future" (TO, 77/TA, 64). (Paraphrasing this argument in the subsequent lecture, Levinas calls it, instead "la relation avec autrui" [TA, 73–74/TO, 82].)[51] The otherness of the feminine is also related to this temporal structure. Eros, the caress, "la volupté" will be considered in terms of "the very event of the future, the future purified of all content, the very mystery of the future"

(TO, 90/TA, 83). In "The Trace of the Other" again, it is the concept of futurity which provides a "concrete" access to the other. According to Levinas, a future in which I shall never participate and which I shall never see nor even foresee, indicates the time of the other: "To be for a time that would be without me, to be for a time after my time, for a future beyond the celebrated 'being-for-death,' to-be-for-after-my-death — 'Let the future and the most far-off things be the rule for all the present days' — is not a banal thought that extrapolates one's own duration; it is passage to the time of the other" (DC, 349/EDE, 192).

In *Totality and Infinity*, the emphasis changes somewhat. Levinas analyzes the "visage" or face and relates it principally to the idea of the infinite, thus indicating the incommensurability of the face with any conceptual resources of the subject. "The relation between the Other and me, which dawns forth [luit] in his expression, issues neither in number nor in concept. The Other remains infinitely transcendent, infinitely foreign" (Ti 194/TI, 211). Levinas relates these notions: "The idea of infinity, the overflowing of finite thought by its content, effectuates the relation of thought with what exceeds its capacity, with what at each moment it learns without suffering shock. This is the situation we call welcome of the face" (Ti, 197/TI, 215).

In the texts which lay the foundations of *Otherwise Than Being*, Levinas returns to the temporal dimension to further describe the face's essential incommensurability. The face is now identified with the unique temporality of the trace ("an immemorial past"; "an irreversible past"; "the presence of that which, strictly speaking, has never been there, of what is always already past"): "In the presence of the other do we not respond to an 'order' in which signifyingness remains an irremissible disturbance, an utterly bygone past? Such is the signifyingness of a trace. The beyond from which a face comes signifies as a trace" (DC, 355/EDE, 198; also DC, 356/EDE, 199).

In these examples, temporal categories are employed to thematize the other's essential incomparability and incompatibility with the subject. They express an approach of the other and the establishing of a relation which disturbs the subject yet which remains beyond the subject's ability to thematize. The other approaches the subject from a temporal dimension which simply cannot be correlated with his. The temporal model, in both the case of futurity and the past of the trace, characterizes the other's transcendence and the other's withdrawal before any attempts to relate to the other.[52]

In *Otherwise Than Being*, the emphasis is less on the transcendence of the other than it is on the incommensurability, expressed in temporal terms among others, of an obligation with respect to the other, a relation to the other specified as the relation of responsibility. Levinas now focuses on the imperious, yet chronologically perplexing character of a responsibility toward the other which antedates the subject that must assume it.

This then raises the problem of the temporal dimension of the relation of difference. As observed, the relation to the other is anterior to and constitutive of the subject's identity and unicity; since the relation is specified as one of responsibility, the subject finds itself involved or implicated in, accused of, or responsible for events which antedate it. Thus the subject is in a position of obligation prior to any commitment made: "it is an assignation of me by another, a responsibility with regard to men we do not even know. The relationship of proximity cannot be reduced to any modality of distance or geometrical contiguity, nor to the simple 'representation' of a neighbor; it is already an assignation, an extremely urgent assignation — an obligation anachronously prior to any commitment" (OB, 100–101/AE, 159).[53] The subject is thus always late for its commitments (OB, 122, 150/AE, 194, 235), always out of phase with regard to obligations and unable to make up for lost time in the exercise of these obligations (OB, 101/AE, 160). The subject finds itself in a situation of indebtedness which antedates any borrowing (OB, 111, 112/AE, 175, 178), of owing more than it possesses (OB, 112/AE, 178), of obedience which antedates any orders received (OB, 13, 139, 150/AE, 28, 219, 235), of obligation which was not freely consented to and which cannot even be remembered (OB, 102, 105, 154/AE, 162, 167, 241), and of relation which has not been chosen, "a bond prior to every chosen bond" (CPP, 123/EDE, 233). In short, the subject is bound by the terms of a contract that it could not evaluate and did not sign.[54]

The logical priority of the relation to the other makes the subject "hostage" to the other. The chronological priority of this relation links the subject to an intrigue which precedes him. A succinct expression of Levinas's original formula for the structurally asymmetrical, nonreciprocable, nonreversible ethical relation follows:

> On the basis of a responsibility always more ancient than the conatus of substance, older than the beginning and the principle, on the basis of the an-archic, the I returned to itself [as] responsible for others — that is to say, as a hostage of the others — that is to say, substituted for others by virtue of its very non-interchangeability — a hostage of all the others who, precisely *qua others* do not belong to the same genus as the I, since I am responsible for them without concerning myself with their responsibility in regard to me for, even of that [responsibility] I am ultimately, and at the outset responsible, the I, I am the man holding up the universe, "full of all things." (HAH, 90–91; see also HAH, 109)

Although not formulated abstractly or theoretically by Levinas, the principle of difference nonetheless informs many of his writings and supports the crux of his argumentation in such complex and original demonstrations as his chapter "Substitution" in *Otherwise Than Being*. Moreover, as observed, the role and function of difference in Levinas's works also distinguishes *Otherwise Than Being* from his other works and from Blanchot's works. While in earlier writings (and in many of Blanchot's works), it functions primarily as one of the vehicles through which Levinas contests totalization, in later work it becomes the principle that accounts for and defines identity, though an identity now conceived in terms other than those of unity, totalization or autonomy. Thus, the curious formula of an imperious and ineluctable, immemorial and incomprehensible, responsibility for the other as the only principle of the self's identity, individuation, unicity, and sameness is both a statement of difference and an expression of Levinas's view of the priority of ethics over all other dimensions of human existence.

If various elements of a theory of difference are formally explored in works by Saussure, Heidegger, and Derrida, Blanchot's and Levinas's texts can be considered case studies of difference. Their texts formulate possible configurations of subjectivity that would derive from difference, and in so doing they present developments of a problem that has been described in the abstract by Derrida: a reexamination of the question of the subject which is traditionally thought in terms of presence, identity, sameness, and unity. While Blanchot explores an "ungrounding" of the subject, Levinas employs the concept of difference both to challenge the primacy accorded to ontology and to elaborate his original view of the priority of the ethical. In subsequent chapters, I will observe how the concept of difference informs other sectors of their writing and thought.

Two

The Problem of Death

Blanchot's persistent preoccupation with the problem of death[1] is saliently underscored by the title of his last published story, a short narrative entitled *The Instant of My Death.*[2] This perhaps autobiographical story recounts an episode during the waning days of World War II during which a young person threatened with imminent execution by retreating German soldiers manages to escape when the commander of the German unit is distracted by a nearby firefight and Russian conscripts motion for the man to escape into a nearby wood. The narrator reflects on the injustice of his good fortune. Three young men in neighboring farms were, in fact, shot and killed by the unit, and the narrator attributes the possibility of his escape to class prejudice. The Russian conscripts, impressed no doubt by the elegance and stateliness of the narrator's house (it is described as "le Château"), are reluctant to execute the house's male inhabitants. The narrator emphasizes and vividly recalls the powerful sensation he experienced as, convinced that he was about to be killed, an intense feeling of lightness invaded him. Like Dostoevsky's Prince Myshkin in *The Idiot* (80–81),[3] Blanchot's narrator records the intense physical sensation elicited by the experience of his imminent execution. There is no attempt to analyze or understand this feeling; it is simply chronicled as a fact, perhaps of a psychological nature, of the sensation aroused by the approach of death. Saved from death by death itself, as he puts it, the narrator retains the indelible impression of an inexplicable sensation of lightness.

Blanchot's interest in the problem of death is, of course, anterior to the war and is a theme that recurs in virtually all of his writings. Blanchot's complicated manner of examining the problem of death can best be approached through consideration of one critical literary essay, "Literature and the Right to Death," in conjunction with analysis of two short narratives, *Thomas the Obscure* and *Death Sentence*. In order to consider the problem of death in Blanchot, however, it is necessary first to observe some formulations of this question in Levinas's early work.

Levinas and the Otherness of Death

A common feature in Levinas's early texts and virtually all of Blanchot's is the presentation of death as the preeminent form of alterity. Death is the basic relation that cannot become a concept or a form of knowledge, both inevitable and ungraspable, in urgent need of comprehension yet resisting attempts to comprehend it.

In the first chapter of the second part of *Being and Time*, Heidegger characterizes an authentic Being-toward-death (*Sein zum Tode, Sein zum Ende*) as an "anticipation" of death as a possibility (*Vorlaufen in die Möglichkeit*) (293–311). In his essay "L'Existentialisme, l'angoisse et la mort," Levinas paraphrases and summarizes Heidegger's analysis in *Being and Time*, translating Heidegger's *vorlaufen* with the verb "s'élancer":[4]

> Heidegger requires a concept of possibility that not be the consequence or the precursor of action and thus he isolates the notion of possibility from action. This allows the notion of possibility to remain possibility such that, when its limits are reached [au moment où elle est épuisée], it is death. In this way, it is death that allows the concept of possibility to be thought and grasped as such: it is

part of this fundamental intuition as the event of existence. . . . Existence occurs in such a way that the being already projects himself forward [s'élance déjà] toward death, and this manner of projecting oneself forward [s'élancer] toward death is, for the being, a possibility in the purest sense of the word. This is because all other possibilities accomplish themselves and become actions while death becomes non-reality, non-being. It is in this sense that Heidegger says that death is the possibility of impossibility. (II, 119)

In *Time and the Other*, Levinas criticizes this posture toward death, for in this view, even as an impossibility death is incorporated into the realm of the possible (TO, 70–71/TA, 57–58). And in a footnote in *Time and the Other*, he corrects Jean Wahl's characterization of Heidegger's view of death as "the impossibility of possibility" in order to phrase it more properly as "the possibility of impossibility" (TO, 70/TA, 92). Levinas also uses this distinction to oppose Blanchot's view of death to Heidegger's. In *Sur Maurice Blanchot*, Levinas, commenting on the association of writing and death in Blanchot's work notes: "Death, for Blanchot, is not the pathos of the ultimate human possibility, a possibility of impossibility, but the incessant repetition [ressassement] of what cannot be grasped, before which the 'I' loses its ipseity. Impossibility of possibility" (SMB, 16).[5]

The emphasis on the absolute otherness of death and the attendant posture of passivity before it is one of the principal articulations of death in Levinas. The expressions that he employs to express this essential passivity, a passivity which is more fundamental than the alternative postures of action and passiveness are the "impossibility of possibility" and perhaps more frequently, variants of the expression "pouvoir de pouvoir." For example, in *Time and the Other*, he writes, "What is important about the approach of death is that at a certain moment we are no longer *able to be able* [nous ne pouvons plus pouvoir]. It is exactly thus that the subject loses its very mastery as a subject" (TO, 74/TA, 62).[6] The act of suicide is thus inherently contradictory; it represents an attempt to restore this "pouvoir," the possibility of action, control, and initiative on death. As Levinas puts it in *Time and the Other*: "Death is never assumed, it comes. Suicide is a contradictory concept" (TO, 73/ TA, 61). In his comments on writing and death in *The Space of Literature*, Blanchot fleshes out the contradiction inherent in the act of suicide[7] and frequently relates, through a pun, its passivity — a "yielding" of power — to the act of writing, through his use of the verb "livrer" or "se livrer" (EL, 16, 17, 22, 27, 118). In *The Writing of the Disaster*, Blanchot returns to this distinction in relation to Heidegger and the problem of suicide, essentially paraphrasing Levinas in opposing Heidegger's view of death as *"possibility of impossibility"* and posing the more appropriate expression of *"the impossibility of every possibility"* (WD, 70/ED, 114–15).[8]

It is interesting that Blanchot adapts this distinction to question the argument of Camus's *The Myth of Sisyphus*, a book of essays which begins with the proposition that "[t]here is only one problem that is philosophically truly serious: it's the problem of suicide" (99). In making consciousness and lucid acceptance of the absurd the way out of the absurd, Camus has, according to Blanchot, relied on an intellectual legerdemain similar to Heidegger's. Blanchot's assessment of Camus's argument is succinct and severe. He emphasizes the logical inconsistency of the striking final line of the essay "The Myth of Sisyphus," "We must consider Sisyphus to be happy [Il faut imaginer Sisyphe heureux]."

> Happy? This assessment is unconsidered and premature. [Voilà qui est vite écrit]. If Camus's book deserves that we not judge it to be an ordinary book, we must also explain why at certain moments it weighs on us and bothers us. It is that he himself does not practice what he preaches [C'est que lui-même n'est pas fidèle à sa règle]; it is that, ultimately, he makes of the absurd not so much something that upsets and destroys everything but something that can potentially resolve things and even fixes everything [ce qui même arrange tout]. In his work, the absurd turns into a solution, a resolution, a kind of salvation. The man who has analyzed the strangeness of his

condition, who has discerned its mechanism, and who endorses his condition [y souscrit] with frankness and lucidity, blinds himself if he seeks to derive from this condition a principle of life [une règle de vie]. He saves himself through his own destruction; he makes a solution out of the fact that there is no solution; he thus exempts the absurd itself from the terrible grip of the absurd. (FP, 70)[9]

But there are other formulations of death in Levinas's early essays, for example, the correlation in *Time and the Other* of the otherness of death to a futurity which is incommensurate with any present. In what again seems to be an argument directed at Heidegger's *Vorlaufen* Levinas states, "this future of death determines the future for us, the future insofar as it is not present. It determines what in the future contrasts strongly with all anticipation, projection, and élan" (TO, 80/TA, 71). And in a play on the words "maintenir" and "maintenant," Levinas relates the impossibility of mastery to the fact that death can never occur in the present: "The now [le maintenant], is the fact that I am master, master of the possible, in a position to grasp the possible. Death is never now [la mort n'est jamais maintenant]" (TA, 59/TO, 72).[10]

Another model of death articulated in temporal terms is the *entretemps* which Levinas uses to describe the temporality expressed by the work of art. More sustained attention will be given to the economy of this concept in chapter 4;[11] however, several of its characteristics are worth noting here. This intertime, meantime, or meanwhile is also characterized in terms of a futurity incommensurate with the present and with any anticipation of the future. It is a futurity which does not cross the interval to the present because the present gets stuck in the interval separating it from the future, hence the determination of the expression by the prefix *entre*. The *entretemps* in "Reality and Its Shadow" is the time of dying, a moment which cannot pass, an event that can only approach, never occur. It specifies, in a temporal sense, the notion of death as impossibility. As something beyond the subject's "pouvoir de pouvoir," death can only be awaited in a waiting for a moment which can never arrive: "This is the anxiety which in other tales [by Edgar Allen Poe] is prolonged like a fear of being buried alive. It is as though death were never dead enough, as though parallel with the duration of the living ran the eternal duration of the interval — the *meanwhile* [*l'entretemps*]" (CPP, 11/LR, 140–41/RO, 786). This formulation provides the thematic structure for the problems of waiting (*attente*) and futurity (*à venir* or *avenir*) which are so frequent in Blanchot's writing.[12]

The concept of the impossibility of death also organizes Levinas's analysis of the *il y a* in *Existence and Existents*.[13] Again responding to Heidegger, Levinas seeks to distinguish the relation to the *il y a* from Heidegger's *Angst*. Characterizing the latter as anxiety or dread before nothingness, Levinas describes the horror of the *il y a* in terms of the horror of an irremissible being, a being not limited by nothingness, the far more terrifying experience of a being that persists even within or beyond nothingness. "That is what is essential in this analysis. The pure nothingness revealed by anxiety in Heidegger's analysis does not constitute the *there is*. There is horror of being and not anxiety over nothingness, fear of being and not fear for being; there is being prey to, delivered over to [être livré à] something that is not a 'something.'"[14] Just as the idea of a death which does not succeed in dying — a death never dead enough — characterizes the *il y a*, this characterization of the *il y a* ends up defining death. This is because the *il y a* both challenges the concept of nothingness as the basis of being ("as an ocean which beats up against it on all sides" EE, 64/DEE, 104) and the association of death and nothingness.[15] So while the expressions "the impossibility of death, the universality of existence even in its annihilation" (EE, 61/DEE, 100) characterize the *il y a*, the *il y a* becomes a model of death: on dying, the character "Phaedra discovers the impossibility of death" (EE, 62/DEE, 102). In his elaboration of the concept of the *entretemps* in "Reality and Its Shadow," Levinas also questions the association of death and nothingness; such an association, he argues, is death seen from without or from afar: "Death *qua* nothingness is the death of the other, death for the survivor."[16]

In various texts, Levinas will attribute this characterization of death to Blanchot, using among others the reference to Edgar Allen Poe which he uses in "Reality and Its Shadow" to characterize the *entretemps*: "Death is not the end, it is the *never-ending of the ending* [*n'en pas finir de finir*]. It is like in certain of Edgar Allen Poe's tales in which the threat gradually approaches and in which the helpless gaze [regard impuissant] measures this still distant approach" (SMB, 16–17).[17]

Thus both the *il y a* and *entretemps*, which introduce complications to categories of Being and time, are associated with the characterization of death in Levinas. This relation of death and of the *il y a* is also a noteworthy and strategically significant concept in Blanchot's long essay "Literature and the Right to Death."

Difference, Dialectic, and Death: "Literature and the Right to Death"

In his monograph *Proximity*, Libertson notes that: "'La Littérature et le droit à la mort' is the scene of Blanchot's extrication of his thinking from that of Hegel" adding that "this movement involves Levinas" (206–7; see also 70–72).[18]

Prior to Heidegger's "anticipation" before death, perhaps the most well-known and most influential articulation of the relation to death is the relation framed dialectically by Hegel in the *Phenomenology of Spirit*. In several passages, specifically in the preface, the analysis of the relation of domination and servitude, and the analysis of the French Revolution and of the Terror of 1793, Hegel describes the sublation of death within the horizon of the spirit. In his *Genesis and Structure of Hegel's Phenomenology of Spirit*, Jean Hippolyte relates the role of death to the general plan of the *Phenomenology*, writing, "Whereas in nature death is an external negation, spirit carries death within itself and gives it positive meaning. The whole *Phenomenology* is a meditation on this death which is carried by consciousness [portée par la conscience] and which, far from being exclusively negative, an end point in an abstract nothingness, is, on the contrary an *Aufhebung*, an ascent" (*Genesis and Structure*, 18/*Genèse et structure*, 23; see also Collin, *Maurice Blanchot*, 208).

Blanchot's long essay "Literature and the Right to Death," which was initially published in two parts, is essentially a long meditation on Hegel and on two of Hegel's best-known commentaries in French, one by Jean Hippolyte — whose translation of the *Phenomenology* Blanchot uses — and the other by Alexandre Kojève (Gasché, "The Felicities of Paradox," 39). The first half of the essay, originally titled "Le Règne animal de l'esprit," refers to a subsection in Hegel's work which analyzes the processes of consciousness achieved by writers, artists, and intellectuals through the relation they establish with their creations, the products of their creative endeavors (PS, 237/PEI, 324). In this part of his analysis, Blanchot paraphrases both Hegel and Hippolyte's commentary of Hegel and adapts the form and general content of Hegel's dialectical arguments to the particular circumstances of the writer and to the literary work (Tommasi, "Per un'esperienza," 48). The purpose is to trace various moments and manifestations of the work of negativity in the different stages of the creative or intellectual processes. While Blanchot does occasionally adjust and modify the basic movement of Hegel's arguments, his general posture is rather mechanical, indicating the pertinence of various forms of negativity to the specific case of literature and of the writer.[19] However, two scenarios entertained by Hegel as only theoretical possibilities are given concrete meaning and positive reality by Blanchot. First, Blanchot continually reenacts the paradox of the origin of the work in Hegel. Second, he gives the phrase "nothing working towards nothingness" [néant travaillant dans le néant] positive meaning (GO, 24/WF, 304/PF, 296, and PS, 239/PEI, 327, *Genèse et structure*, 293).

Blanchot analyzes the paradoxical origin of artistic talent (GO, 24/WF, 303/PF, 296); the end of the artistic process (GO, 24/WF,

304/PF, 296); the work's unique status on its completion and the work or "thing" in itself (GO, 26–28/WF, 306–8/PF, 298–300); the questions of honesty and deceit in relation to the work (GO, 28–31/WF, 307–10/PF, 300–302); the author's intentions with regard to his produced work (GO, 31–33/WF, 311–14/PF, 302–5); the temptations of stoicism, skepticism and unhappy consciousness (GO, 37/WF, 317/PF, 308); and the analysis of freedom and death in the Terror (GO, 38–40/WF, 317–20/PF, 309–10). These analyses generally mirror in form and content Hegelian arguments in the *Phenomenology*. Their purpose is to locate, in various stages of the process of artistic becoming, the presence and essential function of different figures of negativity, nothingness, negation, and disappearance, to name but a few.

Shifting his attention to Kojève's *Introduction à la lecture de Hegel* which he cites in a footnote, Blanchot adapts and compares the Hegelian analysis of work as negativity to the creation of a literary work (Swenson, "Revolutionary Sentences," 15–16, 21–24, 27). In this analysis, the creation of a work of art, specifically a work of literature, will be first compared then contrasted to real work in the world, in this case, the construction of a stove. In its basic formal structure — a literal realization of an abstract idea through the negation/destruction of primary materials which creates a piece of equipment which then enters history and can modify concrete conditions in the world — creating a written work resembles creating a stove; the content of the negation, however, is very different. Because the writer's freedom is absolute and immediate (unmediated), the negation he effects is unmediated, and affects, not the concrete conditions of the real world, but the totality ("His negation is *global*"). Associating this totality with the imaginary allows Blanchot to note a structural similarity of the writer's work of negation and that of revolution.

In his discussion of the French Revolution and of the Terror of 1793, a meditation on Hegel's analysis of the Enlightenment, Blanchot characterizes Sade as the quintessential writer.[20] He appears historically during the Revolution; indeed, according to Blanchot, he identifies himself with both the Revolution and the Terror, he embodies all of the paradoxes that characterize the writer, and embodies, in particular, "the action of a furious negation, driven to blood" (GO, 41/WF, 321/PF, 311). At this juncture, Blanchot quotes, though without attributing it, the passage in the preface of Hegel's work which expresses most succinctly the dialectical sublation of death by the spirit and the consequent elevation of the spirit. Hegel's text reads as follows: "Death, if that is what we want to call this non-actuality, is of all things the most dreadful, and to hold fast what is dead requires the greatest strength. Lacking strength, Beauty hates the Understanding for asking of her what it cannot do. But the life of Spirit is not the life that shrinks from death and keeps itself untouched by devastation, but rather the life that endures it and maintains itself in it. It wins its truth only when, in utter dismemberment, it finds itself" (PS, 19). ["Ce n'est pas cette vie qui recule d'horreur devant la mort et se préserve pure de la destruction, mais la vie qui porte la mort, et se maintient dans la mort-même, qui est la vie de l'esprit. L'esprit conquiert sa vérité seulement à condition de se retrouver soi-même dans l'absolu déchirement" (PEI, 29)]. The second half of Blanchot's essay meditates, through his discussion of literature and literary language, on this formulation of a dialectical relation of life and death ("porter" and "maintenir" being two of the expressions that translate the German *Aufhebung* or *aufheben*). The passage "la vie qui porte la mort et se maintient dans la mort" is quoted four times by Blanchot, though each time without attribution (GO, 41, 46, 54, 61/WF, 322, 327, 336, 343/PF, 311, 316, 324, 330). He also quotes the passage in Hegel's famous analysis of the master and slave dialectic which describes the elevation of the consciousness of the slave through the experience of fear of death. Speaking of the slave's consciousness, Hegel says, "For this consciousness has been fearful, not of this or that particular thing or just at odd moments, but its whole being has been seized with dread; for it has experienced the fear of death, the absolute Lord. In that experience it has been quite un-manned, has trembled in every fibre of its being, and everything solid and stable has been shaken to its foundations" (PS, 117/ PEI, 164).[21]

The first part of "Literature and the Right to Death" is in general a rather servile appropriation of Hegel's arguments, a "fitting" of Hegel's various dialectics to the specific case of literature.[22] The second half, while still very influenced by Hegel (and now by Kojève's commentary), will create a complex dialogue between Hegel's positive dialectic of death and a view that, anticipating somewhat what follows, could be broadly characterized as Levinas's argument concerning the "impossibility of death." This dialogue begins in the discussion of Revolution and of the Terror.

The beginning of Blanchot's essay locates within literature a basic question related to its essence: "literature begins at the moment when literature becomes a question" (GO, 21/WF, 300/PF, 293). At the outset, Blanchot does not identify what the question is; he simply emphasizes how this question has been misconstrued as, for example, denunciation, deprecation or discrediting of art. The question of literature's essence, manifested by literature's questioning of itself, is related to an act of negation intimately and centrally related to literature. Again, this negation is generally misconstrued either in moral terms (the moral emptiness of literature) or in aesthetic terms (its aesthetically illegitimate character). Leaving open, then, the question that is literature, Blanchot turns his attention to the various manifestations of negativity which he develops through the different Hegelian dialectics referred to above. It is not until his analysis of literature and the French Revolution — joined concretely by the figure of Sade — that Blanchot returns to the question to which he alluded in the beginning of the essay. The Revolution and the Terror manifest historically and empirically a relation of life and death, an inhabiting of life by death, a possibility of life *carrying* death, in which life derives from death the possibility of speaking and the truth of speech. The question posed by literature, the question that is the essence of literature, is then the question of this particular relation of life and death.

Hegel's phrase from the preface "la vie qui porte la mort et se maintient dans la mort même" (GO, 41/WF, 322/PF, 311) is actually strikingly inappropriate in this context. While this phrase suggests the positive movement of elevation of consciousness by and through its consciousness of death, the Revolution and the Terror designate, for Hegel, the very failure of this elevation. Enacted in the abstract, the negation of "absolute freedom" is destructive and regressive (PS, 359/PEII, 135; *Genèse et structure*, 445). The far more appropriate citation in this context which Hegel himself makes, would be the dialectic of the master and the slave which restores some positive meaning to the Revolution by suggesting a cyclic view of history in which successive cycles would not be the same (*Genèse et structure*, 447). It is interesting that Hippolyte, in his comments on Hegel's analysis of the Terror, cites the passage from the preface, but precisely to emphasize its contrast with the relation with death in the Terror (PEII, 139, n. 214). Placed in the context of the Revolution and the Terror, the phrase from the preface seems to suggest the opposite of what Hegel intends.[23] The subsequent argument will confirm that this reversal of the Hegelian dialectical movement is what Blanchot intends to relate to literature.[24] This abrupt reversal of the central thesis in Hegel's phenomenology is striking, especially in light of the rather straightforward and unimaginative applications of Hegelian patterns of thought that came before it.

The second portion of Blanchot's essay explores, in a back and forth pattern, models of language and of literature in which, on the one hand, a dialectical relation is established and in which, on the other hand, a dialectical pattern is reversed. The function of "carrying death" is now attributed to language and literature. The very structure of language as a naming is a structure which harbors death because the act of naming implies and carries death (GO, 42/WF, 232/PF, 313).[25] Thus it is possible to affirm both that when one speaks, death speaks in one and that the most authentic form of speech is to say nothing (GO, 43–44/WF, 324–25/PF, 313–14). Playing on the master and the slave dialectic and slightly modifying the phrase from the preface, Blanchot notes that since language confers mastery on the world (GO, 41/WF, 322/PF, 312), everything that has been named has encountered death in the same manner as the slave: "if true language is to begin, the life that will carry this language must have experienced its nothingness, must have 'trembled in the depths; and everything in it that was fixed and stable must have been shaken'" (GO, 43/WF, 324/PF, 314; PS, 117/ PEI, 164). Everyday language accepts this structural tradeoff, the exchange of the potential or deferred death of the object ("deferred assassination" [GO, 43/WF, 323/PF, 313]) for the conceptual stability yielded by the abstract form of the thing which language creates, its meaning. Indeed, in the abstract form of an idea or a concept, the thing is stabilized and defined, free from particularity, from temporal accidents, and from the vicissitudes of change. This is the manner in which the act of naming enacts a successful dialectical operation: the thing is both suppressed and maintained, carried to a higher or more abstract level, that of meaning or that of the concept (GO, 48, 44–45/WF, 329, 325–26/PF, 318, 314–15).

Initially, literary language is defined in relation to everyday language. Demonstrating a certain wariness and skepticism with respect to the procedures of language, literary language effects a certain adjustment. In response to the discrepancy involved in substituting something concrete, a word, for something which has been consigned to abstraction through negation, language adopts two strategies, or really one strategy which involves two stages. It first creates an image by incorporating or including within its procedures the act of negation, since the negated thing is no longer represented directly by a word, rather by what it is not: "Thus is born the image that does not directly designate the thing, but rather, what the thing is not" (GO, 45/WF, 326/PF, 315).[26]

Second, aware that the negation of language has involved the loss, through negation, of the crude, concrete reality of the thing, literary language now turns its attention precisely to that which has been excluded by this procedure and tries to recapture it. It tries to recover and incorporate not only a reproduction of the act of negation itself, as observed above, but that which was originally negated. Blanchot adapts this structure to Hegel's phrase from the preface of the *Phenomenology* the second time it is quoted. Since language involves death (negation), the life of language involves "carrying" death within it. Thus language can be said to be "'the life that endures ("porte") death and maintains itself in it'" (GO, 46/WF, 327/PF, 316). A reversal of Hegel's dialectic is once again being effected as literary language is proceeding from the abstract to a concreteness prior to the distinction of abstract and concrete: "But something was there and is no longer there. Something has disappeared. How can I recover it, how can I turn around and look at what exists *before*, if all my power consists of making it into what exists *after*? The language of literature is a search for this moment which precedes literature" (GO, 46/WF, 327/PF, 316).

Not accidentally, this formulation recalls the structural problems analyzed in chapter 1, specifically in relation to Heidegger (how is one to think a relation prior to Being?) and to Levinas (how does one conceive of a relation prior to unicity and consciousness?), for Blanchot's argument is now informed by Levinas although Levinas will not be cited until later. In order to express what is prior to language, Blanchot writes, literary language turns away from the meaning of words and emphasizes the materiality of language. The word too can provide access to the crude, obscure and anonymous reality prior to the name:

> Yes, happily language is a thing: it is a written thing, a bit of bark, a sliver of rock, a fragment of clay in which the reality of the earth continues to exist. The word acts not as an ideal force but as an obscure power, as an incantation that coerces things, makes them *really* present outside of themselves. It is an element, a piece barely detached from its subterranean surroundings: it is no longer a name, but rather one moment in the universal anonymity, a bald statement

("affirmation brute"), the stupor of a confrontation in the depths of obscurity. (GO, 46–47/WF, 327–28/PF, 317)[27]

The reversal of the Hegelian dialectical pattern that Blanchot effects here involves recognizably Levinasian concepts, themselves a reversal of recognizably Heideggerian ones.[28] The language of an obscure, closed earth ("subsiste la réalité de la terre") evokes some of the basic terms of Heidegger's aesthetic analyses ("Erde" and "Welt" specifically) and the reversal of these terms effected by Levinas, when, for example, in "Reality and Its Shadow," Levinas defines art as the opposite of a clearing or of an opening: "[Art] is the very event of obscuring, a descent of the night, an invasion of shadow" (LR, 132/CPP, 3/RO, 773). Indeed, what literary language now directs itself to is characterized in terms which, through Heidegger's concept of "world," describe very explicitly Levinas's *il y a* and relate it to the impossibility of death:

> [Literature] is not beyond the world, but neither is it the world itself: it is the presence of things before the world exists, their perseverance after the world has disappeared, the stubbornness of what remains when everything vanishes and the dumbfoundedness of what appears when nothing exists. That is why it cannot be confused with consciousness, which illuminates things and makes decisions; it is my consciousness without me, the radiant passivity of mineral substances, the lucidity of the depths of torpor. It is not the night; it is the obsession of the night, it is not the night, but the consciousness of the night, which lies awake watching for a chance to surprise itself and because of that is constantly being dissipated. It is not the day, it is the side of the day that day has rejected in order to become light. And it is not death either, because it manifests existence without being, existence which remains below existence, like an inexorable affirmation, without beginning or end — death as the impossibility of dying. (GO, 47/WF, 328/PF, 317)

Some of Blanchot's most perplexing formulations in this part of his analysis adopt both the form and the language of Levinas's analysis of the *il y a*. Thus the phrase "existence without being" echoes Levinas's analysis in *Existence and Existents*. And, as is the case in the "thought experiment" that Levinas employs to thematize the *il y a*, in which the negation of all beings leads not to nothingness but to an uncanny generality of being (chapters 4 and 5), in Blanchot's argument at this juncture, the negation of meaning, effected by literary language, produces not insignificance but an uncanny, empty generality of meaning: "although the precise meaning of the terms has faded, what asserts itself now is the very possibility of signifying, the empty power of bestowing meaning — as strange impersonal light" (GO, 48/WF, 329/PF, 318).[29] The strategic importance of the intervention of Levinas at this juncture cannot be emphasized enough, for the *il y a* supplies Blanchot with, in effect, a logical device or instrument which enables him to think a non-dialectical or reverse dialectical relation of life and death (Hill, *Blanchot*, 110–11).

Now the basic distinction that Blanchot has drawn between everyday or common language and literary language is fitted to literature itself. Literature has two slopes which can be characterized as "meaningful prose" and poetry in the broad sense ("the people we call poets") (GO, 51/WF, 333/PF, 321). Meaningful prose reproduces the structure of everyday language and, to the extent that it may experience the inadequacy of meaning, will respond by attempting to incorporate the operation of negation in the manner that has been noted previously, presumably by such strategies as adopting the image.

Poetry, on the other hand, focusing on the materiality, the substance of language as such, turns toward the obscure, threatening, unrevealed and unrevealable indeterminacy that is prior to and beneath the world. What is heard through the word is the uncanny otherness of the *il y a*: "an unsettling rustling of insects" (PF, 321/GO, 52/WF, 333). Blanchot will provide a series of examples of the latter, mostly in Ponge, after having noted, though without explanation, that literature always escapes the willful determination of the writer such that when attempting to write "on one slope" one is always already writing on the other. Thus writers such as Ponge and Flaubert, attempting to write clear, meaningful prose, give voice to a much more obscure reality, one whose formulation in terms of "horror" evokes very explicitly Levinas's exposition of the *il y a.* They describe "The horror of existence deprived of the world, the process through which whatever ceases to be continues to be . . . whatever dies encounters only the impossibility of dying . . . existence without being" (GO, 52/WF, 334/PF, 322). The examples that Blanchot provides in this part of his essay, drawn from the set of writers who compose Blanchot's most common literary references — Mallarmé, Ponge, Flaubert, Kafka, Lautréamont, and Sade — represent the closest that the essay will come to literary commentary, interpretation, or criticism.

Blanchot's analysis next effects a transition which is complicated because he has omitted a series of steps. In order to contextualize this transition, it may be useful to recall and summarize the movement of this part of his essay. The principle of the two distinctions (that of everyday language versus literary language, then of meaningful prose versus poetry) is based upon successful dialectical accomplishment in the first case and an unsuccessful accomplishment of this operation or, more fittingly, its apparent reversal in the second. Moreover, the specific context of this dialectic is the structure of language as naming whose basis as negation is predicated upon death. The principle of the first, then, is the annihilation (death) of the thing followed by its recovery in the abstract form of an idea or a concept, and thus within the realm of meaning. In the second case — that initially of literary language, then of poetry — the word does not yield a meaning; rather, it binds language to the threatening indeterminacy of what is prior to the world, a persistence of being beyond being or beyond the alternatives of being and nothingness, and the impossibility of death. The annihilation (death) of the thing through the name thus yields the impossibility of death and it was, as observed, Levinas's *il y a* which supplied Blanchot with this particular formulation.

In his use of these two models in the remainder of "Literature and the Right to Death," Blanchot orchestrates a metaphorical dialogue between Hegel and Levinas, which now focuses principally on death (Hill, *Blanchot*, 112–14). This strategy is attested by the system of references to both writers as well as by the particular arguments which Blanchot confronts. Thus there is the positive accomplishment of the dialectic that Hegel has thematized: "the life of Spirit . . . [is] the life that endures [death] and maintains itself in it," and there is the impossibility of death. Blanchot will provide a set of cultural and literary figures of this concept: immortality in certain religions, the West's cultural concept of "literary immortality" (GO, 58/WF, 340/PF, 327), reincarnation in other religions, and the nightmarish indeterminacy represented in several of Kafka's narratives (GO, 55–57/WF, 337–39/PF, 325–26). The basic argument of all is, simply put, that death both makes and breaks the world. Death works to create the world; in this context, it is present in the successful negation in language which creates meaning, and it assumes unproblematically the place of nothingness when asked to fit within the alternative possibilities of being and nothingness. Yet death also breaks the world; all language and meaning ultimately refer to indeterminacy and indefiniteness and, as an exit from the alternative possibilities of being and nothingness, death opens onto the impossibility of nothingness and the impossibility of dying.

Blanchot now ascribes to literature a dual role parallel to the role that he has just articulated for death. On the one hand, literature "is working towards the advent of the world; literature is civilization and culture" (GO, 56/WF, 338/PF, 326). On the other hand, literature refers "to an existence that is still inhuman" (GO, 57/WF, 339/PF, 327) and refers to the indeterminacy of that which is neither being nor nothingness; "what it does is plunge into this depth of existence which is neither being nor nothingness" (GO, 58/WF,

340/PF, 327). It is in this manner that literary immortality, expressing this second relation of life and death, of being and nothingness, becomes, as it were, a concrete figure of the *il y a*.

The final step of the analysis takes Blanchot's demonstration to a higher, dizzying level of abstraction. Literature has been identified with two contrary movements in close parallel to the two "functions" of death distinguished by both Hegel and Levinas. Like death, literature is related to the positive, creative endeavor of constructing meaning and a world, and yet also to ensuring a relation to the indeterminacy which undermines both. These are not independent or alternating functions. It simultaneously "worlds" and "unworlds" to adapt Heidegger's expressions. In other words, literature is now defined as the relation of ambiguity of these two contrary movements.[30] Literature *is* the relation of these two models, a relation which is itself indeterminate and ambiguous. This makes intelligible Blanchot's previous observation that writers working on one "slope" of literature will inevitably end up on the other since, in a sense, the two slopes are really the same. Thus literature "[plays] everything both ways" (GO, 56/WF, 338/PF, 326); it "[affixes] a negative or positive sign indiscriminately to each of its moments and each of its results" (GO, 59/WF, 341/PF, 328); it involves "all these reversals from *pro* to *contra*" (GO, 60/WF, 342/PF, 329).[31] As if to illustrate his point about ambiguity, the principal assertion of the essay is framed in the form of a series of questions:

> Could it be that the meaning of a word introduces something else into the word along with it, something which, although it protects the precise signification of the word and does not threaten that signification, is capable of completely modifying the meaning and modifying the material value of the word? Could there be a force at once friendly and hostile hidden in the intimacy of speech, a weapon intended to build and to destroy, which would act behind signification rather than upon signification? Do we have to suppose a meaning for the meaning of words that, while determining that meaning, also surrounds this determination with an ambiguous indeterminacy that wavers between yes and no? (GO, 61/WF, 343/PF, 330)

An analogous complication with regard to ambiguity — the ambiguity of ambiguity itself — occurs in Blanchot's analysis of the image. The basic armature of Blanchot's analysis of language there is contained in Levinas's analysis of art's "exoticism" in *Existence and Existents*. In this work, one of the few works explicitly referenced by Blanchot in "Literature and the Right to Death," Levinas distinguishes in the word two axes, so to speak: that of the intelligible, related obviously to meaning and that of the sensory, related to the materiality of the word and to ambiguity. As will be observed in chapter 5, it is this opaque materiality which provides Levinas with a concrete image of the *il y a* (EE, 53–54, 56–57/ DEE, 86–87, 91–92).

Relating this ambiguity back to the problem of death, Blanchot cites for the fourth time Hegel's phrase from the preface of the *Phenomenology*: it too is ambiguous. The "power" of death perpetuates a double "meaning" and a double "direction" of which Hegel has formulated only one: "an irreducible *double meaning*, a choice whose terms are covered over with an ambiguity that makes them identical to one another even as it makes them opposite" (GO, 61/WF, 344/PF, 330). Again, illustrating his point, Blanchot will demonstrate the essential ambiguity of the proposition "death ends in being" ("la mort aboutit à l'être"), interpreting it in accordance with double direction and double meaning.[32]

The intervention of Levinas in Blanchot's analysis of Hegel is particularly significant and strategic because the *il y a* formulates a relation of life and death, being and nothingness, presence and absence contrary to the optimistic elevation in the preface of Hegel's *Phenomenology*. Furthermore, the opposition of these two relations of life and death informs and determines Blanchot's definitions of language and literature; in fact, in the essay's conclusion, their relation defines literature.

In her study of Blanchot, Anne-Lise Schulte Nordholt succinctly states the importance of Hegel for both Blanchot and Bataille: "Hegel's greatness is to have introduced death into thought by making it [death] the movement of truth" (*Maurice Blanchot*, 46). Hegel has accomplished what Schulte Nordholt describes specifically by articulating life and death through the dialectic, producing the very "elevation" which yields the life of Spirit. Since Levinas's *il y a* supplies Blanchot with an alternative, patently non-dialectical, formulation of this relation, it is useful to consider what the character of the relation of life and death within the *il y a* is.[33] While the *il y a* characterizes death and is itself defined as an "impossibility" of death (conceived as nothingness), it strikes one most forcefully that the *il y a* articulates a relation of life and death which is not absorbed by an opposition or negative relation of life, death, being, nothingness, presence, absence, sound, silence, consciousness, and unconsciousness. It thus expresses a between (*Zusammen*, "excluded middle" or "tiers exclu" [SMB, 47, 48, 52; Ei, 48–49/ EI, 47]), or a relation which must be prior to the opposition of these concepts, delineated in Heidegger, for example, as the priority of the "belonging together." Indeed, Levinas's *il y a* appears to formulate a "belonging together" — a "Zusammen-*gehören*" of these concepts which would then account for the prevalence of a vocabulary of residuality, excess, fluidity, and contamination.

It is thus possible to schematize Blanchot's procedures in this essay in the following manner: first oppose to Hegel's dialectical analysis one that establishes a different relation of life and death. For this purpose, he introduces Levinas and the *il y a*, whose principle is difference. In a second step, he analyzes the relation of these two relations; this produces the thematization of the initial opposition in terms of difference. This is what Blanchot calls ambiguity. Thus dialectic is situated with respect to difference; the dialectic becomes an integral and authentic, but local moment within the broader perspective of difference (Libertson, *Proximity*, 71–72; Hill, *Blanchot*, 117).

Despite certain moments of complexity, usually occasioned by an elliptical analytic style (which becomes increasingly so in subsequent essays), "Literature and the Right to Death" is relatively straightforward and provides an excellent example of Blanchot's analytic procedures. The essay develops incrementally, moving back and forth between examples and positions, ratcheting its arguments to progressively higher orders of abstraction. It is very much as Libertson has suggested, the "working through" of a problem — one posed by Hegel and for which the solution will be found in Levinas. Finally, it affords a concrete and clear example of a movement which I think is characteristic of Blanchot: scrutiny of a concept or term leads to the explicit articulation of prior relation and thus to the problem of difference, where the problem of relation as the constitution of terms and definitions is more important than the particular terms and definitions themselves.

Encountering Death: Thomas the Obscure *and* Death Sentence

After "Literature and the Right to Death," Blanchot commonly thematizes the problem of death by rethinking and revising Hegel's phrases from the preface and other portions of the *Phenomenology*. Several notable examples occur in *The Space of Literature*, an analysis of the stoic attitude before death (SL, 101/EL, 122), and in *Death Sentence* (DS, 67/AM, 108). In *The Writing of the Disaster*, Blanchot returns to the theme of suicide and to the problem of the confusion of two types of death, "the *possible* death" and "the death without any name, the death outside the concept — *impossibility* itself" (WD, 68/ED, 112). The movement of this short analysis is interesting in that while Blanchot investigates the psychoanalytical terminology of Serge Leclaire, he retraces the basic steps of his analysis in "Literature and the Right to Death." He poses the problem of death with respect to Hegel and then formulates an explicit rejection of the dialectical relation of death and life ("renders the *Aufhebung* null and void"), observing that "something rings false in the dialectic." Then, representing Heidegger's view of death as Levinas had done, as *"the possibility of impossibility,"* Blanchot corrects it through an explicit rejection of the dialectic and rephrases it, again as Levinas has, as *the impossibility of every possibility*." What is interesting in this short example is the amalgamation of Blanchot's critical revisions of both Hegel and Heidegger. The gesture of suicide, Blanchot argues here (and in *The Space of Literature*), is an attempt to "be master of un-mastery" ["se rendre maître de la non-maîtrise"]. The attempt to convert death to possibility, to construe it, as Heidegger has done, as "possibility of impossibility" is predicated upon: "entrusting itself to the dialectic" (WD, 70/ED, 114). The difference between "the possibility of impossibility" and the more correct "impossibility of every possibility"[34] is precisely the failure of the dialectic, expressed parenthetically: "(betraying, as though demented, the mendacity of the dialectic by bringing it to its conclusion) — revers[ing] the possibility of impossibility into *the impossibility of every possibility* [(démentant, à la façon d'une démence, la dialectique en la faisant aboutir) en *l'impossibilité de toute possibilité*]" (WD, 70/ED, 114–15).

Blanchot developed and nurtured his meditation on death in many fictional works. *The Most High, Thomas the Obscure*, and *Death Sentence* feature the deaths of characters in central or climactic episodes.[35] Similarly, since waiting and forgetfulness are modes of our relation to death, the question figures prominently in the various exchanges of *Awaiting Oblivion* as well as in the narrative of *The Last Man*.

Among these works, the representation of death is perhaps figured most dramatically and most prominently in the accounts of the deaths of Anne in *Thomas the Obscure* and J. in *Death Sentence*. In both of these stories, the narrator witnesses and, in the latter example, intervenes in the death of a female companion.[36] Both stories record with clinical, analytic precision the modifications effected by the approach of death on the consciousness of the dying characters themselves, on the consciousness of those witness to this approach, and on the "space" within which death occurs. The deaths of Anne and J. both serve to make manifest death itself.[37] In particular, the texts chronicle the progressive alteration that occurs as the characters approach the realm of the abstract and the impersonal, approach the absence of time and space, and render this haunting absence manifest and paradoxically present. Both passages demonstrate, often in disturbing detail, the ineluctable failure of the progressively more desperate strategies deployed by consciousness to "carry" death within the horizon of knowledge and of possibility. This is particularly striking in *Death Sentence* since the character J. appears to have died, recovers briefly, then ultimately dies, a situation which clarifies one possible meaning of the title and indicates an evolution of this question toward a higher level of complication with regard to *Thomas the Obscure*.[38]

Blanchot's novel *The Most High* ends with the death of the protagonist Sorge and relates this death to authentic speech (the character's last words are "Now, now I'm speaking" (MH, 252/ TH, 243).[39] In both *Thomas the Obscure* and *Death Sentence*, death does not have the last word; it is neither the end nor the culmination of the narrative. Indeed, the longest single chapter of *Thomas the Obscure* and the longer half of *Death Sentence* record the disruption effected by death in the fictional world of the characters. The deaths of the characters have, in a sense, introduced death into the world and disrupted the world, introducing within it a generality of night, the "other night" of the indeterminacy of being and nothingness, the invasion of an anonymous nocturnal element — recalling Levinas's *il y a* — within which death is impossible. In *Death Sentence*, it has also "carried" with it and into the world the mode of relation to it: first a break or interruption in the narrative, then silence, forgetfulness, and error. The pattern is similar in both works, with *Death Sentence* in particular forming a series of complex intersubjective relations that occur within a dimension whose reference points and parameters have been modified by death. Thus, the narrator's location with regard to other characters in the second half of *Death Sentence* is a complex configuration of proximity and distance, as if separated from them by a window.[40] When characters look at him, like Thomas, he doesn't appear to coincide with himself; on occasion, another character will look at him at a distance from where he appears to be (DS, 68, 70/AM, 109, 112). In *Thomas the Obscure*, the last chapter will record a gradual "return" to the world of the day, of linear time, and of Being.

The ungrounding of the subject that occurs in the first chapter of *Thomas the Obscure* is consistent with the principles of subjectivity in difference, and the logical principles and displacements recorded in the chapter are representative of the various relations into which the character Thomas enters throughout the narrative. In particular, relation with the night, language and silence, the book, various modes of the intersubjective relation, the approach of death, and finally, the return to the "first night" and to the "day" involves a sequence of displacements similar to those observed in chapter 1. They are often expressed through aquatic imagery and metaphors of immersion, inundation, and drowning.[41]

Like the aquatic element, the night, the book, and language in general represent entry into a foreign element. Thus, the night in chapter 2 will appear as the element which supports, immerses, inundates, and invades Thomas and occasions a comparably complex experience of subjectivity. The experience of the book too will "absorb" Thomas (TtO, 25/TO, 27). Again, as in chapter 1, Thomas will apprehend a presence both intimate and distant — "His solitude was complete. And yet, sure as he was that there was no one in the room and even in the world, he was just as sure that someone was there, occupying his slumber, approaching him intimately, all around him and within him" (TtO, 26/TO, 29–30), and he will metamorphose into Kafka's Gregor Samsa (TtO, 28/TO, 32). The analysis of language and intersubjectivity is particularly complicated in *Thomas the Obscure*. The analysis of language reproduces and mirrors the movement of the first chapter in the theme of silence, initially as an interval within language and a condition of meaning, then as medium and element of language whose appearance as such will be effected in various contexts by Thomas. Various modes and functions of silence and silencing are explored, including the silencing of silence when, for example, fearing Thomas's silence, Anne tells him to be quiet and through the positive appearance of silence within language in the form of childish gibberish or frivolous babbling.[42]

In the first chapter of the narrative, the character Thomas emerges from the water intimately related to death; he is neither living, nor immortal but, in a sense, free from the alternatives of life and death: "snatched [arraché] at once from death and from life" (TtO, 37/ TO, 42).[43] Within this general context, the novel investigates another model of death. It is important to emphasize that these two models are neither strictly parallel nor coequal; it is Thomas's relation with death which serves as the context for Anne's relation with death.[44]

The text will record with a striking degree of precision various stages of Anne's progression toward death. This movement involves several components: first and most obviously, Anne's own responses to the approach of death, second, the strategies which those around her employ in response to this approach in order to shield or distance themselves from it, and finally the manner in which death appears in Anne. The double movement, which is in fact only one, of the character's recession into death as the positive form of death's appearance is even more striking in *Death Sentence*. This sequence will appear in Blanchot's analysis of the story of Orpheus as well.

Like J. in *Death Sentence*, Anne appears to make a momentary recovery before beginning the gradual and inexorable process of receding into death. The general thematic premise of this chapter is that as Anne dies, she will effect and make manifest a relationship of life and death; the struggle of dying, the "agonie" is then the initial manifestation of the "work" of death. Various words, gestures, attitudes will alternately reveal on the one hand, life's attempts to negate and "carry" death and, on the other hand, death's gradual undermining of the functions of life, of the strategies of survival, and of the processes of consciousness. This chapter presents, in a sense, and in slow motion, Eurydice's disappearance.

Not manifested by any movement or other signs of effort, a violent and monumental struggle is taking place within Anne that involves Anne's divesting herself of life and of the alternative possibilities of life and death. Those that surround her respond by isolating her and insulating themselves, removing all forms of life from her vicinity. The precautions taken by the living before the approach of death mark a separation, creating consciously or unconsciously a no man's land, a desolate, inhuman, devastated space within which to accommodate death. "Slowly, by a pitiless protocol, they took from her the tenderness and friendship of the world. . . . They had exiled the pleasant seasons, asked the children to cry out in joy elsewhere, called into the street all the anger of cities, and it was an insurmountable wall of shattering sounds that separated her from mankind" (TtO, 78/TO, 85–86). Anne's mother undergoes this transformation as well. Her stone-faced demeanor itself suggests death; her face is described as "terreux" (TO, 86) and she manifests fatigue.[45] Silence is imposed on the vicinity of death; like the friends who gradually stop inquiring about her condition (TtO, 77/TO, 84), her mother silences Anne (who asks her mother if she has been swimming) lest Anne express more than can be accommodated within the space of her dying. "'Be quiet,' said her mother. 'Don't talk, you'll tire yourself.' Obviously, there were no confidences to be shared with a person about to die, no possible relationship between her and those who are enjoying themselves, those who are alive" (TtO, 79/TO, 87). (Her imposition of silence on Anne is comparable to Anne's imposition of silence on Thomas in chapter 7.)

Like Thomas in chapter 2, Anne's condition now mirrors that of Kafka's Gregor Samsa in its thematized passivity. Like Gregor, she has a higher level of awareness or of consciousness than that attributed to her by those around her. She understands those around her but can neither communicate with them nor communicate to them the fact that she understands. Her separation from them is asymmetrical; she now understands, but is unable to express the distance that separates her from the living and the world.[46] She understands that they expect certain behaviors from her but that these behaviors are expressions of the world of the living, representative of the attitude of life before death, not the more fitting situation in Anne's case, of someone far from life and contemplating life's withdrawal. As Anne recedes further and further from the world, the signs of friendship and compassion that Anne extends to her friends express both the remoteness of her location and the distance of their provenance. However, those around her take it as indifference, and "cold reserve" (TtO, 80/TO, 89). Able to assess her situation only from their perspective within the world, her friends misconstrue Anne's words and attitudes; they repeat the clichés of life before the dying: "How insensitive she is becoming; she no longer cares about anything" (TtO, 80/TO, 88); "She's no longer herself, it would be better if she died"; "What a deliverance for her if she died" (TtO, 80/TO, 89 also DS, 17/AM, 32).

Another transformation occurs as Anne enters a realm in which the parameters of time are modified. Those who visit Anne experience this as impatience; they feel "pressed for time" ("to all those who came . . . time was short" [TtO, 81/TO, 90]). Anne, however, begins to harden, she becomes statuesque; her body becomes "the equivalent of a statue" (TtO, 81/TO, 90), "this ideal of marble" (TtO, 82/TO, 92). As Levinas suggests in "Reality and Its Shadow," plastic art, sculpture in particular, expresses another form of time, an "outside" of time which is here manifested in Anne's demeanor and external appearance. (See chapter 4.)

In this realm of progressively greater abstraction, the negation or absence of things, qualities, and feelings becomes the mode of their presence (TtO, 81/TO, 91). Now Blanchot employs an ingenious image to express the particular configuration of being and nonbeing, of being and nothingness that characterizes Anne's location — that of a strange, abandoned, empty city. In the following description, the leitmotiv of the ocean again figures in the context of the image employed by Levinas to describe the *il y a*, a movement of progressive disappearance or elimination of all beings: "During the moments which followed, a strange fortress [une étrange cité] rose up around Anne. It did not resemble a city. There were no houses, no palace, no constructions of any sort; it was rather an immense sea, though the waters were invisible and the shore had disappeared" (TtO, 83/TO, 93). The positing of both the city and its absence, the sea and its invisibility — a conjunction of images which recalls the uncanny imagery of Savannah-La-Mar in Thomas de Quincey's *Confessions of an English Opium Eater* — describes the movement of regression and disappearance, a movement of reverse creation and reverse revelation. This movement is described in terms which recall both the characterization of art in Levinas's "Reality and Its Shadow" (chapter 4) and the purpose of poetic language in "Literature and the Right to Death": "There is no way to express what they were, these shapes, beings, baneful entities — for us, can something which is not the day appear in the midst of the day, something which in an atmosphere of light and clarity would represent the shudder of terror which is the source of the day?" (TtO, 84/TO, 94). Blanchot refers to this as "the conditions of primal creation" (TtO, 85/TO, 96) and "bottomless valleys where the world seemed to have returned to the moment of its creation" (TtO, 84/TO, 94–95).[47]

This image of a city empty of inhabitants and structures also characterizes the space surrounding Thomas. As Anne approaches Thomas in the complex intersubjective configurations analyzed in chapters 6–8 of the story, the same set of images describes the space: "Deserted shores where deeper and deeper absences, abandoned by the eternally departed sea after a magnificent shipwreck, gradually decomposed. She passed through strange dead cities . . . she found a necropolis of movements, silences, voids" (TtO, 61/TO, 66; Bruns, *Blanchot*, 249). In the last chapter, Thomas leads through the various stages of forgetfulness a movement of return to the first night, then to the day. The same image is used, the image records not the movement of disappearance but the

movement of appearing. Aquatic themes and images now underscore the idea of futurity, and the city appears empty because it is
uncreated, not yet edified: "Where, then, was the city? Thomas, at
the heart of the agglomeration, met no one. The enormous build-
ings with their thousands of inhabitants were deserted, deprived of
that primordial inhabitant who is the architect powerfully impris-
oned in the stone. Immense unbuilt cities" (TtO, 115/TO, 133–34).
Parallel to the movement of disappearance into generality is the
gradual freeing from time "le temps, sortant de ses lacs" (TO, 94/
TtO, 84), indicating, for example "the interval of a time simulated
by the fusion of eternity and the idea of nothingness" (TtO, 84/
TO, 95).[48]

Now Blanchot creates in Anne "the paradox of the last hour" as
it is described by Levinas in *Time and the Other*[49] and defines death
as impossibility: "The doctor bent over her and thought that she
was dying according to the laws of death, not perceiving that she
had already reached that instant when, in her, the laws were dying.
She made an imperceptible motion; no one understood that she
was floundering in the instant when death, destroying everything,
might also destroy the possibility of annihilation" (TtO, 84–85/
TO, 96).[50] Yet, at this point, Anne makes one last desperate and
paradoxical gesture: "Now Anne opened her eyes. There was in
fact no more hope. The moment of supreme distraction, this trap
into which those who have nearly vanquished death fall, ultimate
return of Eurydice, in looking one last time toward the visible,
Anne had just fallen into as well. She opened her eyes without
the least curiosity, with the lassitude of someone who knows perfectly well in advance what will be offered to her sight" (TtO, 85/
TO, 97).

This paradox represents an epistemological adaptation of the
ontological paradox of death which Levinas formulates in the following succinct manner: "If you are, it is not; if it is, you are not."
On the one hand, as Anne hovers outside of life, she is now afforded
in the form of a distraction the panoptic perspective that would

allow her to grasp life in its totality, to seize objectively the meaning of life from the perspective afforded by her distance from life. Yet it is a trap since meaning can now only be seized within the space of insignificance that is claiming her: "Like every dying person, she went away observing the rituals, pardoning her enemies, loving her friends, without admitting the secret which no one admits: that all this was already insignificant" (TtO, 86/TO, 97–98). She has a momentary flash of insight and understanding which is promptly absorbed by her silence and her withdrawal from the space of intelligibility and meaning: "she knew now what she had to say to Thomas, she knew exactly the words she had searched for all her life in order to reach him. But she remained silent; she thought: what good is it — and this word was also the word she was seeking — Thomas is insignificant. Let us sleep" (TtO, 86/TO, 98). How Anne's look back can be construed as "suprême retour d'Eurydice" is not straightforward. While her movement with respect to death is analogous to Eurydice's, her "look back" is more consistent with the attitude of Orpheus since Orpheus is the one who wants to "see" the invisible (one will recall that Blanchot titles his analysis of Orpheus, "le *regard* d'Orphée"). In this scene, Anne combines elements of both Orpheus and Eurydice.

The narrative of Anne's death demonstrates and dramatizes many of the elements of Blanchot's analyses of death. Anne's words, gestures, attitudes, and demeanor embody and make manifest a relation of life and death, more specifically, a struggle to make death a possibility and the manner in which it ultimately reveals itself as impossibility. And although Anne's death is also recorded from the perspective of the world or of the day, the text chronicles her recession into a domain in which characteristics of death and life, being and nothingness, presence and absence comingle and co-mix. This space is, as previously observed, comparable to Levinas's *il y a*; it is described through such images as a world prior to creation or what remains after the world's disappearance. The chapter that follows the account of Anne's death is the longest single chapter in the story and chronicles the disruptive effects of Anne's death.

The chapter that narrates Anne's death recalls in its general themes and images, and particularly in its use of aquatic imagery, the first chapter of the narrative. Like Thomas, Anne enters the interval between life and death, being and nothingness, presence and absence, when she hovers between life and death. And, again like Thomas in the first chapter, this interval asserts the priority of a relation of these concepts over their distinction; thus, the "bottom line" of death is neither nothingness, nor absence, nor eternity but an empty, haunting indeterminacy, a generality comparable to Levinas's *il y a*.[51]

*   *   *

Death Sentence, first published in 1948, shares many structural and thematic features with *Thomas the Obscure*. As noted, the first part of *Death Sentence* reproduces in many ways and develops the account of the death of Anne in chapter 10 of *Thomas the Obscure*. The second part of *Death Sentence* mirrors the last two chapters of *Thomas the Obscure*. In both stories, the event of the death of a female companion is analyzed in minute detail. In both cases, the death is attended by the woman's mother and a character named Louise; a friend in *Thomas the Obscure* (TtO, 85/TO, 97) and the dying woman's sister in the case of *Death Sentence* (DS, 14/ AM, 26). In both cases, a substantial part of the narrative is devoted to analysis of the effects and aftereffects of the death. The character's death destabilizes the world or introduces into the world a logical complication. The general thematic movement of both narratives could be simplified as follows: the character dies, death appears, and the appearance of death marks a disruption within the world, such that death and life, being and nothingness, presence and absence now appear in a relation which is prior to their distinction. (This movement is also comparable to the thematic movement of the first chapter of *Thomas the Obscure*.) The complicated second half of *Death Sentence* takes place within such a problematic dimension. While *Thomas the Obscure* concludes with a return to the world of the day, in the conclusion of *Death Sentence* the narrator appears to be drawing another female acquaintance within this space. The perplexing "viens" with which he addresses her is addressed from a position outside of time [je dis éternellement]; it carries the mysterious weight of the "venir" or "à venir" in Levinas's formulation of death: "Death is never assumed; it comes [elle vient]."[52]

Many features also distinguish *Death Sentence* from *Thomas the Obscure*. Unlike *Thomas the Obscure, Death Sentence* is narrated in the first person and situated with respect to precise dates and specific historical events.[53] These events relate on several occasions to the narrated events, in particular to the Munich crisis of October 1938 and the bombing of Paris. Although it is far more historically precise than *Thomas the Obscure, Death Sentence* is a much sparser narrative than the former; it is an obscure, enigmatic, and lapidary story.[54]

The thematic structure of the first part of the narrative, which records the movement toward death of the narrator's companion, who is referred to only as J., again recalls the thematic movement of the legend of Orpheus. In fact, what the first part of *Death Sentence* examines and develops is called in *Thomas the Obscure*, the "suprême retour d'Eurydice" (Hillis- Miller, "Death Mask," 191, 198). The character J. appears to have died yet responding to the narrator's call makes a brief recovery before, with the narrator's assistance, taking a lethal dosage of narcotics and passing away.[55]

One feature that accounts for the particular difficulty of *Death Sentence* is its signifying in the manner of Levinas's trace or of Baudelaire's "forest of symbols." J.'s words, attitudes, expressions, and general demeanor express sometimes positively, sometimes

negatively the struggle of her agony.[56] As in Anne's case, she sometimes expresses her resistance to the "work" of death and at other
times her inexorable yielding to this work. Furthermore, her words
and expressions, like Anne's, "carry" the remoteness of their location and express certain characteristics of their provenance. Both
positively, by her words yielding to death, or negatively, by her
attempts to resist death, she expresses and makes appear the work
of death.

In all likelihood, J. is dying of consumption. On a simple, physical level, the struggle of life and of death within her takes the concrete form of her fighting for breath. Her breathing becomes
manifest, audibly and concretely through its negation, interruption,
and hindrance by violent fits of coughing, gagging, and choking.
The alteration of her voice or the unusual inflection of her words
(DS, 21/AM, 37), the "weak cry" (DS, 20/AM, 36) which she makes
as she seems to awaken from death, and, ultimately, her death rattle
(DS, 28/AM, 49) and the "rasping breath of her" (DS, 29/AM, 50)
become the first positive manifestation of the work of death. Thus,
these sounds represent her increasing inability to perform the basic
biological function of life and are the positive form of death, the
appearance of death in her. As J.'s condition worsens and appears
hopeless, her mouth no longer seems to belong to her: "that mouth
open to the noise of agony, did not seem to belong to her, it seemed
to be the mouth of someone I didn't know, someone irredeemably
condemned, or even dead" (DS, 28/AM, 49). As J. recedes and
"passes away" what appears in her place is an "other" ("la bouche
d'une autre").[57]

Her words, often perplexing or meaningless in themselves, indicate her fluctuation between life and death, and reveal her "coordinates." Indeed, it is as if, like in Baudelaire's "Correspondances,"
death emits through J. various signals, some decipherable — if not
completely intelligible — others not. J. expresses, for example, her
temporal and spatial remoteness from the world of the narrator.
Thus, as she emerges from her initial lapse into death, her first

impulse is to seek to restore the parameters of time, to articulate the present with a past. With a certain anguish in her voice, she asks the narrator, "How long have you been here?" (DS, 20/AM, 37). She also indicates that she has no recollection of the events of the night. "I asked her what those interesting things were that she had said she would talk to me about on my return. Then she had a sort of fit of absent-mindedness and distantly answered: 'Yes, when you come back I'll talk to you about it'" (DS, 22–23/AM, 40). Like the disjunction experienced by Thomas in the first chapter of *Thomas the Obscure*, J. experiences a temporal lag or delay in relation to the narrator ("à votre retour je vous en parlerai"), while the narrator expresses her delay spatially, "elle répondit d'un peu loin."

In the same scene, the narrator observes that prior to regaining consciousness, J. appears to have opened her eyes onto a horrifying scene which, while it is instantly forgotten as J. returns to consciousness "perfectly natural, gay and almost recovered" (DS, 20/AM, 36), is then partially remembered, or rather, at the limit of recollection — about to be recalled. J. then experiences the apprehension that the narrator himself is a link to this awareness prior to consciousness, to this immemorial past: "But I think I was also struck by [the voice's] uneasy inflection: as she asked me how long I had been there, it seemed to me she was remembering something, or that she was close to remembering it, and that at the same time she felt an apprehension that was linked to me, or my coming too late, or the fact that I had seen and taken by surprise something I shouldn't have seen" (DS, 21/AM, 37). Her question and the anguish in it manifest an attempt to establish a path for consciousness back to what precedes it: an attempt to secure and ground the present. Hence, for J., the narrator's presence could both involve seeing what should not have been seen and being too late to see anything at all. Then, in a reversal of this situation, the fact that the following night the narrator does not leave her side, begins to clarify for J. the events of the previous night. She begins to "know," "discover," and "learn of" the events of the previous night: "'Why, she said coldly, 'are you staying *precisely* tonight?' I suppose she was beginning to know as much as I did about the events of the early morning, but at that moment I was frightened at the thought that she might discover what had happened to her; it seemed to me that would be absolutely terrifying for anyone to learn who was naturally afraid of the night" (DS, 24/AM, 42). J.'s movement toward death suggests a regression into generality and abstraction or, more specifically, a conjunction of the concrete and the abstract. Like the character Anne in *Thomas the Obscure*, J. becomes, from the narrator's point of view, statuesque; her immobility is that of a "recumbent effigy and not of a living being. . . . She who had been absolutely alive was already no more than a statue" (DS, 19–20/ AM, 35). On the other hand, what J. perceives is a movement toward abstraction comparable to the "foundering" into the image that will be examined more fully in chapter 4. Contemplating a bouquet of flowers brought to her by the narrator, she expresses both their spatial disjunction — they appear to be moving around her room — and an absence of particularity that can only be understood as a movement toward abstraction in her characterization of a "perfect rose" or "une rose par excellence" (DS, 24–25/AM, 43–44; Londyn, *Maurice Blanchot romancier*, 41, 51).

The indication of a "rose par excellence" signals J.'s location at this juncture within a sphere of abstraction and generality. At various moments of her movement toward this sphere her hands manifest a convulsive, paroxysmal struggle (DS, 20/AM, 35), and she clutches desperately at the narrator's hand (DS, 23, 26, 30/AM, 41, 46, 51); however, in this same movement she does not tolerate human contact. Repeating Christ's phrase to Mary Magdalene on his emergence from the grave, *noli me tangere*, she rudely rebuffs the narrator's attempt to comfort her. This incident, presumably reported to the doctor by the nurse, is doubtless what occasions his exclamation "Oh, good heavens" ("Ah! par exemple") (DS, 26/ AM, 46). (The doctor is a believer and displays in his office a reproduction of the shroud of Turin in which he discerns Veronica's likeness behind that of Christ [DS, 9/AM, 19; Madaule, *Une Tâche sérieuse?* 95; Hill, *Blanchot*, 153]).

This play of abstraction and concreteness, presence and absence, indicates a relation of being and nothingness that is prior to their distinction and informs many of the most perplexing elements of the story. In the second part, other characters will be alternately apprehended either as statuesque (DS, 38, 69/AM, 65, 111) or abstract, usually in the form of a *pensée* (DS, 32, 39, 60, 68/AM, 55, 67, 98, 109). The perplexing leitmotiv of the handprint, one of the elements that concretely links the two parts of the story, gives form to the relation of abstraction and concreteness which produces the image (chapter 4). The handprint and the mortuary mask in the case of Nathalie represent an attempt to fix the invisible element; it secures the "empreinte" thus making the element appear in its solidity and positivity. It is, of course, an image of the face and of the hands, like the Shroud or like Veronica's cloth. But it is also the positive form of the relation of being and nothingness; it fixes the image, giving form to the collapse into image and abstraction. The print makes solid the element in which one exists and holds one's individual shape within it. In effect then, the handprint is the opposite of the "rose par excellence." While the rose collapses into abstraction, leaving behind an alluring, perfect-looking image, bereft of the imperfections of concreteness and particularity, the print anticipates this movement and attempts to negate it. It represents an attempt to forestall the collapse into impersonality, generality, anonymity and neutrality. (The print is obviously related to both particularity and specificity of the person. It is made all the more so since the print of J.'s hand is taken by the narrator to a chiromancer in order to have its lines read [DS, 10/AM, 21].)

Within this dimension of abstraction and generality, suggested by the indication of a "rose par excellence," J. now enters a state of semi-conscious, wakeful vigilance comparable to the "impersonal vigilance" which Levinas ascribes to the subject in relation to the *il y a* (EE, 60/DEE, 98). Though she appears to be sleeping, in fact she has an acute awareness and perception of what surrounds her, even of that which is not manifest. Thus, she appears to awaken abruptly to comment somewhat coldly on the narrator's whispered conversation with the nurse then to lapse back into her apparent slumber. "When the nurse came to talk to me — in a low voice and about nothing important — J. immediately awoke and said in a cold way, 'I have my secrets with her too.' She went back to sleep at once" (DS, 26/AM, 46). Then, demonstrating an intimate understanding of the narrator's innermost anguish about his miraculous calling of J. back to life, she again awakens, looks at the narrator and gives expression to his feelings and his thoughts: "[J.'s look] seemed to understand me profoundly: that is why I found it friendly, though it was at the same time terribly sad. 'Well,' she said, 'you've made a fine mess of things'" (DS, 27/AM, 47). And although she appeared unconscious when her nurse enquired about giving her a shot, she shows that she was aware of the particular enquiry when she awakens subsequently and answers her. It is in this state of neutral vigilance that J. points to the narrator while telling her nurse "Now then, take a good look at death" (DS, 28/AM, 48). This may suggest the narrator's imminent role in administering the lethal dose of narcotics in a shot, or it may designate a broad and general involvement of the narrator with death, in which the narrator is comparable to Thomas.[58]

At this juncture, Blanchot examines J.'s temporal location in more detail and provides one of his most succinct commentaries on impatience.[59] In her initial movement toward death, J.'s temporal attitude was that of awaiting:[60] "she would die, she was almost dead, the wait had not begun at that moment; at that moment it had come to an end; or rather the last wait had gone on nearly the duration of the telephone call" (DS, 19/AM, 34). While earlier in the narrative it is principally J.'s mother who experiences impatience in J.'s presence (DS, 8/AM, 17–18), it is now J. herself who feels pressed for time:

> Extreme impatience rose from her whole being. If at first I was a little hurt by her coldness towards me, that did not last; I sensed too clearly the reason for that impatience, for that fever, for the surging of all her strength; I saw how, by a quicker movement than anything we could do, she kept one step ahead of the blows that were trying to do away with her. We were all very slow creatures and she needed to move like lightning to save her last breath, to escape the final immobility. (DS, 29/AM, 51)

It is as if each temporal unit is undergoing linear distortion such that it cannot pass sequentially into the subsequent unit. This collapse of the moment into an absence of time is made manifest by J.'s reaction to it; her impatience with the apparent slowness of those around her.

Here, as elsewhere and particularly in his analysis of the myth of Orpheus, Blanchot's narrative suggests that impatience manifests an attempt to restore temporal intervals, boundaries, and limits on an absence of time, on what Blanchot will call elsewhere, the interminable and the incessant. Waiting and impatience correspond to two characteristics of the same principle: a relation of linear time, structured in units and intervals, and the absence of time. Waiting corresponds to the distortion or stretching of the moment, the fracturing or collapse of the present into a moment that will not and cannot pass; this is the futurity that Levinas describes as the time of dying, the *entretemps*, the temporality expressed by statues and by plastic art and which will be considered more fully in chapter 4. Impatience, on the other hand, manifests an attempt to negate or control this collapse by structuring the interminable, by seeking to restore temporal parameters where they have dissipated.

J.'s impatience will express itself in her final request: "*Immediately* afterwards she said to me in a low and *rapid* voice: '*Quick*, a shot'" (DS, 30/AM, 51–52, my emphasis). The lethal dose of narcotics administered by the narrator in response to this request allows J. to die in the day. Her death marks a break in the narrative, an interruption, a gap. But it is not an end of the narrative nor is it a moment of "truth." Indeed, the second part of the narrative, which — like chapter 11 of *Thomas the Obscure* — chronicles the effects of J.'s death, begins by marking emphatically the themes of error, silence, and forgetfulness.

Even more clearly and more emphatically than in *Thomas the Obscure, Death Sentence* formulates a temporary suspension of death, an "arrêt de mort" which affords a glimpse at its work. In his analysis of the *il y a*, Levinas employs the image of reverse creation and formulates a subject in a hypostasis. He calls the present the act of emergence from the *il y a* and the constitution of the self in this emergence.[61] This positioning involves a paradoxical temporality, a moment in which, positioning itself out of nothing, the present must precede itself. Levinas uses the word "arrêt" to characterize this movement: "The 'halt' of the present [L''arrêt' du présent] is the very effort of taking a position, in which the present joins with itself and takes itself up [se rejoint et s'assume]" (EE, 80/DEE, 137). All of these elements can be located in Blanchot's *Death Sentence*. As in the case of the character Anne, J.'s gradual lapse into death characterizes a movement of reverse creation, a gradual movement toward nothingness and toward the absence of time. This nothingness, however, like Levinas's *il y a*, reveals itself to be more than nothingness. In it appears an impossibility of nothingness, a perpetuity of dying, and J. both experiences and demonstrates the experience of its generality, its horror, its absence of temporal parameters, and its vigilance outside of time. Like the event of Levinas's hypostasis, J. temporarily emerges from this generality, anonymity, and neutrality. In her brief "return" to life, she positions herself as a hypostasis and a subject; she is "the subject that pulls itself up [s'arrache] from the anonymous vigilance of the *there is*" (EE, 82/DEE 140). This action too is an "arrêt," the temporary interruption, the brief arresting of death, which, almost in the manner of an optical instrument, affords a look at its work.

The theme of the suspension of death and of the suspension of the instant of death is central to the narrative published recently by Blanchot and alluded to at the beginning of this chapter. Indeed, in a play on the word "instant" in his title and the expression "en instance," Blanchot concludes the short narrative effecting the change from the instant of his death to the "unfinished business" of his death: "What remains is only the feeling of lightness which is death itself or, more precisely, the instant of my death, henceforth indefinitely suspended [Seul demeure le sentiment de légerté qui est la mort même ou, pour le dire plus précisément, l'instant de ma mort désormais toujours en instance]" (IM, 20).[62] It is interesting that this short narrative — which mentions Hegel and decries the injustice in the execution of young peasants in his locality when, as in the case of the narrator of *The Instant of My Death*, "The Lords had been spared" (IM, 15) — has none of the triumphant quality of Hegel's slave having trembled before the "absolute master" and through this having attained a higher level of consciousness. In the second half of *Death Sentence*, Blanchot returns to Hegel's phrase from the preface of the *Phenomenology* and conspicuously inserts the word "falsehood" [mensonge]. ("Because that life transforms the life which shrinks away from it into a falsehood. [Car cette vie transforme en mensonge la vie qui a reculé devant elle]" [AM, 108/DS, 67]). Similarly, Blanchot's short narrative invokes Hegel in order to mark again, explicitly or implicitly, Blanchot's rejection of Hegel's thematization of death. There is no superior understanding, only the sense of "unfinished business." The instant is inhabited by an "instance" and an inexplicable sensation of lightness recalled years later. The "moment of truth" is not a moment of truth.

THREE

Two Stories of the Encounter: Orpheus and Ulysses

The previous chapter focused on the question of death as a relation with an ungraspable otherness. Its relation to the question of the artwork can be assessed through consideration of Blanchot's readings of the myths of Orpheus and Ulysses, two narratives recording "close encounters with death" as Gregg puts it (*Maurice Blanchot*, 46). In the encounter that no one may survive or the descent from which no one may return, Ulysses appears to succeed where Orpheus appears to fail. Had Orpheus devised a more clever subterfuge to recover Eurydice, had he engineered a strategy such as that of Perseus to see what cannot be seen or that of Ulysses to hear what cannot be heard, his adventure might have been very different. Because the trajectories in these encounters are both parallel and opposite, consideration of both stories affords a concise assessment of how stories involving death relate to the problem of the artwork.[1] Both of these stories also afford a clear view of Blanchot's particularly creative logic, and of the confluence of his thought with that of Levinas, for both Orpheus's failure and Ulysses's success have another overlooked dimension.[2]

Orpheus and Inspiration

The reworking of the story of Orpheus is one of Blanchot's most original, elegant, and subtle demonstrations. This short essay is for Blanchot the central concern of *The Space of Literature*.[3] In it, Blanchot analyzes the nature, source, and origin of artistic inspiration; typically, as he does so, all of these notions undergo substantial revision.

Conventionally, literary or artistic inspiration is articulated as a relation with alterity in the form of another being, a muse, whose voice invests the artist in the second of the two meanings of "parole soufflée" that Derrida explores in his analysis of Artaud (*L'Ecriture et la différence*, 262; Libertson, *Proximity*, 142–43). This configuration involves two related but distinct dimensions of inspiration: the otherness of the muse herself and the attitude of passivity of the artist who receives the inspired idea, message, or wisdom. The notion of art as initiative, activity, and power is thus removed from the domain of the artist, whose role is passive and whose control is solely technical, and restored at the level of the muse herself. In other words, the predicates of power are conserved but situated within the alterity of the muse; otherness is thus still construed as another *power*.[4]

Blanchot's analysis of the story of Orpheus addresses this model indirectly, answering the questions: How does one find literary inspiration? What is the origin of literary inspiration? (More simply, when or under what conditions does inspiration occur?) The responses to these questions will take the form of a dense, multifaceted complex, and remarkably elegant model.

The elements of the story of Orpheus that interest Blanchot are part of the central episode recounted in Virgil's *Georgics*, to wit, the failed attempt to retrieve Eurydice from the underworld. In characteristic fashion, Blanchot tells the story following the traditional sequence of events, then retells it according to a second, far less conventional logic, and then interprets it according to the essential ambiguity revealed in the two tellings. As in "Literature and the Right to Death" and elsewhere, this pattern is comparable to what one might call a reverse dialectic.

The first, conventional version of Orpheus's story is the story of a tragic failure. Orpheus conceives a plan to recover Eurydice from Hades; he devises a strategy and agrees to certain mandatory procedures, that is the injunction not to turn around and look at Eurydice until he has returned with her to the light of the day and the world. At the level of the plan, the strategy is sound enough and not particularly complex. Yet in the execution of the plan, something goes wrong and Orpheus fails. He fails first because he has forgotten the procedures. This forgetfulness is accounted for first in terms of desire (he wishes to see Eurydice) and second, impatience (he does not wait until the appropriate time — the definitive exit from the underworld — to look at her). Both this desire and his impatience are related to an uncharacteristic carelessness on the part of Orpheus, an insouciance, as Blanchot puts it.

In the retelling of a story according to a second set of less obvious criteria, Blanchot most commonly identifies the apparently negative factors of the initial version, grounds their positivity, accounts for them in a fuller manner, and establishes their necessity. Thus, the retelling of the story of Orpheus highlights, among other factors, Orpheus's forgetfulness, his impatience, and his carelessness.

Initially, Blanchot will probe both the apparent and hidden meanings of this forgetfulness. Although forgetfulness is one of Blanchot's densest concepts (since it is the positive form of recollection that we have of the other),[5] Orpheus's forgetting functions rather simply here. Orpheus forgets his initial goal, what Blanchot calls his "oeuvre," because in the course of his mission of recovery, it has been preempted by a second, forbidden imperative to see Eurydice. This secondary motivation ultimately preempts Orpheus's mission and undermines his strategy of recovery. This is how Blanchot puts it:

> But if he did not turn around to look at Eurydice, he still would be betraying, being disloyal to, the boundless and imprudent force of his impulse, which does not demand Eurydice in her diurnal truth and her everyday charm, but in her nocturnal darkness, in her distance, her body closed, her face sealed, which wants to see her not when she is visible, but when she is invisible, and not as the intimacy of a familiar life, but as the strangeness of that which excludes all intimacy; it does not want to make her live, but to have the fullness of her death living in her. (GO, 100/SL, 172/EL, 228)

Blanchot further develops the necessity of Orpheus's forgetting, explaining that "Orpheus forgets the work he has to accomplish, and he has to forget it, because the ultimate requirement of his impulse is not that there should be a work, but that someone should stand and face this 'point' and grasp its essence where this essence appears, where it is essential and essentially appearance: in the heart of the night" (GO, 99/SL, 171/EL, 227–28). Forgetting, then, is the positive form of experiencing the second motivation.

Several modifications have occurred. First, the goal of Eurydice's recovery has been replaced by the exigency of the journey itself; hence, there is effected a reversal of end and means. This reversal suggests, as Blanchot makes very clear, that along with the recovery of Eurydice, what Orpheus seeks, and perhaps seeks principally, is the forbidden knowledge of death. To see Eurydice not in the "diurnal truth" but in her "nocturnal darkness" is to seek an understanding (seeing) of death in its otherness.[6]

From the perspective of his initial plan and strategy (the perspective of the day), Orpheus's failure is evaluated according to two factors: first, in terms of its inevitability (since the descent itself is transgressive), and second, in terms of the impatience that (motivated by his desire) has undermined his mission.

The day first condemns the mission itself. According to this logic, since the descent to Hades is in itself transgressive, looking at

Eurydice is inevitable. In other words, the principle of Orpheus's entire undertaking is madness, motivated by an essential lack of measure. The project itself thus undergoes an *ex post facto* revision according to the law of the day that now second-guesses it, condemns it as folly, and assesses that it had to fail from the outset. The temporal occurrence, the "event" of Orpheus's actual turning and looking is, itself, revised: "It is inevitable that Orpheus defy the law forbidding him to 'turn around,' because he has already violated it the moment he takes his first step towards the shadows. This observation makes us sense that Orpheus has actually been turned towards Eurydice all along" (GO, 100/SL, 172/EL, 229).

Now the day appears to reverse itself and makes a second, apparently contradictory judgment. It assigns the blame instead to Orpheus's impatience: "Passing judgment on what Orpheus undertakes to do, the day also reproaches him for having shown impatience" (GO, 100/SL, 173/EL, 229). Blanchot's analysis of Orpheus's impatience is tricky and has confounded many of his commentators.[7] The problem is twofold: first, midway through the analysis, Blanchot effects an important but easily missed transition from the logic of the day to the logic of the work such that Orpheus's impatience, labeled a mistake in the first context is ultimately acknowledged as a "correct impulse" within the second. Second, the revision of the concept of impatience occurs prior to Blanchot developing an interpretive context (the logic of the work) in which this revision is intelligible. (He does this subsequently in a section of the essay entitled "Inspiration.")

According to the logic of his plan (of the "day"), Orpheus failed in the temporal dimension of its execution. He would not wait until he had exited the underworld to turn around and look at Eurydice. The progress out of the depths of the underworld was too slow for him. Hence, the failure is attributable to his impatience. Orpheus experiences this as an inadequacy and atones for it as a fault (his carelessness). But why could Orpheus not wait? The initial explanation of Orpheus's desire is now supplemented by a second one.

The experience of the underworld, the experience of the approach of death is an experience of time's absence.[8] Initially at least, impatience is the impulse to restore temporal parameters where they do not exist; patience, in this context, is a ruse which successfully secures timelessness by reestablishing, through technical means, some sort of temporal measure: "Impatience is the mistake made by a person who wishes to escape the absence of time; patience is the trick that tries to master this absence of time by turning it into another kind of time, measured in a different way" (GO, 101/SL, 173/EL, 230). Patience, in this analysis, is thus analogous to the successful ruse devised by Ulysses who succeeds (initially at least) at the very point where Orpheus has failed.

How, then, is the impatience to be understood as a "correct impulse"? As noted above, the context within which the following is clearest is only developed in the subsequent section of Blanchot's essay where the positivity of inspiration is established. The revision of impatience is an excellent example of the nondialectical logic that Blanchot frequently employs.[9] The impatience that is initially the fatal flaw in the execution of Orpheus's strategy, and is thematized in opposition to the patience that would have expressed itself in a technical solution to master the absence of time, becomes precisely what gives Orpheus access to a more authentic or truer form of patience: "[T]rue patience does not exclude impatience; it is the heart of impatience, it is impatience endlessly suffered and endured."

Impatience is the positive form in which Orpheus has experienced the approach of death in its temporality (or lack of temporality since it is the absence of time). By motivating his transgressive gaze, it has allowed Orpheus to see death's approach in the form of Eurydice's disappearance. Orpheus's impatience occasioned this encounter to the extent that his mission to recover Eurydice was at the outset doubled by "this one concern: to look into the night at what the night is concealing — the other night, concealment which becomes visible" (GO, 100/SL, 172/EL, 229). Finally, this

impatience leads Orpheus to true patience, the patience of enduring endlessly the loss of Eurydice. (True patience is thus not a higher
form of patience which through opposition and synthesis sublates
impatience; true patience must instead be understood as an involvement of patience with impatience that is prior to the opposition of
the two.)[10]

To this point, Blanchot's course in the essay has been to highlight the reasons for Orpheus's failure, then to show that, far from
being accidental or incidental, this failure actually occurs in accordance with a necessity dictated by what he calls the logic of the
work: "Orpheus . . . forgets the work he is to achieve, and he forgets it *necessarily*" (my emphasis, SL, 171/GO, 99/EL, 228). The
various consequences of Orpheus's gaze are also necessary: "this
desire, and Eurydice lost, and Orpheus scattered are necessary to
the song, just as the ordeal of eternal worklessness ("désoeuvre-
ment") is necessary to the work" (GO, 101/SL, 173/EL, 230).

The lengthy analysis of inspiration that follows revises Orpheus's
failure and defines inspiration through it, formulating the positivity of Orpheus's quest as evoked by the concept of impatience:

> And everything happens as if, by disobeying the law, by looking at
> Eurydice, Orpheus was only yielding to the profound demands of
> the work, as though, through this inspired gesture, he really had
> carried the dark shade out of Hell, as though he had unknowingly
> brought it back into the broad daylight of the work.
>
> To look at Eurydice without concern for the song, in the impa-
> tience and imprudence of a desire which forgets the law — this is
> *inspiration*. Does this mean that inspiration changes the beauty of
> the night into the unreality of the void, makes Eurydice into a shade
> and Orpheus into someone infinitely dead? Does this mean that
> inspiration is therefore that problematic moment when the essence
> of the night becomes something inessential and the welcoming
> intimacy of the first night becomes the deceptive trap of the *other*
> night? This is exactly the way it is. All we can sense of inspiration
> is its failure, all we can recognize of it is its misguided violence.
> But if inspiration means that Orpheus fails and Eurydice is lost

twice over, if it means the insignificance and void of the night, it also turns Orpheus towards that failure and that insignificance and coerces him, by an irresistible impulse, as though giving up failure were much more serious than giving up success, as though what we call the insignificant, the inessential, the mistaken, could reveal itself — to someone who accepted the risk and freely gave himself up to it — as the source of all authenticity. (GO, 101–2/SL, 173–74/EL, 230–31)

The difficulty of the preceding paragraphs resides in what Blanchot mentions only briefly, almost in passing. (Again, the non- or reverse dialectical pattern, in the involvement of failure and authenticity is palpable here.) The emphasis is now on the positivity of Orpheus's experience. The gaze — originating in impatience, forgetfulness, carelessness — occurred in accordance with a second imperative unknown to Orpheus, the nocturnal contemplation of Eurydice. But what actually happened is more complicated. There was first the motivation for the gaze which was impatience, second, the gaze itself in which, expecting to see Eurydice in her nocturnal otherness, Orpheus saw only her disappearance. This disappearance is immediately interpreted by Orpheus as the failure of the mission of recovery. However, the disappearance of Eurydice into the void is ultimately, though still unbeknownst to Orpheus, the very "truth" of the nocturnal encounter that he was seeking. It is in this way that, as Blanchot puts it, "through the inspired gesture, he really had carried the dark shade out of Hell, as though he had unknowingly brought it back into the broad daylight of the work."

It thus becomes clear why Blanchot revises the negative elements of the initial strategy so as to account for their necessity; the factors that are both causes and effects of the failure of the initial plan represent the positive form of the second imperative's accomplishment. Inspiration's positive form, generally speaking, is that of a *necessary failure.*[11]

Used to define inspiration, Blanchot's rethinking of Orpheus's adventure situates the artist's work outside of and beyond the artist's power and initiative. We readily and intuitively accept the notion that the work of art always somehow (but can we really explain how?) exceeds the artist's purposes, intentions, and plans. Blanchot's Orpheus provides a model for how this happens. The artist's power, initiative, and mastery are confidently directed toward a specific purpose, goal, or aim. Yet, the artist reaches a point at which that aim is lost, the purpose lost sight of, the goal betrayed. He loses his bearings and fails to accomplish what he has set out to accomplish. He experiences this as failure and atones for it as such, yet it is through this failure that the artist is put in touch with the authentic "event" of inspiration, a purpose that was unknown to him as he set out. Through the failure that is inspiration, he has accomplished something that is beyond his ability to conceive, plan, and execute.

Inspiration and the Trace

Artistic inspiration as a consequence of failure, as an accomplishment which exceeds one's powers of conception, planning, and execution recalls the early elaboration of one of Levinas's richest concepts, the trace. In the essay "L'Ontologie est-elle fondamentale?" Levinas thematizes the trace in response to the existentialist philosophers' equation of action and responsibility. The trace suggests a responsibility that exceeds intentionality: "The act was not pure; I left traces. Wiping away these traces, I left others. . . . Thus we are responsible beyond our intentions. . . . That is to say that our consciousness, and our mastery of reality through consciousness, do not exhaust our relationship with reality, in which we are present with all the density of our being" (en, 3–4/EN, 14–15/II, 124). The subsequent essay "The Trace of the Other," gives much fuller development to the notion of trace. In distinguishing the trace from the sign (although he points out that a trace is also a sign) Levinas writes,

> But when a trace is thus taken as a sign, it is exceptional with respect to other signs in that it signifies outside of every intention of signaling and outside of every project of which it would be the aim. When in transactions one "pays by check" so that there will be a trace of the payment, the trace is inscribed in the very order of the world. But a trace in the strict sense disturbs the order of the world. It occurs by overprinting. Its original signifyingness is sketched out in, for example, the fingerprints left by someone who wanted to wipe away his traces and commit a perfect crime. He who left traces in wiping away his traces did not mean to say or do anything by the traces he left. (DC, 356–57/EDE, 199–200/CPP, 104)

Levinas goes on to characterize the trace, the trace's "divinity," and its resistance to conventional phenomenological categories. The trace is one of the modes of "presence" of the other. Levinas also characterizes the trace as the paradoxical presence of a movement which is the passage into a remote past of that which was never present:[12] "A trace is a presence of that which properly speaking has never been there, of what is always past" (DC, 358/EDE, 201/CPP 105).

The obvious pertinence of the structure of the trace to Blanchot's analysis of Orpheus resides in the trace's absolute excess. In this lies the main difference between the sign — always the expression of an intention even if unplanned, ill-conceived, or poorly executed — and the trace, understood as that mark left by the one who has attempted to cover his tracks. The trace, while a positive presence, a concrete event or mark, thus easily mistaken for a sign and an accomplishment, remains wholly outside of the intentions, desires, plans, and power of its author. Its author, in a pun that Blanchot will frequently employ, has no authority over the trace. The structure of the trace, so described, accomplishes the same purpose as Blanchot's narrative of Orpheus's inspired gaze; it situates the trace, like inspiration, radically beyond the artist's dominion of power and control. In this sense, the artist's inspired work is always in the form of a trace.

Curiously, in this essay Blanchot evokes the relevance of his analysis to works of art only in terms of the artistic masterpiece's retaining a vestige of the Orphic encounter, a vestige whose form is precisely that of the trace: "As we look at the most certain masterpiece, whose beginning dazzles us with its brilliance and decisiveness, we find that we are also faced with something which is fading away, a work that has suddenly become visible again, is no longer there, and has never been there. This sudden eclipse is the distant memory of Orpheus's gaze, it is a nostalgic return to the uncertainty of the origin" (GO, 103/SL, 174/EL, 232). What Blanchot characterizes in the form of the trace, "something" which without having ever assumed the form of visibility, is receding from view like a "sudden eclipse," is precisely — although Blanchot tells us only indirectly, metaphorically — the moment at which the work has escaped its author's intentions. It is the moment at which, against the background of the work's technical brilliance, evidence of its author's confident mastery and "decisiveness," something else is introduced into the work, something whose appearance is furtive yet refers us to the work's "origin" in uncertainty and inspiration.

This model of inspiration, like Levinas's trace, both accounts for the work's positivity, its appearance within the economy of the real, and attests the artwork's essential relation to and investment by something that radically exceeds this economy. The artwork itself is thus also evidence, a testimonial, a trace of alterity. Although neither Levinas's nor Blanchot's models are wholly new, both are remarkably ingenious. Through the single, simple actions they describe and analyze, they account for the domain of power, effectivity, control, and intentionality which always asserts its pre-eminence. Yet both locate the "origin" of the work of art or the trace, the origin of inspiration, at the point where the limits of this domain are reached. At this point, a second, no less real but far more problematic and elusive dimension of experience, whose principle is not power, emerges. Hence the work of art is situated within an economy of power and yet is always irreducible to that economy.

Baudelaire's prose poem "The Artist's *Confiteor*" formulates a comparable model of the work of art's origin. The poem begins with a lengthy thematization of a complex structure of subjectivity accounting for the subject's involvement with and susceptibility to the exterior (in this particular poem, various manifestations of nature). This account is achieved metaphorically: the subject is alternately penetrated by the exterior and overflowing the boundaries of the self into the outside: "all these things think through me, or I think through them" (*Parisian Prowler*, 4/*Oeuvres complètes*, 278). While this structure of subjectivity is congruent with models in both Bataille and Blanchot, it is the poem's conclusion that is of particular interest here: "Studying the beautiful is a duel in which the artist shrieks with fright [crie de frayeur] before being defeated" (*Parisian Prowler*, 4/*Oeuvres complètes*, 278–79). In as much as one can identify the artwork with this shriek or "cri," this model also, situates the work within an economy of power and control (a duel), yet locates the authentic artistic "event" at the moment when the limits of this economy are reached. Like Levinas's trace and Orpheus's inspired, careless gaze, his necessary failure, Baudelaire's scenario accounts for the positivity, the empirical existence of the artwork at the same time that it locates it beyond any intentionality of conception, planning, purpose, power, or execution.

If the initial analyses of "The Gaze of Orpheus" appear to correspond to some of Levinas's concepts, the penultimate section of Blanchot's essay recasts many elements of the story in Bataillian terms. In light of this section and in light of the analysis of the necessity of Orpheus's gaze, the relatively minor importance accorded in Blanchot's analysis to the concepts of prohibition and transgression as Bataille has defined them is striking; indeed, initially at least, Blanchot characterizes Orpheus's gaze more in terms of betrayal than in terms of transgression. Now, however, in the section "Gift and Sacrifice," Blanchot formulates the principal elements of the story of Orpheus in explicitly Bataillian terms of expenditure, loss, the sacred, the profane, prohibition, transgression, and sacrifice. This interpretation has been emphasized by Libertson and following Libertson by several of Blanchot's commentators. The logic of prohibition and transgression elaborated by Bataille in his study *L'Erotisme* provides one of the most succinct examples of the relation of difference. Considered in Bataille's terms, the night that contains Eurydice is the sacred night that can yield to the power of the song; Orpheus's gaze is the transgression that is also a gift and a "perte sans profit."[13]

Blanchot's Conclusion

Blanchot's essay ends with a short but difficult paragraph that explicitly grounds the origin of writing in inspiration. He tells us that writing begins with the gaze of Orpheus and recalls both the motivations and consequences of the gaze. Only through this inspired, desiring, but insouciant gaze can one reach the origin of the artwork (in inspiration), that which consecrates the song. Then Blanchot introduces a temporal complication. In order to arrive at the moment at which he would turn toward Eurydice (the moment that is the origin of art), he needed to already possess art; put in terms of Orpheus's song, to arrive at the origin of the song, he needed to already possess the song. Blanchot immediately translates this paradox, and, uncharacteristically, tells his reader quite explicitly what it means in terms of writing: "This means: one can only write if one arrives at the instant towards which one can only move through space opened up by the movement of writing. In order to write one must already be writing" (GO, 104/SL, 176/EL, 234).

Blanchot presents here a complicated temporal structure related to art. The song and the loss of Eurydice are two events which logically must have preceded each other. The unique event of the origin is composed of two moments or events, the two moments of the Orphic adventure, which cannot be placed in chronological order since each must precede the other logically and chronologically; writing's origin is thus an impossible origin, a moment which must always precede itself. Stated more concretely, writing must occur prior to the point at which writing might begin and conversely, writing can begin only if and when it is preceded by writing.

Blanchot's analysis of Orpheus thus here demonstrates its own internal logic. We may ask, "What is the origin of artistic inspiration?" yet, as we seek to answer it, we find that it undergoes an important revision, that the tools that we employ to clarify this question — such concepts as logical and chronological originarity — are modified. Why and according to what principle does this modification occur?

In "Literature and the Right to Death" Blanchot has thematized this problem by way of Hegel: "From his very first step, Hegel virtually says, a person who wishes to write is stopped by a contradiction: in order to write, he must have the talent to write. But gifts, in themselves, are nothing. As long as he has not yet sat down at his table and written a work, the writer is not a writer and does not know if he has the capacity to become one. He has no talent until he has written, but he needs talent in order to write" (GO, 23/ WF, 302–3/PF, 295).

Blanchot is referring to, and rewriting ("Hegel virtually says, [Hegel dit à peu près]"), a passage from the *Phenomenology* in which Hegel fleshes out the internal contradiction in the notion of the beginning of an action or work: "The individual who is going to act seems, therefore, to find himself in a circle in which each moment already presupposes the other, and thus he seems unable to find a beginning" (PS, 240/PEI, 327–28). In "Literature and the Right to Death," Blanchot appears to accept Hegel's resolution of this contradiction, as explained here by Hippolyte: "But this is circular only in theory, not in actual action. If 'action is the development of spirit as consciousness' (PE, I, 327; PG, 287; PM, 422), all the moments interpenetrate and, properly speaking, action has no beginning." (*Genesis and Structure*, 303/*Genèse et structure*, 293). In the case of the literary work, Blanchot will introduce a modest but significant adjustment whose purpose is to challenge the progressive, organic development of consciousness through the work: Blanchot notes that "the same is true for each new work, because everything begins again from nothing" (GO, 24/WF, 303/PF, 296).

If in "Literature and the Right to Death" the circularity of the origin is implicitly dismissed as a purely theoretical problem (as characterized by Hippolyte), this theoretical problem returns most insistently to conclude the analysis of "The Gaze of Orpheus." Indeed, the operation of consciousness through action and the work is an excellent example of a finely tuned dialectic, not hindered by the apparent logical circularity of its initial moment. Blanchot introduces to the notion of origin a constitution through difference. The "moment" as such is a compound or composite, and the two elements that Blanchot has identified as its constitutive moments must be understood in a relation that is prior to their distinction hence the impossibility of according to either priority over the other. Articulating the origin of writing according to the concept of difference is characterized by Blanchot as a "leap" which, like the leap of suicide (SL, 104/EL, 127), is comparable and parallel to the spring or leap (*Satz*) out of representational thinking that Heidegger articulates in his analysis of identity in terms of prior relation. But it also suggests the association of originarity and leap that Heidegger analyzes in the word *Ursprung* in his essay "The Origin of the Work of Art" (*Der Ursprung des Kunstwerkes*). While the references to other authors are more subtle than in essays like "Literature and the Right to Death," clearly Hegel and Levinas are present in Blanchot's model, contributing both positive and negative elements to it. Blanchot's essay weaves an intricate pattern, constructs a complex, multidimensional model of artistic inspiration, the "origin" of the work of art.

Inspiration, like death, is ultimately a relation with otherness. Unlike the relation with the alterity of death, however, we survive the experience of inspiration and construct a testimonial of the experience in the form of the work.[14] This much is generally attested, as observed initially, in the classical model involving the muse. In addition, inspiration is an encounter that cannot be planned or arranged; this passive attitude too is, in various degrees, contained in the muse's relation to the artist. The muse, of course, is traditionally figured as a being; similarly, the Baudelairian model of artistic inspiration implicitly recognizes the other as another being since the artist is engaged in a duel with it. However, Blanchot's story of Orpheus avoids construing the other as another being. In Blanchot's analysis, the event of artistic inspiration is removed from the domain of power, the muse's or anyone else's. Blanchot's model most successfully thematizes the encounter with the other in inspiration that occurs authentically on the other's terms, beyond power and through the failure of power.[15]

In both its form and its theme, inspiration in Blanchot's analysis is comparable to Levinas's analyses of the idea of the infinite and, interestingly, of desire. Both desire and the idea of the infinite, according to Levinas, involve a relation to an otherness whereby the self or I "thinks more than it thinks."[16] Like the responsibility that Levinas describes, the work of art is ultimately a "pouvoir fait d'impuissances" (EDE, 197/DC, 354).

Ulysses and the Sirens

A complete analysis of stories of the encounter needs to consider the model articulated through Orpheus's adventure against a story which records an encounter that in its initial phase succeeded precisely where Orpheus failed. This is the story of Ulysses and of his encounter with the Sirens, analyzed by Blanchot in the essay "Le Chant des Sirènes" (1954).

Again Blanchot's reflection is consistent with Levinas's and has no doubt informed it. In his analysis of the trace in the essay "The Trace of the Other" (1963), Levinas, revising and indeed reversing the movement of the Hegelian concept of the *oeuvre* that interested Blanchot in "Literature and the Right to Death," uses the opposition of the story of Abraham and the myth of Ulysses: "*A work conceived radically is a movement of the same unto the other which never returns to the same.* To the myth of Ulysses returning to Ithaca, we wish to oppose the story of Abraham who leaves his fatherland forever for a yet unknown land, and forbids his servant to even bring back his son to the point of departure" (DC, 348/ EDE, 191, Levinas's emphasis).[17]

Blanchot's analysis of Ulysses' encounter begins with speculation concerning the nature of the alterity of the Sirens and the manner of their approach. In considering what exactly constitutes the otherness of the Sirens, Blanchot begins by investigating the nature of their song: "what sort of song was the Sirens' song?" (GO, 105/ TSS, 59/LV, 9). Its initial provenance — and power of attraction — is the "au-delà": it is "an inhuman song," "one that remained in the margins of nature," "foreign to man," "awakening in him that extreme delight in falling which he cannot satisfy in the normal conditions of his life" (GO, 105/TSS, 59/LV, 9). A second theory, presented as speculation ("But, others say"), situates its provenance within the economy of the real, not within the "au-delà"; rather within the "en-deçà." It is not the otherness of the beyond, it is instead the otherness within.

> But, others say, there was something even stranger in the enchantment: it caused the Sirens merely to reproduce the ordinary singing of mankind, and because the Sirens, who were only animals — very beautiful animals because they reflected womanly beauty — could sing the way men sing, their song became so extraordinary that it created in anyone who heard it a suspicion that all human singing was really inhuman. . . . There was something marvelous about the song: it actually existed, it was ordinary and at the same time secret, a simple everyday song which they were suddenly forced to recognize, sung in an unreal way by strange powers, powers which were, in a word, imaginary: it was a song from the abyss and once heard

it opened an abyss in every utterance and powerfully enticed whoever heard it to disappear into that abyss. (GO, 105–6/TSS, 59/ LV, 9–10)

Although Blanchot presents both of these possibilities as speculative ("some say . . . others say . . ."), it is clear, even at the outset, that he tends toward the second interpretation; he subsequently confirms this when he characterizes Ulysses as "the one who enters into a relationship with the force of the elements and the voice of the abyss" (GO, 110/TSS, 63/LV, 15). Thus, the alterity of the Sirens relates less to the economy of a beyond or an unexplored than to the economy of the abyss or, as Levinas would put it, the hither side ("en-deçà"), the world of shadow; it is an obscurity that is not a limit of illumination's efficacy, but a function of illumination.

Next Blanchot turns his attention to the navigation that leads to the Sirens. Recalling that the victims of the Sirens were intrepid sailors, Blanchot again speculates on the causes of their failure. Some, apparently, committed Orpheus's mistake; yielding to impatience, they claimed to have reached their destination too soon: "It has always been possible to believe that those who approached it were not able to do more than approach it, that they died from *impatience*, from having said too soon: 'Here it is; here is where I will drop anchor'" (GO, 106/TSS, 60/LV, 10, our emphasis). Others, instead, no doubt navigating confidently toward the beyond, missed the mark: "Others have claimed that, on the contrary, it was too late: the goal had always been overshot" (GO, 106/TSS, 60/LV, 10). Figured as an actual destination, a point in space, the Sirens are always a point missed; they can be approached, not reached. While one can secure the approach to the Sirens with technique and the confidence that stems from courage in confronting danger, something always goes awry. This inadequacy, this inability to secure their location or position within the real, is subsequently attributed to the Sirens themselves, hence the negative characterizations of the Sirens as evil, deceptive, fraudulent, nonexistent. Hence, too, the initially positive — though heavily ironical — characterization of Ulysses' accomplishment in conquering them: "the good sense of Ulysses was enough to do away with this puerile nonexistence" (GO, 106/TSS, 60/LV, 11). The analogy of this movement with the temporal approach of the other, as Blanchot demonstrates it in terms of the "other night," is readily apparent. In the essay "The Outside, the Night" which precedes "The Gaze of Orpheus" in *The Space of Literature*, Blanchot thematizes — through metaphors of navigation among others — a comparable attempt to secure the approach of the other night in the form of a temporal event or an "instant" at which one would pass from the first night to the other night. The one who might wish to secure the first night with respect to the other night would need to be able to avoid this instant: "Thus it is that moment which he must avoid, just as the traveler is advised to avoid the point where the desert becomes seductive mirage. But such prudence is useless here. There is no exact moment at which one would pass from night to the other night, no limit at which to stop and come back in the other direction. Midnight never falls at midnight. Midnight falls when the dice are cast, but they cannot be cast till Midnight" (SL, 169, 116/EL, 225, 146). Like the approach to the Sirens, the approach to midnight is experienced as an imminence and an approach or as a limit crossed, a past event whose occurrence has, despite our vigilance and attentiveness, passed without our knowledge in the manner of Levinas's trace.

In marked contrast to these unsuccessful approaches to the Sirens, Ulysses finds a technical solution both to the approach and to the encounter with the Sirens. While Orpheus descends to the underworld where he reenacts the loss of Eurydice, Ulysses draws the Sirens into the realm of the real; there, they die. Blanchot notes that "Ulysses' attitude, the amazing deafness of a man who is deaf because he can hear, was enough to fill the Sirens with a despair which until then had been felt only by men, and this despair turned them into real and beautiful girls, just this once real and worthy of their promise, and therefore capable of vanishing into the truth and depth of their song" (GO, 107/TSS, 60/LV, 11). The Sirens and living men are two principles that, like Captain Ahab and the whale, Moby Dick, cannot coexist, yet (therefore) their encounter is inevitable: "Each wants to be everything, wants to be the absolute world, which would make it impossible for him to coexist with the other absolute world, and yet the greatest desire of each is for this coexistence and this encounter" (GO, 110/TSS, 63/LV, 16). To Orpheus's carelessness, impatience, and forgetfulness are opposed the cunning, calculating trickery of Ulysses, the technical means to solve the problem of the Sirens whereby Ulysses forces the Sirens to accept his terms in the encounter. Ulysses thus emerges victorious, intact from an experience that no one can survive.

Now, however, Blanchot qualifies this conquest in two ways. First, he ridicules Ulysses' victory, tellingly, in the Hegelian terms of the slaves' gaining mastery over their master: "this happy and confident cowardice, rooted in a privilege which set him apart from the common condition, the others having no right to such elite happiness but only to the pleasure of seeing their leader writhe ludicrously, grimacing with ecstasy in empty space, but also a right to the satisfaction of gaining mastery over their master" (GO, 107/ TSS, 60/LV, 11). This comment confirms the parallel with Levinas's explicit association of the trajectory of Ulysses' journey and the Hegelian movement of the *oeuvre*.

Second, Blanchot revises the conventional interpretation of this encounter as a unilateral victory for Ulysses. It is only an apparent, provisional victory. Its true meaning is a defeat for Ulysses: "Even once the Sirens had been overcome by the power of technology . . . Ulysses was still not free of them. They enticed him to a place which he did not want to fall into and hidden in the heart of the *Odyssey*, which had become their tomb, they drew him — and many others — into that happy, unhappy voyage which is the voyage of the tale — of a song which is no longer immediate, but is narrated, and because of this made to seem harmless, an ode which has turned into an episode" (GO, 107/TSS, 60–61/LV, 12). There is here a clear, symmetrical reversal of the story of Orpheus. Where Blanchot revises the failure of Orpheus so as to demonstrate its necessity in accordance with the work's logic, the victory of Ulysses is first discredited then shown to be a defeat, also in accordance with the logic of the work. While Ulysses's technical solution to hearing the Sirens' song results in drawing them into the realm of the real where they die, the Sirens, through their death, draw Ulysses where he did not wish to go, into another song, into the tale, into the heart of the *Odyssey*. The death of the Sirens, their conquest by Ulysses, is only the first act of a drama which now far surpasses and encompasses the sharp mind and strategic ability of Ulysses; it is ultimately the song that has won. When considered according to the Hegelian terms of Levinas's formula, the adventure of Ulysses represents a totalization and conquest of the other by the same, a scenario for which Levinas offers the alternative of the story of Abraham. Yet Blanchot senses a complication within the sequence of Ulysses' story; the victorious totalization of the other is only a moment, a step followed by the more significant one in which Ulysses' glorious conquest is itself absorbed by the song. Ulysses may have conquered a song, but it is *the* song, the *Odyssey*, ultimately, that has the last word.

Novel and Tale

In the subsection entitled "The Secret Law of the Tale," the scenario of Ulysses' approach of and encounter with the Sirens serves as the context for a distinction in aesthetic terms between the novel and the tale (Laporte, *Maurice Blanchot*, 67; Hill, *Blanchot*, 143). This relation is sketched out rapidly by Blanchot; more fully developed is a temporal analysis of the tale for which this distinction initially provides the framework. The approach of the Sirens is related to the form of the novel, the encounter itself to the tale. The novel's basis is the world of mastery, power, and technique that secures the approach to the other, but more specifically, the novel's basis is the sequential, linear time of actual navigation in space; in other words, the temporal parameters that inform the novel are secure and logical, they are those of the familiar, everyday "world." In contrast to the novel, "the tale is usually about an exceptional event, one which eludes the forms of everyday time and the world of the usual sort of truth, perhaps any truth" (GO, 109/TSS, 62/LV, 14). The form of the tale is related to the encounter as an event which does not "occur" according to or within the same temporal parameters of the approach. This thesis is further developed in the conclusion of the essay.

The central argument of Blanchot's analysis relates the temporal and logical relation within the tale. He has already suggested, though not really developed, the thesis that, when correlated as the approach and the encounter, the novel and the tale are in a paradoxical relation in which each must precede the other. On the one hand, the tale will tend to become the novel ("Once the tale has become a novel" [GO, 108/TSS, 61/LV, 12]), on the other hand, the origin of the tale arises from the novel, "The tale begins at a point where the novel does not go, though in its refusals and its rich neglect it is leading towards it" (GO, 108/TSS, 62/LV, 13). The counterintuitiveness of this relation, moreover, is precisely the point Blanchot is pursuing. He spells out the "secret law" of the tale in the following manner:

> Yet if we regard the tale as the true telling of an exceptional event which has taken place and which someone is trying to report, then we have not even come close to sensing the true nature of the tale. The tale is not the narration of an event, but that event itself, the approach to that event, the place where that event is made to happen — an event which is yet to come and through whose power of attraction the tale can hope to come into being too.
>
> This is a very delicate relationship, undoubtedly a kind of extravagance, but it is the secret law of the tale. The tale is a movement towards a point, a point which is not only unknown, obscure,

foreign, but such that apart from this movement it does not seem to
have any sort of real prior existence, and yet is so imperious that
the tale derives its power of attraction only from this point, so that
it cannot even "begin" before reaching it — and yet only the tale
and the unpredictable movement of the tale create the space where
the point becomes real, powerful, and alluring. (GO, 109/TSS, 62/
LV, 14)

The rest of Blanchot's essay with minor exceptions is an attempt to explicate the logic of these two paragraphs through various restatements and examples. Before examining Blanchot's
various examples and reasonings, it is worth noting the apparent
thematic and logical analogy of this argument to the conclusion of
Blanchot's analysis of the story of Orpheus. The origin of the tale
is, as an impossible origin, congruent with the origin of writing as
Blanchot has presented it in the subsection of "The Gaze of
Orpheus" entitled "The Leap." Now thematized as a differential
relation — such that neither term can be accorded logical or chronological priority over the other — the tale is composed of an event
and the telling of that event. To paraphrase Blanchot: the tale is the
telling of an event, the telling of which causes that event to occur.
In the conclusion of his analysis of the story of Orpheus, Blanchot
writes: "one can only write if one arrives at the instant towards
which one can only move through space opened up by the movement of writing" (GO, 104/SL, 176/EL, 234).

To demonstrate this, Blanchot proposes two analytical examples.
First, he imagines an amalgamation of Ulysses and Homer. "What
would happen if instead of being two distinct people Ulysses and
Homer comfortably shared their roles, and were one and the same
presence?" (GO, 109/TSS, 62/LV, 15). This amalgamation reproduces and develops the correlation of the form of the novel with
the approach, and the form of the tale with the encounter. The role
of Ulysses becomes that of the navigator who guides the approach;
the role of Homer is that of Ulysses within the space of the encounter, in other words, that of the poet, who tells of the encounter

and of the approach. In the initial understanding of this scenario, it is the encounter with the Sirens that effects the transition or "metamorphosis" from Ulysses to Homer: "To listen to the Song of the Sirens is to cease to be Ulysses and become Homer" (GO, 110/ TSS, 63/LV, 15). However, in a second moment, Homer's priority over Ulysses is suggested since "only in Homer's story does the real encounter take place" (GO, 110/TSS, 63/LV, 15). Commenting on the logical difficulty of thinking these two propositions simultaneously, Blanchot provides another example of an impossible, or differential origin: "This seems obscure, it is like the embarrassment the first man would have felt if, in order to be created, he himself had had to pronounce in a completely human way the divine *Fiat lux* that would actually cause his eyes to open" (GO, 110/TSS, 63/LV, 15; Libertson, *Proximity*, 272).

Second, Blanchot will apply this reasoning to another story involving navigation toward a fateful encounter, Melville's *Moby Dick*:

> Of course it is true that only in Melville's book does Ahab meet Moby Dick; yet it is also true that only this encounter allows Melville to write the book, it is such an imposing encounter, so enormous, so special that it goes beyond all the levels on which it takes place, all the moments in time where we attempt to situate it, and seems to be happening long before the book begins, but it is of such a nature that it also could not happen more than once, in the future of the work and in that sea which is what the work will be, having become an ocean on its own scale. (GO, 110/TSS, 63/LV, 15–16)

The encounter must have preceded the telling, yet it can only occur through the telling, as a result of the telling. Anticipating the objections that might derive from the counterintuitiveness of this relation, Blanchot concludes his essay with an analysis of the encounter that accounts for the "ambiguity" of this temporal pattern.

The Ambiguity of the Present

Like "Literature and the Right to Death," Blanchot's readings of the stories of both Ulysses and Orpheus progress toward ambiguity.[18] He begins with the commonsensical explanation that an event took place in the actual lives of authors such as Nerval, Melville, or Proust. A fateful meeting, an encounter with another person, a chance occurrence that triggers a memory — this event motivates its representation by various means in a work of art intended to communicate the experience. Blanchot immediately rejects this experiential model as simplistic. Coordination of the simple sequential chronology and linear causality of this interpretation does not adequately represent the encounter's disruptive and complex nature. So Blanchot returns to the encounter with the Sirens and asks: What was it that actually *occurred* in the encounter? What happened at the problematical *point* of the encounter? Of what does the actual experience of the encounter consist? These questions lead to another fundamental question concerning the configuration of time that is revealed in the moment of the encounter.

> All the ambiguity arises from the ambiguity of time which comes into place here and which allows us to say and to feel that the fascinating image of the experience is present at a certain moment, even though this presence does not belong to any present, and even destroys the present which it seems to enter. It is true, Ulysses was really sailing, and one day, on a certain date, he encountered the enigmatic song. And so he can say: now — this is happening now. But what happened now? The presence of a song which was still to be sung. And what did he touch in the presence? Not the occurrence of an encounter which had become present, but the overture of the infinite movement which is the encounter itself, always at a distance from the place where it asserts itself and the moment when it asserts itself, because it is this very distance, the imaginary

distance, in which absence is realized, and only at the end of this distance does the event begin to take place, at a point where the proper truth of the encounter comes into being and where, in any case, the words which speak it would originate. (GO, 112/TSS, 65/ LV, 18–19)

The time of the encounter is not adequately represented by the concept of the present. The encounter introduces an interval, a distance, a deferral, or an opening (*ouverture*) into the concept of the present (note how Blanchot, through clever puns on the words "overture" and "movement," introduces musical terminology to describe the excess of the song's event over the notion of the present). In the present of the encounter, the present does not coincide with itself, or, rather, the encounter takes place within the space of the present's noncoincidence with itself (because, Blanchot will argue, the encounter is this very noncoincidence). This temporal structure recalls the instant or moment "désormais toujours en instance" of Blanchot's last narrative, and suggests as well the temporality of the *entretemps* in Levinas's essay "Reality and Its Shadow" (1948) and the "fissile" characteristic of the present described in "Enigma and Phenomenon" (1957) (CPP, 68, 69/EDE, 210, 211). The *entretemps* or "intertime" is precisely this interval within the present; it describes a configuration of the temporality of the other and, most pointedly in Levinas's analysis, of the temporality of death. It is also the specific temporality of the encounter such that, as Levinas writes: "The great 'experiences' of our life have properly speaking never been lived" (CPP, 68/EDE 211).[19]

The present as internally riven and mediated derives from its differential constitution, a temporal structure observed in both Derrida's essay "La Différance" and Blanchot's analysis of the origin of writing. The theme of an interval within the present also recalls very recognizably the structure of mediation within identity observed in Heidegger's analysis of the "Principle of Identity" to the extent that the present of the encounter is construed as a "*belonging* together" of two moments; the present is a relation and, according to Blanchot, the encounter enacts that relation.[20]

This particular structure of time manifests itself in the "present" of the encounter, a temporal unit that splits itself into at least two identifiable components: on the one hand, a lag or delay, an "always already," an "always too late" ["toujours déjà passé"] and, on the other hand, a deferral, an "always yet to come."[21] Such a division of the present is precisely the paradoxical temporality that Blanchot has formulated in various contexts, most directly in the temporality of the tale and in the navigation toward the Sirens, represented as a destination either approached or overshot but never reached. Both Blanchot and Levinas illustrate their numerous thematizations of this temporality with literary examples. Levinas cites Edgar Allen Poe: "The characters of certain tales of Edgar Allen Poe must have found themselves in this empty interval. A threat appears to them in the approach of such an empty interval; no move can be made to retreat from its approach, but this approach can never end" (LR, 140/CPP, 11/RO, 786). Blanchot ends his analysis of Ulysses with a short quote from Goethe: "'*[I]n another age you were my sister or my wife*' — this is the nature of the event for which the tale is the approach" (Blanchot's emphasis, GO, 113/TSS, 65/LV, 19). Goethe's short quote, while not intuitively complex, illustrates very well the complicated conjunction of proximity and distance, of an approach that is both too late and experienced as the approach of a recurrence.

Such a multifaceted characterization of the time of the encounter has also been thematized poetically by Baudelaire. While Blanchot and Levinas generally elaborated their concepts independently of Baudelaire (references to Baudelaire in both authors are not conspicuous), the poem "To a Passerby" thematizes precisely the structure of the temporality of the encounter that has been observed here. It records with remarkable accuracy, in both spatial and temporal terms, an approach and disappearance of the passerby; furthermore, the transition from one to the other "occurs" in such a way that she disappears without ever having been present. On the other hand, the encounter has disrupted, literally redefined the time of the poet ("I am suddenly reborn from your swift glance") such that Blanchot's short commentary on Goethe's verse could be applied to Baudelaire: "This event upsets relations in time, and yet affirms time, the particular way that time happens, the tale's own time which enters the narrator's duration in such a way as to transform it" (GO, 113/TSS, 65/LV, 19).[22]

The figure of Ulysses represents a particularly striking intersection of the thought of both Blanchot and Levinas. For both thinkers, Ulysses serves as a cultural figure who embodies the Hegelian logic of the *oeuvre* and dialectic of culture, whereby the Same having undergone a temporary alienation returns to itself in an active identification, enriched by a conquest, assimilation, or appropriation of the other. Blanchot disparages Ulysses' victory over the Sirens through the Hegelian terms of domination and servitude. Similarly, for Levinas, Ulysses embodies both the egology of the subject in Western thought as well as its perennial allergy to the other, and Levinas presents the alternative trajectory of the story of Abraham. As he has done with the myth of Orpheus, Blanchot revises the victory of Ulysses. First, the victory is cast as only a provisional one. Following from the first point, Blanchot observes that Ulysses does not emerge intact from the encounter since through the encounter he has also become Homer. Ulysses may think that he emerges intact with a forbidden knowledge that he can attribute to the successful execution of his plan, yet the encounter has also effected a metamorphosis. The encounter with alterity is thus an alteration which does not and cannot simply lead back to the Same (Hippolyte, *Genèse et structure*, 372-73).

Blanchot employs both the story of Orpheus and the story of Ulysses to construct an encounter with the other that both escapes the intentions of its author and alters the subject without construing the other as power able to alter the subject. Both stories define the work of art as an activity outside of the jurisdiction of individual power and initiative ("fait d'impuissances"), in which, as in the case of Levinasian desire and infinitude, one is invested with something for which one cannot account, and put in the position of thinking more than one can think.[23]

Through the encounter, both stories investigate the problem of time. Both the encounter as a punctual event and inspiration's origin figured as a moment are formulated in accordance with a complex, composite structure of the instant or the present. This interpretation of the present as riven, mediated, and composed of prior elements, where, moreover, the relation has precedence over the elements, provides a striking example of a thematization of time through the concept of difference. The following chapter will investigate the manner in which the work of art manifests this complex structure of time.

FOUR

Encountering the Image

I have observed that many of Blanchot's and Levinas's analyses, unmistakably influenced by Hegel, appropriate his terms, images, and concepts, and then revise or adjust them. This revision records a movement that is nondialectical and either does not produce totalization or produces a problematical totalization which can only be understood in terms of difference. Blanchot and Levinas also respond to Heidegger's ontological analyses, in particular on the origin and the role of the artwork. Again, they appropriate then lead away from the conclusions of the initial text. This has been observed briefly in the consideration of "Literature and the Right to Death."

In a series of well-known papers on aesthetics which will not be summarized here, Heidegger proposes a model of art as an act of founding, grounding, and taking measure.[1] Art is a relation with the other whose purpose or accomplishment is ultimately a securing of the world with respect to that otherness. Art mediates between the world and an otherness that is cast in various terms: the otherness of the gods or the divine, of the "earth" prior to a "world."[2] The poet's action, fraught with risk and heroic since the poet is engaged in uncharted regions, is basically an action of conquest similar to that of Ulysses; it is a reduction of the other to the laws of the same. The otherness of the gods, of an earth (prior to world) is reduced or reified. The acts of grounding, founding, and taking measure are acts of integration within a sphere of intelligibility or understanding, within what Heidegger calls a "world." In Heidegger's scenario, the poet encounters the other and integrates the otherness of the other into the uses, purposes, and projects of the world (Hill, *Blanchot*, 77–91).

The terms that Heidegger uses, founding, grounding, taking measure, clearing, illumination, as well as metaphors of equipment, technology, and tools are evoked with various degrees of explicitness in a whole set of analyses of both Blanchot and Levinas (in which, generally, the latter's tend to inform the former's although the lines of influence go both ways as the pattern of cross referencing in their works suggests). In general, aesthetic examples are often evoked in Levinas's early writings to introduce a certain complication into the basic vocabulary of phenomenology. Levinas's questioning of ontology, prior to leading him to the complex ethical analyses in *Otherwise Than Being*, is related to aesthetics; such a basic ethical concept as that of the face, for example, is initially formulated as, "Isn't art an activity that gives things a face?" (en, 10/EN, 22/II, 133).[3] Blanchot adapts and develops Levinas's analysis in his aesthetic investigations.[4] The complication that art introduces with respect to the question of being is perhaps best seen in relation to a concept that is basic in both aesthetics and phenomenology, that of the *image*.[5]

The Image

The journal *Les Temps modernes* is a curious venue for the publication of one of Levinas's early essays on the work of art, attested not just by the positions that Levinas defines in his essay but by a defensive preface to the article signed by the editor (T.M.) of the journal which situates the essay with respect to the views about art that Sartre has developed in his study *What Is Literature?*[6] "Reality and Its Shadow" (1948) adopts the uncharacteristic rhetorical form, for Levinas, of the manifesto; its final subsection is entitled: "Pour une critique philosophique." Prior to this concluding section, the essay outlines a view of art not only completely incompatible with Sartre's[7] but also very different from the view developed by Heidegger in "The Origin of the Work of Art." Levinas demonstrates that the categories of being and time are not adequate to the work of art and essentially reverses the relation that Heidegger has established between art and truth.

Prior to investigating the complication introduced by the artwork to the category of Being, Levinas situates the work of art against the intellectualism of Heidegger's view of art and the appropriation of the artwork by the world of action and political engagement in Sartre by removing the artwork from the sphere of the concept. While normally associated with a "beyond" beyond cognitive understanding (as in the Heideggerian model alluded to above), the artwork, Levinas argues, is instead related to the opposite tendency. Art is neither a clearing, nor an illumination, nor a revelation, nor, he writes with an intended pun, a creation; it is an event of obscuring.

> To go beyond is to communicate with ideas, to understand. Does not the function of art lie in not understanding? Does not obscurity provide it with its very element and a completion sui generis, foreign to dialectics and the life of ideas? Will we then say that the artist knows and expresses the very obscurity of the real? But that leads to a much more general question, to which this whole discussion of art is subordinate: in what does the *non-truth* of being consist? Is it always to be defined by comparison with truth, as what is left over after *understanding*? Does not the commerce with the obscure, as a totally independent ontological event, describe categories irreducible to those of cognition? We should like to show this event in art. Art does not know a particular type of reality; it contrasts with knowledge. It is the very event of obscuring, a descent of the night, an invasion of shadow. To put it in theological terms, which will enable us to delimit however roughly our ideas

> by comparison with contemporary notions: art does not belong to the order of revelation. Nor does it belong to that of creation, which moves in just the opposite direction. (LR, 131–32/CPP, 3/RO, 773)

Hence the notion of the concept is inadequate to art since the concept is always the thing illuminated and grasped within understanding; a more adequate notion, he suggests, is that of the image. Prior to providing a working definition of the image (beyond its opposition to the concept), Levinas explores various models of noncognitive, nonconceptual apprehension. The common principle of these modes of apprehension is that they do not involve power but, as he puts it, a "fundamental passivity" (LR, 132/CPP, 3/RO, 774). He borrows from ethnography the concept of a "participation" as in religious rites or sacrifices.[8] He comments on the manner in which we respond to rhythm ("rhythm represents a unique situation where we cannot speak of consent, assumption, initiative or freedom, because the subject is caught up and carried away by it" LR, 132/CPP, 4/RO, 775)[9] or music in general ("in listening [to music] we do not apprehend a 'something,' but are without concepts" LR, 133/CPP, 5/RO, 776). He proposes the (non)cognitive model of a "waking dream," the "captivation or incantation of poetry and music . . . a mode of being to which applies neither the form of consciousness, since the I is there stripped of its prerogative to assume, its power, nor the form of unconsciousness, since the whole situation and all its articulations are in a dark light, *present*" (LR, 133/CPP, 4/RO, 775). Finally, he insists on the irreducibility of such a mode of apprehension to the opposition of the conscious and unconscious mind instead describing "a sphere situated outside of the conscious and the unconscious" (LR, 133/CPP, 4/RO, 775).[10]

Having established this relation, Levinas turns his attention to the image itself. Its economy derives from a being's noncoincidence with itself; a simple, autonomous conception of identity is not sufficient to contain being. In order to establish the economy that produces the image, Levinas employs an argument that is very similar to Heidegger's analysis of mediation within identity. "There is then a duality in this person, this thing, a duality in its being. It is what it is and it is a stranger to itself, and there is a relationship between these two moments. We will say the thing is itself and is its image. And that relationship between the thing and its image is resemblance" (LR, 135/CPP, 6/RO, 778). Resemblance is not a relation of an original and its copy, nor is it a relation of a thing with something else that looks like the original; resemblance is a basic instability in the form of a doubling of the original itself. This doubling — resembling — is what engenders the image. In Levinas's example of this "phenomenology" of the image, the original seems at a spatial or temporal distance from itself, somewhat in the manner of the various disjunctions effected in the characters Thomas, Anne, and J. observed in chapters 1 and 2: "The original gives itself as though it were at a distance from itself, as though it were withdrawing itself, as though something in a being delayed behind being" (LR, 135/CPP, 6–7/RO, 779).[11]

The economy and logic of the image is then applied to various aesthetic examples, caricature, picturesqueness, fable, allegory,[12] and visual art (primarily pictures and painting). All of these examples are analyzed in terms of reality's doubling of itself in the movement of resemblance. They all express an object's noncoincidence with itself, a nontotalization or an incomplete totalization, a kind of excess over itself and over its identity, the object constituted in difference. This, as might be expected, yields an essentially ambiguous view of reality: on the one hand, reality, being, the absolute are disclosed in truth, revealed in reason, illuminated in intelligibility and understanding, and yield to the appropriation of cognition through conception and causality. On the other hand, through this fundamental doubling of the real, another dimension of reality, being, or the absolute appears, one that is resistant to such appropriation — the dimension of reflection, resemblance, shadow, and obscuring.[13] This movement of doubling is related again to the initial distinction of the "en deça" as opposed to the "au-delà," the latter being, according to Levinas, always predicated upon totalization and related to disclosure in truth.

The analysis of the image thus provides a foundation for Levinas's initial dissociation of art from cognition. Art is not a primitive, incomplete, foundational, or prior mode of cognition. It is not an event that is, in its full and proper development, subsumed by knowledge and cognition; its necessity derives from an economy that remains essentially foreign and irreducible to cognition. The image and the concept derive from parallel and incompatible necessities explained by the relation of difference.

The concept of difference is applied at several distinct levels here. First, difference is the principle of resemblance, that is of reality's, being's, or the absolute's noncoincidence with itself; difference is the principle of the two distinct modes or, as Levinas puts it, of the "two contemporary possibilities of being" (LR, 136/CPP, 7/RO, 780). Because the real is grounded in difference — mediation within identity — it appears in two distinct phenomenal modes: as thing, being, or original on the one hand and as shadow, image, or reflection on the other. Second, while the principle that governs the first category (that of being or thing) is totalization, which guarantees concept, cognition, intelligibility, dialectic, and power, the principle that governs the image is, again, difference. Hence the image is a relation of difference of being and nothingness, just as participation (the relation to the image) is a relation of difference of subject and object, or of modes of conscious and unconscious apprehension, a "waking dream" as Levinas puts it.[14] The image is "foreign to dialectics" (LR, 131/CPP, 3/RO, 773), and the relation to it is "a fundamental passivity" (LR, 132/CPP, 3/RO, 774). Finally, although this anticipates to some degree the manner in which Blanchot will develop Levinas's analysis, the relation of these two modes of thing and image on the one hand and of dialectic and difference on the other hand, is, itself a relation of difference. Thus, Blanchot argues, this opposition will be formulated as a relation of difference; just as power will confuse itself with powerlessness and passivity, the concept will confuse itself with the image.

The various levels of the concept of difference in this analysis parallels Georges Bataille's analyses of the sacred and the profane in his *L'Erotisme*. These analyses, like Blanchot's earlier essays, present Hegelian concepts and then move away from them. Thus difference characterizes the formlessness that is prior to the distinction of sacred and profane, then characterizes the sacred in opposition to the profane (predicated instead on totalization, effective negativity, power, and so on). Finally difference accounts for the subsequent relations of sacred and profane in the complex relation of prohibition and transgression and, specifically, in the idea of a prohibition that makes transgression attractive and, paradoxically, inevitable, "l'interdit est là pour être violé" (71) as Bataille says.[15]

Time and the Work of Art

The concept of difference in "Reality and Its Shadow" initially describes concepts that are not thinkable in the oppositional terms of either/or (being or nothingness, presence or absence, subject or object, conscious or unconscious, and so on). This occasionally means situating principal concepts *between* such pairs of terms, as noted in the characterization of participation in terms of a "waking dream." In another attempt to thematize participation as a relation which does not fit the dichotomy of subject and object, Levinas qualifies the image as "interesting" in the etymological sense of *inter esse*: "An image is interesting, without the slightest sense of utility, interesting in the sense of *involving*, in the etymological sense — to be *among* things which should have had only the status of objects" (LR, 133/CPP, 4/RO, 775).[16]

The between that cannot be thematized within groups of opposed concepts is also what organizes Levinas's reflection on time and the artwork in this essay. At the outset, in the opposition of the "au-delà" and the "en deça," Levinas has raised the possibility of opposing a "beyond" of time or timelessness to an "en deça" of time which would be situated within the "interstices" of time (LR, 131/CPP, 3/RO, 773). The penultimate subdivision of "Reality and Its Shadow" explores this conception of time now characterized as the intertime, the *entretemps*.[17]

In describing this particular form of time, the time of the image, Levinas analyzes the temporality expressed in plastic art, particularly in the statue although he also mentions painting, as well as in narrated works. Levinas observes that in the statue, "the instant endures infinitely" (LR, 138/CPP, 9/RO, 782), the time expressed by plastic artworks is that of an "eternally suspended future" (LR, 138/CPP, 9/RO, 782, 783). The temporality of the narrated work is slightly different. It involves the fixity of repetition: "the infinite repetition of the same acts and the same thoughts" (LR, 139/CPP, 10/RO, 784). Levinas dissociates this fixity very explicitly from any intimation of totalization, the concept, dialectic, truth, or power: "Such a fixity is wholly different from that of concepts, which initiates life, offers reality to our powers, to truth, opens a dialectic. By its reflection in a narrative, being has a non-dialectical fixity, stops dialectics and time" (LR, 139/CPP, 10/RO, 784). Levinas here applies to the general problem of time in the narrative the economy of the image or of resemblance.

Thus the temporality revealed by the artwork appears in two guises revealed by plastic and narrated works: first as the infinite endurance of the instant or the eternal suspension of the future, an always still to come; second, as an infinite repetition, an always already, a temporal resemblance or a temporal doubling, or in another formulation — interesting because it mirrors rigorously the characterization of the image — a delay of time behind itself.[18] Levinas assimilates these two interpretations by insisting on the essentially plastic nature of the narrated work, and he investigates the space "between two well-determined moments" (LR, 139/CPP, 10/RO, 784) in order to characterize the *entretemps*. Through the figure of Niobe, a passing allusion to Zeno, a brief analysis of the temporality of death, and reference to Edgar Allen Poe, Levinas will develop this analysis of the temporality of the plastic artwork as an empty, eternal interval.[19] Levinas remarks that if being is able to cross such an interval, as it does so, its shadow or its image remains immobilized or trapped in this inhuman time (Llewelyn, *Emmanuel Levinas*, 10). Moreover, "The eternal duration of the interval in which a statue is immobilized differs radically from the eternity of a concept; it is the meanwhile [*l'entretemps*], never finished, still enduring — something inhuman and monstrous" (LR, 141/CPP, 11/RO, 786). This temporality is opposed to a temporality of confident initiative, action, and accomplishment; it is, instead, the time of powerlessness and "nightmare" (LR, 139/CPP, 9/RO, 783).

Thus the application of difference to the present or to the moment leads to the interval within the moment and to the present's noncoincidence with itself (via delay, doubling, or repetition). When one considers the present moment as a totality, one finds that it is riven by an internal mediation, a monstrous, empty interval. When one seeks to consider the moment in a linear or logical sequence as a moment distinct from other moments, a present in relation to a past moment or to a future moment, one observes that the two moments are so related that their relation is prior to and more fundamental than the unicity that can be accorded to either term.[20] Hence, the experience of the present is that of an inextrication of the present and the future which takes the form of an always or still yet to·come, the approach of a point or imminence of an event that remains eternally suspended, an "avenir" that is always and only "à venir": "An eternally suspended future floats around the congealed position of a statue like a future forever to come. The imminence of the future lasts before an instant stripped of the essential characteristic of the present, its evanescence" (LR, 138/CPP, 9/RO, 782). The present and future are related in such a way that neither can assert priority over the other. Each deprives the other of its essence while retaining its qualities; it is a relation without totalization because it is prior to totalization. This temporality is the temporality of waiting, and patience and impatience need to be understood in this context.[21]

One can account for the temporality that Levinas has derived from the narrated artwork, "the infinite repetition of the same acts and the same thoughts," according to either of the two models of difference: as mediation within identity or as relation prior to identity. The experience of time as "always already past," as endless recurrence, and as repeated loss are among the forms that this temporality takes.

Levinas states that, contrary to the common view that the plastic artwork effects a stoppage of time, a technical capturing of the instant, or a freeze frame of the present, the artwork is instead the expression of an other time, of the temporality of the other. This accounts for the strategic importance in the essay of the analogy of the temporality of death and the temporality of the artwork. Similarly, art manifests an otherness of being which cannot be thought in terms of an opposition of being and nothingness, or being and nonbeing. The otherness expressed by art is not the otherness of a "beyond," of a region not yet encountered or secured by the concept. It is an otherness that is prior to, opposed to, and yet within the concept. Art derives both from the economy of an obscurity that is prior to the clearing and illumination of the concept as well as from the economy of the shadow that is a function of that very illumination. Such a view of art is thematized somewhat less rigorously but through strikingly similar concepts and metaphors by Artaud.[22]

"Reality and Its Shadow" is, as noted at the outset, a relatively early essay in Levinas's career. It does not have the elegance of some of his later analyses. The thematization, for example, of a "between" (inter, entre, interval, logic of a "tiers exclu") in this essay is either abandoned or used more metaphorically in subsequent formulations of difference since the notion of "between" rests on the assumption of the two totalities which define it. Yet the essay makes apparent two tendencies in Levinas's writings: first, it explicitly demonstrates the attempt to move away from concepts and categories that are informed by phenomenology (Hegel, Heidegger, and Sartre).[23] Second, it illustrates the strategic importance and the role of difference in effecting this move. Levinas's essay as a whole and his analysis of the image and the economy of resemblance in particular will serve as both an introduction to and conceptual framework for some of Blanchot's most complex analyses in *The Space of Literature*.

Blanchot and the Image

In "Literature and the Right to Death," Blanchot defines the image by adapting Hegel to his reflection on literature and aesthetics. In this context, the operative principle of the image is negativity. Literary language demonstrates awareness of the inconsistency involved in representing the absence of a thing with a word which is, itself, a concrete, real thing. Literary language thus creates the image, which is not a representation of the thing but a representation of what the thing is not.[24]

The initial analyses of *The Space of Literature* similarly adapt Levinasian concepts to the aesthetic questions that interest Blanchot. The particular problem of the image is adapted and developed by Blanchot in the penultimate and concluding sections of the first essay of *The Space of Literature* entitled "Essential Solitude" as well as in an appendix section entitled "The Two Versions of the Imaginary." As some of Blanchot's richest analyses and also some of his most complicated, these are worth detailed and sustained attention.

The image is first thematized in the context of the concept of fascination, a mode of perception whose principal features are that it is passive and nonconceptual and that it exceeds the dichotomy of subject and object. In contrast, the intentional *visée*, the act of seeing, as a condition of cognition as well as one of its principal metaphors is a voluntary, transitive action of a subject performed on an object. One of its conditions is adequate separation of the two by means of a spatial interval. This assures the effectiveness of the intentional act by presupposing the autonomy of the subject and guaranteeing his power to totalize the object. In his definition of fascination, Blanchot revises all of these characteristics:

> Why fascination? Seeing implies distance, the decision that causes separation, the power not to be in contact and to avoid the confusion of contact. Seeing means that this separation has nevertheless become an encounter. But what happens when what you see, even though from a distance, seems to touch you with a grasping contact, when the manner of seeing is a sort of touch, when seeing is a contact at a distance? What happens when what is seen imposes itself on your gaze, as though the gaze had been seized, touched, put in contact with appearance? Not an active contact, not the initiative and action that might still remain in a true touch; rather, the gaze is drawn, absorbed into an immobile movement and a depth without depth. What is given to us by contact at a distance is the image, and fascination is passion for the image. (GO, 75/SL, 32/ EL, 25)[25]

Blanchot insists that fascination, like Levinas's trace, is an act situated beyond a "subject's" power and initiative. It is a mode of seeing that is not an expression of power but rather of powerlessness or impossibility.[26] In the following description of fascination as an excess over blindness and sight, one will note how Blanchot uses double negation to effect a characterization that is patently not dialectical: "Fascination is the gaze of solitude, the gaze of what is incessant and interminable, in which blindness is still vision, *vision that is no longer the possibility of seeing but the impossibility of not seeing*, impossibility that turns into seeing, that perseveres — always and always — in a vision that does not end: a dead gaze, a gaze that has become the ghost of an eternal vision" (GO, 75/SL, 32/EL, 26; my emphasis).

If the one who perceives in fascination is without power and is not a subject, the thing perceived is not an object: "It can be said that a person who is fascinated does not perceive any real object, any real form, because what he sees does not belong to the world of reality, but to the indeterminate realm of fascination" (GO, 75/ SL, 32/EL, 26). What is perceived is an image, or, rather the object's "foundering" ("s'abîmer" and "s'effondrer") into its image, that is the distance that is "the unlimited depth that lies behind the image, a depth that is not alive, not tractable, absolutely present though not provided, where objects sink ["s'abîment"] when they become separated from their meaning, when they subside ["s'effondrent"] into their image" (GO, 75–76/SL, 32/EL, 26).

Fascination, as Blanchot analyzes it, is a specific instance (analyzed in terms of vision, subject, and object) of the relation that Levinas has described as participation and rhythm. And, as in the case of Levinas's participation, the irreducibility of the relation to terms of conscious and unconscious perception, irreducibility to categories of subject and object, an essential passivity, and a foreignness to cognition describe and define fascination.[27] The description of fascination as a collapsing of the interval or distance, as a "contact à distance" is also anticipated by Levinas's characterization of the *inter esse*, "to be among things which should have had only the status of objects" as an "exteriority of the inward" (LR, 133/CPP, 4/RO, 775).

The image itself corresponds very precisely to Levinas's use of the term and its economy is that of what Levinas calls resemblance. However, at this juncture, Blanchot is using both the image and fascination principally to characterize the element or "milieu" of fascination. The element or domain opened up by fascination and manifested through the image is, as shall be seen below, a field for which Levinas's *il y a* provides the general context and for which Blanchot will identify and analyze specific instances and characteristics. For the essential anonymity of Levinas's *il y a*, for example, Blanchot substitutes the neutral presence or impersonality. Like the analysis of "Reality and Its Shadow," which characterizes art as the expression of a fundamental alterity of the concept, Blanchot's fascination is situated in the space of an "en deça"; it is foreign to revelation, to meaning, to presence in space, and to the temporal concept of the present. "What fascinates us, takes away our power to give it a meaning, abandons its 'perceptible' nature, abandons the world, withdraws to the near side of the world [se retire en deça du monde] and attracts us there, no longer reveals itself to us and yet asserts itself in a presence alien to the present in time and to presence in space" (GO, 75/SL, 32/EL, 25). To write is to enter into the element of the image and of fascination; this corresponds with Levinas's general characterization of art. I will return to this characterization considering its fuller context in Levinas's *il y a*.

Blanchot's essay ends with a long footnote in which he wonders "out loud" if literary language in general cannot itself be related to this economy of the image. Does literature not effect the distance of language with respect to itself that is the image with respect to the object (Fynsk, in Gill, *Maurice Blanchot*, 81)? Could literature then generally be understood in terms of the economy of the image as "image de langage" instead of as "un langage imagé?" These questions lead Blanchot to briefly investigate the economy of the image, which he then defers to the appendix essay, "The Two Versions of the Imaginary."

The Versions of the Image

Blanchot's analysis of the image is complicated. It relies heavily on Levinas's analyses in "Reality and Its Shadow" and "Il y a" yet makes certain modifications and contributes a degree of complexity to both.[28] Blanchot analyzes the economy of resemblance that produces the image in Levinas in a series of examples which range from concrete and empirical to highly abstract in two separate contexts: first, *disappearance* and second, *resemblance*. The first is an excess over the categories of being and nothingness, presence and absence. The second is the reflection or doubling of the thing, the object's noncoincidence with itself.

The concept of disappearance is actually an amalgamation of two Levinasian analyses: first, the economy of resemblance that has been noted, second, the "thought experiment" that Levinas uses in the beginning of "Il y a" (Sitney, afterword to GO, 183–84; Critchley, *Very Little . . . Almost Nothing*, 56). The image is related to the movement of disappearance of the world and the persistence of something because this disappearance can only be incompletely accomplished. Blanchot's articulation of these two Levinasian analyses is complex because he has joined the spatial and temporal metaphors used to describe resemblance. In "Reality and Its Shadow," Levinas describes resemblance as either an object's *distance* from itself or *delay* behind itself (LR, 135/CPP, 7/RO, 779). Blanchot associates both of these in the movement of disappearance such that it is the delay that manifests the distance: "After the object comes the image. 'After' means that first the thing must move away in order to allow itself to be grasped again. But that distancing is not the simple change of place of a moving object, which nevertheless remains the same. Here the distancing is at the heart of the thing" (GO, 80/SL, 255/EL, 347). As objects disappear, their images lag behind and are momentarily delayed, somewhat like the smile of Lewis Carroll's Cheshire cat.[29] Disappearance, as an articulation of difference and as a movement or a passage from being to nothingness, from presence to absence thus affords a momentary glimpse of the image. This "thought experiment" is Blanchot's attempt to record the positive perception of the image.

Another adjustment that Blanchot brings to Levinas's analysis is to define two contexts ("two versions") of the image. As a relation of presence and absence, of being and nothingness, the image necessarily lends itself to a certain ambiguity and contradiction. The economy of the image is both the leftover or persisting presence of something that has disappeared and the movement of disappearance, the foundering into nothingness of something present. Hence one can conceivably interpret the image as a securing of a thing's absence or as the opposite, as the fundamental instability of the thing, its permanent threat of collapsing into the abyss. In this way, Blanchot's two versions of the image reproduce the distinction that Levinas has drawn between the concept (the securing version of the image) and Levinas's image (the obscuring, destabilizing version of the image). This is one of the features that makes Blanchot's analysis more confusing than that of Levinas. On the other hand, this confusion is one of Blanchot's principal points; he is particularly interested in the persistent tendency to take the second version of the image for the first, that is to assume with regard to the image attributes of stability, power, effectivity, and control where they insistently are not.[30]

Thus, the first version of the image is that it is a "limit next to the indefinite." Notwithstanding the tentative nature of this limit ("mince cerne"), it has a pacifying, humanizing, cleansing, appropriating, purifying function. It serves the purposes of power, control, and affirmation since even in the essentially unstable form of the image, the formless, the indefinite, the endless, and the limitless acquire form, consistency, and closure and achieve a temporary, tentative totalization. As such, the image's nature appears to be *formal*. However, its true nature is related not to form but to substance and depth. The following passage, in which Blanchot plays on the opposition in French of "forme" and "fond" and on the multiple meanings of the word "fond" — as content or substance as opposed to form or style, as depth (or rather as the deepest or remotest part), as base or basis, and as the essential, constitutive part or truth of something — also illustrates the perverse difficulty of Blanchot's style since a transition that marks a crucial opposition is signaled, in the French text, only by a semicolon:

> The image can, when it awakens or when we awaken it, represent the object to us in a luminous *formal* aura; but it is nonetheless with *substance* that the image is allied — [(L'image) peut bien, quand

elle s'éveille ou quand nous l'éveillons, nous représenter l'objet en une lumineuse auréolle *formelle*; c'est avec le *fond* qu'elle a partie liée] — with the fundamental materiality, the still undetermined absence of form, the world oscillating between adjective and substantive before foundering [s'enfoncer] in the formless prolixity of indetermination. (SL, 255/EL, 346/GO, 80; Blanchot's emphasis)

Blanchot illustrates this movement with a brief, empirical analysis of fascination. Again, he plays repeatedly with multiple meanings and the suggestive potential of his words:

> But when we are face to face with things themselves — if we fix upon a face [si nous fixons un visage], the corner of a wall — does it not also sometimes happen that we abandon ourselves to what we see? Bereft of power before this presence suddenly strangely mute and passive, are we not at its mercy? Indeed, this can happen, but it happens because the thing we stare at [la chose que nous fixons] has foundered, sunk into its image [s'est effondrée dans son image], and the image has returned into that deep fund of impotence to which everything reverts [ce fond d'impuissance où tout retombe]. (SL, 255/EL, 347/GO, 80)

First, Blanchot is clearly emphasizing the various meanings of the verb "fixer" used twice in these two sentences. Its principal meaning in this context of staring or looking fixedly is clearly associated with other meanings of stabilizing, determining, specifying, and establishing.[31] The movement of collapse into the image is expressed through the verb "effondrer" constructed on the word "fond," thus relating the action of sinking to a collapsing of the foundation. The action emphasizes sinking into an abyss, since Blanchot will use the noun "fond" to specify the movement.[32] Finally, the movement is expressed as a reverting, a falling back to a "fond d'impuissance"; this movement is expressed with the verb "retomber" whose suggestion of the noun "tombe," while only morphological, is thematically consistent with the movement described since the movement is associated with death. This association is subsequently developed in the context of the analysis of the cadaver, of burial rituals, and of grave sites.

The example is instructive since it begins by acknowledging the transitive gaze and its predicates of fixity and stability — the ability or power to secure — then records its displacement by fascination — a "reversal of power into participation," as Levinas might say, whence "we abandon ourselves to what we see, . . . we are at its mercy, powerless" (GO, 80/SL, 255/EL, 347) — and links this to the disappearance or foundering of the object into the image and into nothingness. The purpose of the example and of the multiple meanings of the word "fixer" is thus clear. It articulates the two versions of the image; the relation that has been observed between the thing and its image now describes the relation of the first image and the second image.

Invoking resemblance and reflection, Blanchot next accounts for the image according to an economy of difference: "In the image, the object again touches something it had mastered in order to be an object, something against which it had built and defined itself" (GO, 81/SL, 256/EL, 347). This example's use of a relation of difference in its reasoning, is probably clearer than the example itself. The object is itself a relation and does not coincide with itself, yet in order to be an object, that is, in order to disclose itself as an object in meaning and truth, the object must resolve this non-coincidence, "master" this indeterminacy. The collapse of the object into the image reverses this movement but, more importantly, in this reversal, reveals the constitution of the object itself in difference.

While Blanchot's analysis of the image has a distinctly Levinasian inspiration, his adjustments and modifications to Levinas's models and examples are notable. The logic of difference that accounts for the relation of image with respect to the object also accounts for the relationship between the first image (Levinas's concept, the version of the image which is appropriated by cognition) and the second image (Levinas's image, which is a collapsing, a fascination, and a passivity). This significant step situates the economy of cognition within the economy of the image as a moment of this economy, the economy of power within the broader and prior economy of powerlessness, and the economy of the dialectic within the economy of difference as a relation of difference.[33] This relation, latent in Levinas's analysis, is identified and developed by Blanchot. Indeed, it is a particular interest of Blanchot's and a characteristic procedure in his texts to show how one image is always taken for the other, how powerlessness is consistently mistaken for power and how passivity is always assumed to be effective control.[34]

Image and Cadaver

The second half of Blanchot's analysis focuses on the economy of resemblance through an exploration of the peculiar phenomenology of the cadaver. The purpose of this analysis, again inspired by Levinas with important thematic affinities to certain sectors of Bataille's thought, is to link the image and resemblance to the question of death.

In the essay "Il y a," Levinas speaks of the cadaver as horrible because of its excess over categories of being and nothingness. The inability of the cadaver to assume the simple status of a thing or object is manifested in its "return" to haunt, to become a ghost. (Levinas plays on the meanings of "revenir" and on the gerund "revenant" which signifies ghost. This word play recalls the word play observed in Blanchot on the word "retomber.") While Levinas does not explicitly characterize the ghost in terms of image or the economy of resemblance, such a characterization is implicit in his description. Significantly, in order to characterize implicitly the logic of resemblance which describes the relation of cadaver and ghost, Levinas uses the verb "porter," one of the verbs which traditionally expresses *aufheben*, the action of dialectical resolution. He writes, "A corpse is horrible [Le cadavre c'est l'horrible]; it already bears in itself [Il porte en lui] its own phantom, it presages its return. The haunting spectre [le revenant], the phantom, constitutes the very element of horror" (EE, 61/DEE, 100). (Levinas's phrase recalls the phrase "La vie qui porte la mort et se maintient en elle" which punctuates "Literature and the Right to Death.") The movement Levinas analyzes in the cadaver runs directly counter to the movement that Hegel thematizes in the preface of the *Phenomenology*. Bataille too, in *L'Erotisme*, speaks of the horror inspired by the cadaver. In Bataille's analysis the horror of the cadaver is related to an excess over categories of being and nothingness which Bataille expresses through the image of "contagion" in both biological and ontological terms. The act of burying the dead manifests, in Bataille's view, a response to this disruptive "violence" of the cadaver (51–55).

Blanchot will investigate the phenomenology of the cadaver in two parts: first, by noting the association effected by the cadaver of being and nothingness, second by formulating this relation in terms of resemblance. As noted, the most immediately striking characteristic of the cadaver is its irreducibility to the conventional categories of phenomenological thought. Although the cadaver may initially appear in the mode of thingness, thingness is obviously not adequate to describe it. The cadaver concretely juxtaposes presence and absence, and indicates a "bridge" between here and nowhere. Blanchot characterizes in the same way the essence of solitude as the realm of fascination, the absence of time, and the action of the image (GO, 73–74/SL, 30–31/EL, 22–23).

> What is there, in the absolute calm of what has found its place, nevertheless does not realize the truth of being fully here. Death suspends relations with the place, even though the dead person relies heavily on it as the only base left to him. Yes, the fact is that that base is lacking, place is missing, the cadaver is not in its place. Where is it? It is not here and yet it is not elsewhere; nowhere? but the fact is that then nowhere is here. The cadaverous presence establishes a relation between here and nowhere. (GO, 81/SL, 256/ EL, 348)[35]

The cadaver's resemblance also complicates its relationship to such categories. This is the second axis of Blanchot's investigation.

Blanchot begins with an empirical observation, noting that the word "resemblance," when applied to a cadaver, has a particular meaning. Mourners will find that, at a certain juncture, the relation to the cadaver seems to withdraw from the realm of interhuman relations. At that point, Blanchot says, mourners will note that the cadaver begins to resemble itself. The resemblance is thus not a relation or comparison with the deceased prior to his death. It is, instead, a relation of noncoincidence of the cadaver with itself, in the form of a doubling, a reflection, an image. Hence the cadaver actualizes the two contexts of the relation of difference; it indicates both a prior relation of being and nothingness, and it indicates a mediation within identity. The cadaver then effects a second disruption in the notion of place. Explicitly associating the verb "errer" and the noun "erreur" as if the latter were a gerund of the former, Blanchot implies that the cadaver becomes a wanderer, in a movement similar to Levinas's "returner" or "revenant."[36] And in the inspiration of Levinas's image, this wanderer is also an "error" since he does not disclose himself in truth or in the context of cognition, the concept, or knowledge.

This tendency of the cadaver to wander, to return, is the corollary of what Bataille has called contagion or violence. In the Hegelian inspired anthropological or ethnological context of Bataille's *L'Erotisme*, human consciousness manifests itself first as a consciousness of death. Historical evidence of this can be found in the archaeological record in procedures for burial, the assignation of certain sites for the remains of the deceased, and the construction of various types of funereal monuments (36, 48–55).

Blanchot notes that the disruption caused by the cadaver is not limited to space but applies to time as well. In addition to the abyssal foundering of being, the cadaver's wandering introduces another time. Blanchot will, like Bataille, investigate burial traditions and practices for clues of these attributes. He finds them in the reality which funerary rituals manifest an attempt to *negate*.

Finally, an end must be put to what is endless: one does not live with dead people under penalty of seeing here sink into an unfathomable nowhere, a fall that is illustrated by the fall of the House of Usher. The dear departed, then, is conveyed to another place, and undoubtedly the site is only symbolically at a distance, in no way unlocatable, but it is nevertheless true that the here of here lies, full of names, of solid constructions, of affirmations of identity, is preeminently the anonymous and impersonal place, as though, within the limits drawn for it and in the vain guise of a pretension capable of surviving everything, the monotony of an infinite erosion were at work obliterating the living truth that characterizes every place, and making it equal to the absolute neutrality of death. (GO, 84–85/SL, 259/EL, 353)

The resting place, the cemetery, is characteristically marked by monuments, solid structures of marble or granite with inscriptions in stone which are affirmations of place, identity, and time. Yet the true nature of the cemetery is that of the anonymous and impersonal, the collapse into the indeterminacy of nowhere, nothingness, and the infinite. Thus the appearance of solidity and permanence is a "vain guise," the location only apparently or symbolically marginal or "off to the side" ("à l'écart") since it is, ultimately, the truth and basis of *every* place. In this problematic space, the infinite erosion of space and place, of person and identity, of solidity and totalization, and of sequential and linear time is occurring. Thus the principles observed in connection with the cadaver mirror the different facets of the image. As the image places "a limit on the indefinite," the necessity to move the cadaver corresponds to the need to put a "term to the interminable." Likewise, the collapse of the object into the image in fascination mirrors the foundering of here into nowhere that occurs in the burial site, a foundering which funereal procedures, inscriptions, and monuments attempt to forestall.

The Image and the Artwork

The cadaver as a case study of resemblance and of the image establishes concretely two relations which will be explored subsequently: the relation of the image and death and the relation of the image and the artwork. The latter is derived from Hegel and associates funereal monuments with early forms of art, particularly classical art. This leads Blanchot back to the two versions of the image, now analyzed concretely in aesthetic terms as an ambivalence that haunts classical art, as if classical art concealed a repressed side, an ominous, disruptive reality.

Initially Blanchot recalls the two versions of the image. The image is not the truth of the thing and is not in the service of the truth. It is a withdrawal from the space of meaning and truth. The image can be misappropriated and made to serve the truth of the world; in this relation, its true nature is reversed. Furthermore, one image can be taken for another.[37] This is possible because of the very structure of the image. In an analysis that parallels the analysis of the ambivalence of naming in "Literature and the Right to Death," Blanchot notes, "Certainly we can always recapture the image and make it serve the truth of the world; but then we would be reversing the relationship that characterizes it: in this case, the image becomes the follower of the object, what comes after it, what remains of it and allows us to have it still available to us when nothing is left of it, a great resource, a fecund and judicious power" (GO, 85–86/SL, 260/EL, 354). Thus the true movement of receding into image, which removes the object from power, is misunderstood as the movement that yields the object to us in the form of its image. The object's resemblance, its noncoincidence with itself in the form of reflection and image — thus what makes it withdraw from the horizon of appropriation — is interpreted in a linear, temporal manner such that the object has priority over its image.

According to Blanchot, this appropriation of the image is characteristic of classical art. Here again, Blanchot appears to be adapting and developing Levinas's argument in "Reality and Its Shadow." In the latter essay, Levinas notes that classical art attempts to effect the totalization that resemblance prevents by dissimulating, covering, or absorbing the image (in the following quote, referred to as "caricature"): "The art called classical — the art of antiquity and of its imitators, the art of ideal forms — corrects the caricature of being — the snub nose, the stiff gesture. Beauty is being dissimulating its caricature, covering over or absorbing its shadow" (LR, 137/CPP, 8/RO, 781). Referring to the reversal observed above, Blanchot writes, "Classical art, at least in theory, implied it too, glorying in bringing back resemblance to a figure and the image to a body, in reincorporating it: the image became vitalizing negation, the ideal labor through which man, capable of denying nature, raised it to a higher meaning, either in order to know it, or to take pleasure in it through admiration" (GO, 86/SL, 260/EL, 354–55).

Thus, in classical art, the image can be appropriated as the vitalizing negation, can perform the securing, founding and grounding function that, in the Heideggerian analysis, is the essence of art. The image — evidence of the object's noncoincidence with itself — is covered over, suppressed, totalized, incorporated; in Levinas's words, the image, reflection, shadow, or caricature is absorbed. Similarly, resemblance, the object's excess over itself, becomes the figure of imitation which imposes on resemblance the logic of a relation of two constituted entities — original and copy. Thus it imposes a logic of totalization on a movement whose principle is difference.

Classical art thus appears to be a ruse, a strategy which secures and manipulates the image, annexing it to the service of meaning or aesthetic appreciation. But classical art cannot quite get away with the ruse without an inadvertent concession to the true nature of the image. One of the tenets of classical art, generally assumed to guarantee its truth ("vérifier"), is universality. This appeal to universality affirms the image because its principle is impersonality, anonymity, the indeterminacy of the void: "impersonality was also the troubling site of encounter where the noble ideal, concerned for values, and the anonymous, blind and impersonal resemblance exchanged places and passed for each other in a mutual deception" (GO, 86/SL, 260–61/EL, 355).

The analysis of classical art, like the analysis of the cadaver, functions as a case study. It develops the analysis of the cadaver and builds on its conclusions, illustrating again the tendency to mistake one image for another. The image that lets itself be appropriated in truth is taken to be the truth of the image. However, like the grave site which manifests an attempt to secure certain principles against their inexorable erosion and collapse, classical art attempts to turn impersonality into universality, hence to base a guarantee of truth and veracity on the principle of impersonality which is, itself, the impossibility of truth. The appropriation of the image in classical art is thus only apparently successful and in fact indicates the true nature of the image and our tendency to misunderstand this nature. While the image lends itself to the illusion of power, security, and mastery, its true meaning withdraws it from this domain and is, ultimately, this withdrawal; the image's principle shows itself to be the passivity of fascination, indeterminacy, and anonymity.

It is evidence of the all-powerful nature of God to make man in his image and resemblance (Gen. 1:26–27). But lest one take the story of Genesis either as a model of art and artistic creation, or, more generally as a model of power through the image, Blanchot makes a series of adjustments and reversals (Sitney, Afterword to GO, 184). First, God is removed from the picture. "Man is made in his own image" means that man's identity or totalization (the "making" of man) is based on the principle of resemblance or of difference. This "making" through the image is explored in psychoanalytical terms by Lacan in his analysis of a "mirror stage" in psychological development. And, lest one jump too quickly to the conclusion that this relation can, in turn, produce totalization (by dialectical means for example) Blanchot directs our interpretation of the phrase: "Man is made in his own image: this is what we learn from the strangeness of the resemblance of cadavers. But this formula should first of all be understood this way: *man is unmade according to his image*" (GO, 85/SL, 260/EL, 354). The image is not a moment whose basis, principle, or horizon is totalization or power. Man's "making" in the image is an "unmaking" to the precise extent that it removes totalization, power, effectivity, cognition, and truth as bases of man's existence. Man's constitution is a constitution in difference.

Duplicity and Ambiguity

I have observed on several occasions and in various contexts that Blanchot's analyses characteristically evolve toward ambiguity.[38] Ambiguity is generally either the principle (explicit or implicit) of their development, the point toward which they tend, or both. Because ambiguity expresses the relation of difference, it forestalls the dialectical relation that Blanchot is perpetually challenging. The analysis of the image is a particularly salient example; not only does it evolve toward ambiguity, it makes this ambiguity, itself, ambiguous. This thematizes a second or higher order of ambiguity.

Initially the two versions of the image[39] are related to the two opposite interpretations of negativity in "Literature and the Right to Death." Blanchot describes these as "the fact that death is sometimes the work of truth in the world, sometimes the perpetuity of something that does not tolerate either a beginning or an end" (GO, 86/SL, 261/EL, 355). Thus, on the one hand, the image can be appropriated as a "vitalizing negation" (GO, 88/SL, 262/EL, 358; a term Blanchot has already used to characterize classical art, GO, 86/SL, 260/ EL, 354). On the other hand, the image is that inevitable referral to a neutral double, to impossibility, and to passivity,

to the movement of foundering and collapse that he has described
so dramatically. The articulation of the two versions of the image
in a relation of "either/or" is itself a gesture that belongs to the first
of these two possibilities. The phrase, particularly the verb he uses,
"pacifier par un ou bien ou bien" (EL, 358/GO, 88/SL, 262), recalls the "vitalizing" function of the image which he has initially
described as "d'apaiser, d'humaniser" (EL, 346/GO, 79/SL, 255).
As suggested above, the logic according to which the two types of
image are distinguished is now applied to the relation itself; thus,
there are two articulations, two versions of this relation.

Blanchot thematizes three levels of ambiguity. I will discount
the first since he situates it on the level of the world and describes
what we might call polysemy. The second level of ambiguity is
what has been observed above; the two versions of the image
essentially alternate, vie for space, eclipse or displace each other
continually in a "movement that involves infinite degrees" (GO,
88, 87/SL, 261, 262/EL, 357, 356), such that even if one is always
mistaken for, preempting, or undermining the other, they remain
essentially separate instances. The moments of this alternation are
expressed in the form of "sometimes . . . sometimes" and turn into
"either/or":

> Here, what speaks in the name of the image "sometimes" still speaks
> of the world, "sometimes" introduces us into the indeterminate re-
> gion of fascination, "sometimes" gives us the power to use things
> in their absence and through fiction, thus keeping us within a hori-
> zon rich in meaning, "sometimes" makes us slip into the place where
> things are perhaps present, but in their image, and where the image
> is the moment of passivity, having no value either significative or
> affective, being the passion of indifference. (GO, 88–89/SL, 263/
> EL, 358–59)

Expressed in this way such a relation secures the indeterminacy of
the two moments. It subordinates indeterminacy to initiative and
control by introducing the possibility of choice. Thus while ambi-

guity has provided the basis for the choice, it vanishes through the initiative of choice.

Blanchot then formulates another relation, a second version of ambiguity (which, in the terms of the essay, is a "third level" of ambiguity, also referred to as "essential ambiguity"). This is a relation in which the "sometimes . . . sometimes" alternation and either/or opposition becomes a relation of "always the one and the other" such that the indeterminacy is maintained. In other words, indeterminacy is established as the ultimate basis of determinacy, and as its permanent, though unacknowledged, partner. Here difference is substituted for negativity to account for ambiguity. All meaning becomes image and, as such, is void.

The logic of the essay might suggest a relation of the two types of ambiguity similar to the two types of image: first an alternation and confusion of the one for the other, the tendency to interpret the second (indeterminate ambiguity) as the first (ambiguity determined through choice), then the establishing of a relation that is prior to and more fundamental than their distinction. Instead, Blanchot ends by briefly thematizing ambiguity in terms of Heideggerian dissimulation. According to such an interpretation, ambiguity would be that part of dissimulation that cannot be subsumed as negativity; it is thus a left over, a remainder of dissimulation (Libertson, *Proximity*, 52–55; Hill, *Blanchot*, 77–91, 122–27).

Although the concluding section of the essay indicates the pertinence of Heideggerian concepts to Blanchot's analysis, its principal inspiration is clearly Levinas. It can be considered with only slight exaggeration a reading and development of Levinas's study through Levinas's own concepts.[40] It develops logically and organically, introduces empirical or intuitively straightforward examples, and proceeds incrementally toward ever greater levels of abstraction, initially focusing on analysis of the concrete object and ending by thematizing the relation between two different types of relation.

As observed at the outset, Blanchot's initial analysis of the image derived from Hegel and its logic was that of negativity. However, the logical principle of the major avenues of this analysis — the investigation of the relation of object and image, then of the two types of image, then of the two types of ambiguity — is the concept of difference. It first accounts for the two terms, second, defines the second in relation to the first, finally accounts for their relation, then for the relation of this relation. Thus, for example, the logic of difference initially accounts for the image according to the economy of resemblance or the principle of an object's non-coincidence with itself. The relation of difference then accounts for the image as such (as a relation of being and nothingness, presence and absence, here and nowhere, and so on). Finally the logic of difference explains the relation of the two types of image that Blanchot has described and, in a last step which ratchets this essay to a high level of abstraction, explains the two types of ambiguity.

Encountering the Image

The analysis of the image forms a locus in which the investigations of phenomenology and aesthetics converge in a particularly rich way.[41] As has been observed, it is also a context in which one can appreciate the rich mutual influences of Blanchot and Levinas and, in particular, Blanchot's tendency to formulate in subtle and creative ways the aesthetic dimensions of concepts which he derives from Levinas. For both Levinas and Blanchot, the analysis of the image is a context in which aesthetics challenges and forces a substantial revision of principles of phenomenology. One manner in which this can be observed concretely is the displacement of negativity and dialectic by difference.

Thus the image in both Blanchot and Levinas relies on examples from aesthetics but goes beyond the domain of aesthetics to record fundamental complications in ontology and in phenomenology. It bases the economy of the real in a realm of fascination and passivity.

The encounter with the image is an encounter within being that takes one out of being to a relation of being and nothingness that is prior to being. More precisely, the encounter with the image records a movement from an economy of being where negativity and totalization ground the relation of being and nothingness to one in which difference accounts for it. While, for example, Ulysses' encounter with the Sirens takes place within time, it leads Ulysses to another time, not outside of time, but outside of the present, in the interval of the present's noncoincidence with itself, an "inter-time," the time of the other, the time of difference.

If the image describes a relation of being and nothingness, it also describes, as noted, this relation as prior to the distinction of being and nothingness. Yet what "is" prior to the distinction of being and nothingness? What can "be" prior to being? This logical problem provides the context for Levinas's analysis of the *il y a*. As I shall observe in the following chapter, the Levinasian *il y a* will furnish the essential features of Blanchot's figures of neutrality, impersonality, and "other night," and the encounter with the other night reproduces and develops many of the features that have been identified in the encounter with the image.

FIVE

Encountering the Other Night

In the previous chapter, I observed that both Blanchot and Levinas analyzed the image (and its various corollary forms of shadow, reflection, resemblance, obscurity) as an instance in being that was not reducible to being or, more generally, to the distinction of being and nothingness. Although the image initially appears to follow the object and thus appears to be secondary to the object in a linear temporal sequence, the image ultimately attests a distance or a displacement within the object such that its totalization and identity are understood to be, themselves, secondary and momentary effects of difference. This is consistent with the initial instability which indicates a complication in the opposition of being and nothingness. Though at first it appears in the guise of a temporary deficiency, or a secondary inefficiency, it reveals itself to be more fundamental than the opposition in question because it indicates and manifests a relation that is prior to the opposition.

It is this essential *priority* of the involvement of being with nothingness that serves as the basis of Levinas's investigation of the *il y a*. This analysis first appeared in an essay (published in *Deucalion* I in 1946) and was subsequently integrated in the book

Existence and Existents (1947). In the latter work, the essay forms the initial exposition of the book and the second subsection of a chapter of the book entitled "Existence without World." The first division of this chapter, entitled "Exoticism," is devoted to aesthetics, and its basic argument is parallel with "Reality and Its Shadow" (1948). Noteworthy in this arrangement is the structural importance of the essay "Il y a," the initial pages of which serve as the introduction of the larger work, and the main body of which is indicated by Levinas in the preface to the work's second edition as the book's center of gravity ("morceau de résistance"). Furthermore, the problematic of the *il y a* is introduced by analyzing the exoticism of the work of art.

The general problem of a complication in the distinction and opposition of being and nothingness represents a very broad sector of Blanchot's thought; this is also one of the areas in which the reciprocal influence of Blanchot's and Levinas's analyses is widest-ranging and most visible. At two critical junctures of "Literature and the Right to Death," Blanchot attests Levinas's *il y a* (GO, 51, 55/WF, 332, 337/PF, 320, 324) while, of the four footnotes in *Existence and Existents* (a dearth attributed in the preface to the unusual and difficult conditions of the book's writing), two situate the book with respect to the essay "Il y a" and the other two to Blanchot's fictional works *Thomas the Obscure* and *Aminadab*. The reference to *Thomas the Obscure*, moreover, cites the second chapter of the story as a particularly salient example of the characteristics of the *il y a*. Furthermore, Levinas repeatedly notes the similarity of the *il y a* to certain of Blanchot's key terms such as "le dehors," le "neutre," the "remue-ménage" or murmur of being.[1]

A comprehensive examination of all of these concepts and of their various contexts would prove impractical within the horizon of the present study. In order to observe the elaboration, evolution, and the complex moments of this concept in the texts of both Blanchot and Levinas, I will limit my consideration to one of its defining characteristics — its obscurity or nocturnality. In those texts where Levinas is concerned more with the encounter or "experience" of the *il y a* than with the act of positioning with respect to it that he will call hypostasis, the encounter of the *il y a* is preeminently a nocturnal encounter. And just as Blanchot defines two versions of Levinas's image, he will elaborate, in some of his most dramatic analyses "two versions" of the night: the first night and the other night.[2]

Exoticism and the Il y a

In an inspiration that again appears to run counter to Heidegger's views of the work of art as founding, Levinas in *Existence and Existents* elaborates a view of the artwork as a tearing of an object from the world (Bruns, *Maurice Blanchot*, 58). The artwork does not secure or integrate; it is instead a movement away from the world, an exoticism in the etymological sense, a *wresting* from the world (the verb "arracher" in various forms occurs seven times in this short essay). The context of this argument is consistent with that elaborated by Heidegger; however, the movement runs directly counter to the movement of Heidegger's essays. As Levinas writes: "A painting, a statue, a book are objects of *our* world, but through them the things represented are extracted ["s'arrachent"] from our world" (EE, 52/DEE, 84). The artwork effects thus an alienation of the world. The privilege of sensation over cognition in the experience of an artwork does not suggest that sensation is a precondition of perception and cognition; rather it indicates a fundamental foreignness with respect to cognition and to perception which, Levinas argues, is always perception of and within a world (DEE, 77/EE, 49; LR, 134/CPP, 5/RO, 776). Ingeniously, Levinas then explores the converse of this argument. The alienation effected by the artwork explains why objects which strike one as intrinsically foreign objects, for example, which belong to antiquity or to archaic civilizations, will, without being works of art, produce an aesthetic effect.[3]

Using examples from Rodin and from modern painting (which will often incorporate or juxtapose, in the form of collage for example, real objects with painted ones), Levinas observes modern art's tendency to thematize a brute, crude materiality, the elemental strangeness and density that are prior to the world, that are left over at the end of the world, and, more importantly, that remain resistant to illumination, appropriation, and integration (Bruns, *Maurice Blanchot*, 60–61; Llewelyn, *Emmanuel Levinas*, 34). Levinas identifies this brute formlessness with the *il y a*: "The discovery of the materiality of being is not a discovery of a new quality, but of its formless proliferation [grouillement informe]. Behind the luminosity of forms, by which being[s] [les êtres] already relate to our 'inside,' matter is the very fact of the *there is*" (EE, 57/ DEE, 92). This form and matter opposition recalls the "forme" and "fond" opposition described previously in the context of Blanchot's analysis of the image and articulates the relation of elemental materiality to exteriority (exoticism) and to obscurity.

Il y a

The definition of the *il y a* in the preceding subsection as matter, material, or substance could be misleading if removed from the aesthetic context in which it is located. Here, the *il y a* represents the intrusive presence of something which has resisted form and formal clarity. In relation to the formal characteristics of the artwork, this materiality represents the "en deça" which was described in the consideration of the image in chapter 4. It is left over, excessive, non-assimilable, intrusive, and conspicuously present. Rather than being the "very fact of the *il y a*," it is one example of its apprehension.

The *il y a* is described through a thought experiment which, according to Llewelyn, Levinas borrows from Husserl (*Emmanuel Levinas*, 27–28), although its logic is also analogous to a demonstration of Bergson's to which Levinas alludes and to which he makes several adjustments to help define the *il y a*. If one imagines a negation corresponding to the totality of being, what would remain following its accomplishment? Levinas first thematizes this as a movement of reverse creation, a *return* to nothingness of all beings. What remains is the *il y a*. The expression interests Levinas because it expresses existence without using the verb "to be" (thus "there is" while perhaps the only way to translate "il y a," is not an adequate translation and I have not adopted it here) and it expresses it impersonally and idiomatically.[4] Much of the chapter defining the *il y a*, "Existence sans existant," is an exploration of various metaphors characterizing this abstraction both positively and negatively. Prior to being and nothingness is an "atmosphere," a "field of forces," a presencing of absence, a murmuring silence, an indeterminacy, an anonymity, an impersonality, a density of the void.[5] Among the readers of Levinas, Ciglia and Chalier have proposed interesting and creative characterizations of the *il y a*. Noting that Levinas often attributes to Heidegger his discovery of the pure "verbality" of Being, Ciglia coins an interesting expression to characterize the *il y a*. He speaks of "the remarkable conceptual shift [la remarquable torsion conceptuelle] which takes place in the displacement of the difference between Being and the being" (in *Les Cahiers de la nuit*, 153). Chalier astutely relates the *il y a* to the Hebrew expression *tohu-wa-bohu* used to characterize what existed prior to God's creation of the world and which supplies the etymology of the French word *tohu-bohu*.[6]

Encountering the Il y a

The apprehension or encounter of the *il y a* is an "event" which, as Levinas points out, adjusts the concept of experience: "We could say that the night is the very experience of the *there is*, if the term experience were not inapplicable to a situation which involves the total exclusion of light" (EE, 58/DEE, 94; Davis, *Levinas*, 35). Subsequently, Levinas develops the nocturnal character of the *il y a*; its principal feature is obscurity: "Darkness is the very play [jeu] of existence which would play itself out even if there were nothing. It is to express just this paradoxical existence that we have introduced the term 'there is'" (EE, 64/DEE, 104).

Levinas develops the *il y a* in terms evocative of the aesthetic analysis presented in "Reality and Its Shadow." The *il y a* in both form and function is analogous to the image and shadow, in a sense combining features of both the image and the shadow. The *il y a* corresponds to Levinas's attempts in "Reality and Its Shadow" to derive and describe terms that do not correspond to being or time or to the various divisions they imply (*entretemps, inter-esse*, and so on). Both art and *il y a* are defined as an obscuring, both characterized as a movement reversing the movements of creation and revelation (by extension, both are characterized as prior to the world), both are described as movements that cannot be formulated in dialectical terms (EE, 58/DEE, 94–95; LR, 136, 139/CPP, 7, 10/RO, 780, 784), both involve noncognitive modes of perception for which Levinas will make use of Lucien Lévy-Bruhl's concept of "participation," and both, finally, will lead Levinas to a thematization of the impossibility of death.

In this essay Levinas emphasizes the experience of the *il y a*, an experience, as noted above, that implies revision of the word "experience" itself. Levinas specifies the nocturnal encounter with the *il y a* as nocturnal terror: "Le frôlement de l'*il y a*, c'est l'horreur" (DEE, 98/EE, 60). The noun "horreur" occurs eighteen times in this short essay; if one counts English and French occurrences of the noun "horrible" and the verb "horrifier" one arrives at twenty-one usages of the word in a thirteen-page chapter! The noun "frôlement" is equally interesting and not adequately translated by "rustling" since it indicates an indirect mode of tactile sensation, something less than a grasping. And this "less than" has a distinctly clandestine connotation: indeed, the nouns "frôleur" and "frôleuse" denote sexual perversion, particularly the former. The verb "frôler" opposes itself to the up front, diurnal directness of grasping and seizing in precisely the same manner as the caress, which Levinas analyzes in the context of the phenomenology of eros and which he also relates to obscurity.[7] That the *il y a* "discloses" itself in the manner of a "frôlement" makes it analogous in terms of sensation to the visual perception of the image.

Levinas distinguishes this nocturnal terror from anguish of death, which Levinas first formulates in the general, universal context of ethnology with a reference to the work of Lévy-Bruhl on so-called primitive cultures (EE, 61/DEE, 99–100). He then distinguishes it from existential nausea (EE, 61/DEE, 100) and from existential anguish related to nothingness (EE, 62/DEE, 102), and finally, from the Heideggerian anguish of being-toward-death (EE, 63/DEE, 102; TA, 57/TO, 70). He proceeds to analyze it in various guises and through a series of examples, accounting for the lexical concentration observed above. These examples are concrete and empirical and involve a broad range of literary examples, most prominently *Phaedra, Macbeth*, and *Hamlet* though Levinas will also evoke authors in the fantastic tradition such as Hoffmann, Rimbaud, and Maupassant and the Realist and Naturalist writers Huysmans and Zola. Finally, as noted above, Levinas acknowledges Blanchot's story *Thomas the Obscure*.[8]

Three distinct features of the terror of the *il y a* derive from the indeterminacy of the world, the indeterminacy of the self, and the impossibility of death.

At one level, the *il y a* is both the movement of the world into indeterminacy and the encroaching approach and "presencing" of this indeterminacy. In many ways, it reproduces in the general context of being the movement from the object to the image; in the *il y a*, it is all of being that founders into the formlessness of the void, and this formless anonymity, in turn, invades intrusively and menacingly. While one can still speak of space in the form of a field of forces, an anonymous, impersonal field, "champ sans propriétaire et sans maître," this space cannot be secured. There is no taking its measure: "But the points of nocturnal space do not refer to each other as in illuminated space; there is no perspective, they are not situated. There is a swarming [grouillement] of points" (EE, 58–59/DEE, 96). The indeterminacy itself threatens taking the form of a formless menace, a threatening, anonymous, obscure invasiveness against which there is neither refuge nor recourse; one can neither counter this threat nor withdraw from it. Fluid metaphors, similar to those observed in *Thomas the Obscure* characterize this invasion: "disscudre" (EE, 94), "suinter" (DEE, 97), "nager" (DEE, 97), "submerger" (DEE, 94, 95, 99; Gregg, *Maurice Blanchot*, 109–10). The related term "grouillement" (DEE, 96) is used as well in the previous chapter to qualify this uncanny materiality of being in order to provide an initial definition of the *il y a* as swarming (EE, 59) or proliferation (DEE, 92/EE, 57). It indicates excess with respect to the static status of objects. It describes the swarming action of flightless insects, of worms, and particularly, of maggots; thus it suggests the horrific motion of a dead animal, for example, to whose body maggots impart their own movements. Such an interpretation, though implicit in the word "grouillement," corresponds to the analysis in this text of the cadaver's doubling of himself in the spectre or ghost, and depicts metaphorically the related analysis of the impossibility of death and the horror of immortality.

Levinas next analyzes the dispossession of subjectivity in the *il y a* according to two related axes. First, a dispossession of self cannot be avoided: "Before this obscure invasion, it is impossible to take shelter in oneself, to withdraw into one's shell. One is exposed" (EE, 59/DEE, 96). Dispossession also strips the self of its initiative and power, retaining only its passive vigilance. Here, again, one observes Levinas making use of Lévy-Bruhl's concept of participation to describe an excess over the oppositions of subject and object, and of interior and exterior. "Horror is somehow a movement which will strip consciousness of its very 'subjectivity.' Not in lulling it into unconsciousness, but in throwing it into an *impersonal vigilance*, a *participation*, in the sense that Lévy-Bruhl gives to the term" (EE, 60/DEE, 98; EN, 56/en, 45). Again, the alternatives of identity and its destruction, of consciousness and unconsciousness do not adequately represent the status of subjectivity in the *il y a*. Rather, Levinas seeks terms that indicate an excess over or an intermediary of these alternatives. Although he does not use the term "rhythm" to characterize subjectivity in the *il y a*, it would be an appropriate description.[9] A comparison of Durkheim and Lévy-Bruhl marks the distinction sought here by Levinas. The former retains the subject and object distinction in the experience of the sacred, while the latter's concept of (mystical) participation articulates an identity deprived of its "privacy," an identity whose relation with an exterior is prior to its unicity and which is constituted through difference.

The most striking consequence of Levinas's analysis of the *il y a* is the impossibility of death. The influence of this analysis on Blanchot's "Literature and the Right to Death" has been described in chapter 2. Here one notes the corollary, now in the context of Being, of the temporal analysis of the *entretemps* in "Reality and Its Shadow." Were one to articulate these two analyses simply and literally, one might suggest that the *il y a* is the space of the *entretemps*, and the *entretemps*, the temporality of the *il y a*.[10] As noted, the *il y a* appears to correspond in a much more general manner to the various specific terms that Levinas employs in "Reality and Its Shadow," to indicate an excess over the categories of being and nothingness such as the "inter-esse" or characterizations such as the exteriority of the interior. The *il y a* is the more general but prior characterization of this excess or rather the indication of excess as prior to the distinction of being and nothingness.

The indication of *il y a* as prior to and more fundamental than the distinction of being and nothingness when articulated with the association of death and nothingness situates death, not in the context of nothingness with negativity as its principle, but in the context of the *il y a* with difference as its principle. "A presence of absence, the *there is* is beyond contradiction; it embraces and dominates its contradictory. In this sense being has no outlets" (EE, 64/

DEE, 105). Death is thus neither annihilation nor nothingness; it is neither an exit from being nor the horizon of existence. Its interpretation as such is an attempt to mobilize death within the world of the possible, an attempt to which the *il y a* gives the lie (Ciglia, in *Les Cahiers de la nuit*, 157–58; see chapter 2). In critical moments of horrible realizations, Phaedra, Hamlet, and Macbeth discover that behind death as nothingness, as the possibility of exit from being, there is still being, a perpetuity of existence: "Phaedra discovers the impossibility of death, the eternal responsibility of her being, in a full universe in which her existence is bound by an unbreakable commitment, an existence no longer in any way private" (DEE, 102/EE, 62). One indication of this horror is precisely the image, the ghost, the fact that the cadaver is never at rest but returns to haunt the shadows, to wander or err, as Blanchot puts it. "Spectors, ghosts, sorceresses are not only a tribute Shakespeare pays to his time, or vestiges of the original material he composed with; they allow him to move constantly toward this limit between being and nothingness where being insinuates itself even in nothingness, like bubbles of the earth ('the Earth hath bubbles')" (EE, 62/DEE, 101).

These numerous important intersections of the analysis of the *il y a* with the analysis in "Reality and Its Shadow," the introduction of the *il y a* by way of an example from aesthetics, and the prominent role of literary references in this essay associate art with the *il y a*. These connections can be summarized in the following, somewhat schematic form. Like the *entretemps*, the *il y a* is revealed and first analyzed through art, specifically plastic art. Both art and the *il y a* are related to an obscuring, to a refractoriness to illumination, and to reverting to a state prior to creation; indeed, both rely on the metaphor of reverse creation. In the case of both art and the *il y a*, Levinas indicates the inadequacy of subject/object, conscious/unconscious, interior/exterior distinctions and explores various models of noncognitive perception to characterize subjectivity: among them, Lévy-Bruhl's mystical participation, but also impersonal vigilance, waking dream, and rhythm. Both art and the *il y a* involve a complex relation of difference within time and being which has dramatic implications when applied to the conventional association of death and nothingness and to death as "outside" of, or beyond time. Finally, as observed, the economy of the image is related to the *il y a*. The image is a moment of the *il y a*; conversely, the *il y a* is the basis, telos, and "truth" of the image.

The concept of the *il y a* informs, in addition to *Existence and Existents*, major axes of the analyses in *Time and the Other* and *Totality and Infinity*. The place of aesthetics and the relationship of the *il y a* to aesthetic categories is not as prominent in Levinas's subsequent works. The *il y a* is retained primarily as the background against which an act of emergence is accomplished that produces a subject, a hypostasis, in the act of nomination or identification that constitutes the present. Reversing the movement of the analysis of exoticism, Levinas now uses the act of wresting, and the verb "arracher" to describe the event of hypostasis (EE, 60, 82/DEE, 98, 140; DF, 293/DL, 408; Ciglia, in *Les Cahiers de la nuit*, 155). The three works referred to above chronicle and analyze along generally parallel paths the constitution of this subject and its trajectory toward the other. While the *il y a* remains to disrupt and "haunt" the subject in its journey, it is to the latter that Levinas will direct his attention (Ciglia, *Les Cahiers de la nuit*, 153, 155; Critchley, *Very Little . . . Almost Nothing*, 77–78).

If Levinas seems at this juncture to depart from aesthetics, Blanchot, in *The Space of Literature* especially but also elsewhere (*The Book to Come, The Infinite Conversation*) will take up where Levinas leaves off, exploring the implications of Levinas's definitions with respect to art in general and to writing in particular. Thus Blanchot's analyses of solitude and of the writer's relation to the work, his extensive reflection on the comportments of suicide, the role of the *neutre* and the impersonal, his analyses of night and sleep, will continually adapt and adjust Levinas's arguments in both form and substance to the domain of writing, much as he adapted Levinas's concept of the image in "The Two Versions of the Imaginary" and his reflection on the impossibility of death in "Literature and the Right to Death." In what follows, I will consider an example of this in one of Blanchot's most original and most dramatic essays, his thematization of the "other night."

Writing and Solitude in Blanchot

As I have noted, Blanchot's adaptation of the analysis of the *il y a* to aesthetic problems in *The Space of Literature* is wide ranging and attested by his references to both *Existence and Existents* and *Time and the Other*. Hypostasis, emergence from the anonymity and formlessness of the *il y a*, is thematized by Blanchot in a series of guises to characterize, for example, the act of writing in the analysis of the relation of the work and the book. In a thematization that reproduces the basic terms of Levinas's hypostasis while reversing its direction, in Blanchot's analysis to write is to enter into a relation with an essential anonymity, a formlessness, an *entretemps* expressed here as: "l'interminable, l'incessant." This relation is a passivity, a fascination, a yielding of power. In a series of puns on the words "livre" and "auteur," Blanchot characterizes writing as a delivering of oneself ("livrer," "se livrer") and a yielding of authority: "What he is to write delivers [livre] the one who has to write to an affirmation over which he has no authority" (SL, 26/EL, 16/GO, 68).[11]

In a series of analyses that examine the particular form of the writer's mastery over the act of writing, Blanchot proposes that the ability to write resides in the ability to impose silence on an interminable murmur. It is to break with the indeterminacy of impersonality and the absence of time. Various models of this relation are proposed and various consequences of this situation thematized in terms of specific characteristics and definitions of literary art.

The "préhension persécutrice," or involuntary prehension is one model of the type of power that Levinas has described in terms of the trace or that Blanchot, perhaps more successfully, examines in the story of Orpheus. He imagines a "sick" hand that cannot stop writing, a hand stuck, as it were, in a type of *entretemps* conspicuously characterized by the metaphor of shadow and the economy of resemblance: "The hand moves through a time that is hardly human, that is neither the time of viable action nor the time of hope, but rather the shadow of time which is itself the shadow of a hand slipping in an unreal way toward an object that has become its shadow" (GO, 67/SL, 25/EL, 15).[12] The writer's mastery and ability are the capacity to stop this movement. It is the power to break, to emerge from the indeterminacy, the anonymity or impersonality, the incessance, and the murmuring of this realm of fascination and the absence of time. Hence a writer's tone, for example, is defined by Blanchot as the particular form of silence that the writer is able to impose on this murmuring. "Tone is not the voice of the writer, but the intimacy of the silence he imposes on speech, which makes this silence still his own, what remains of himself in the discretion that sets him to one side" (GO, 70/SL, 27/EL, 18). Just as writing fiction involves a concession to anonymity and impersonality in the substitution of the third person for the first person, the creation of fictional characters attempts to negate this anonymity and preserve a personal form. Fictional characters are thus directly analogous to the inscriptions and monuments in the cemetery. Their truth resides in what they attempt to negate or deny: anonymity and formless, impersonal indeterminacy. And, in an argument that anticipates the versions of the image analyzed in chapter 4, Blanchot relates this impersonality to the universalizing claims of French classical art, where impersonality in the guise of the universal serves as the guarantor of the work's truth (GO, 70/SL, 28/EL, 19). Similarly, the diary form manifests an attempt to secure the personal truth threatened by this relation; its logic too is that of the tomb. Curiously, the diary uses writing as an attempt to secure although writing is this very destabilizing relation. Thus the recourse to the diary is somewhat like attempting to use the poison one has ingested as an antidote.

The analysis of the involuntary prehension is uncharacteristically weak in Blanchot's analyses of art. Libertson wonders at some length what to make of the abrupt, incomprehensible reversal apparent in Blanchot's recourse to Hegelian negation in defining the work of art (*Proximity*, 131–33, 275). In Libertson's view, the logic of silence as mastery is both "disturbingly foreign to," and continually preempted by all of Blanchot's other demonstrations, specifically that of Orpheus. And Libertson concludes that this particular demonstration, as well as several others in *The Book to Come*, reveal — even after the "extrication" represented by "Literature and the Right to Death" (*Proximity*, 206) — a "genuine temptation by the Hegelian concepts" (*Proximity*, 133).

One possible solution to this riddle might be found in Levinas, who, perhaps more than Hegel, informs this model of art as interruption. Indeed, the structure of the involuntary prehension reproduces the structure of hypostasis — whereby a subject constitutes itself out of and against the formless anonymity of the *il y a* in an event which is not a negation of it — and adapts it to the act of writing. One clue might be Blanchot's concept of "essential solitude" in this general context. As noted above, in Levinas, the hypostasis produces a subject in the form of a solitude (TO, 39, 54–58/TA, 18, 35–39). Blanchot's analysis of essential solitude reverses the movement of Levinas's hypostasis, such that for Blanchot, essential solitude is the movement toward the space of formless anonymity, incessance, and neutrality. Blanchot's use of solitude suggests that Levinas, the *il y a*, and hypostasis, more than Hegelian negation, form the context of the analyses in *The Space of Literature*.[13]

Just as Blanchot adapts Hegel's arguments in the *Phenomenology of Spirit* to writing and to literature in the first part of "Literature and the Right to Death," in *The Space of Literature*, Blanchot appears, in many cases, to be adapting Levinas's analyses of the *il y a* to the context of writing and of the literary work. The examples of the involuntary prehension and essential solitude suggest that Blanchot is more convincing when he adapts the inevitable and terrifying return of the *il y a* to the context of writing, rather than the act of emergence which produces a subject in Levinas and would, analogously — according to the model of the involuntary prehension — produce a written work.[14]

The particular positioning of the writer with respect to the work, the various relationships of the writer to the impersonal and the incessant reproduce and often reverse the sequence of the emergence of a solitude from the anonymous vigilance of the *il y a*. Thus, the *il y a*, in the various forms such as neutrality, impersonality, incessance which Blanchot will give it, tends to assume more the role of a disarming and disruptive encounter which undermines the subject.[15] As noted, Levinas accorded particular attention to the apprehension of the *il y a* as an experience of nocturnal terror. This nocturnal encounter, the experience of the *other* night, is one of Blanchot's most striking and most dramatic analyses.

The Other Night

Blanchot's "other" night initially indicates the writer's relation with impossibility (Libertson, *Proximity*, 106, 140). It defines the writer's relation with a sphere where power and initiative cease to be operative principles. It appears to be a concrete instance, a specific, intuitive example of the "thought experiment" that Levinas employs at the beginning of the analysis of *il y a*. The other night is what persists following the disappearance of things in the night. It may be useful to recall how Levinas has characterized the nocturnal quality of the *il y a*.

> When the forms of things are dissolved in the night, the darkness of the night, which is neither an object nor the quality of an object, invades like a presence. In the night, where we are riven to it [or, preferably: "fixated to it" ("rivés à elle")], we are not dealing with anything. But this nothing is not that of pure nothingness. There is

no longer *this* or *that*; there is not "something." But this universal absence is in its turn a presence, an absolutely unavoidable presence. It is not the dialectical counterpart of absence, and we do not grasp it through a thought. It is immediately there. There is no discourse. Nothing responds to us, but this silence; the voice of this silence is understood and frightens like the silence of those infinite spaces Pascal speaks of. (EE, 58/DEE, 94–95; see also EI, 45–51/ Ei, 47–52)

Blanchot formulates the other night in remarkably similar terms: "But when everything has disappeared in the night, 'everything has disappeared' appears. This is the *other* night. Night is this apparition: 'everything has disappeared'" (SL, 163/EL, 215). For the one approaching the other night, "the void is now a presence coming toward him" (SL, 169/EL, 224).

Blanchot's characterization of the other night reproduces a pattern observed in his demonstrations of negativity, the image, and the different levels of ambiguity. In several instances Blanchot revises certain concepts in such a way as to thematize two sides, two operations (two versions or two levels) of each concept. Blanchot often sketches a complex, shifting relation of these two sides or operations, and ascertains the persistent tendency to confuse one for the other. This pattern is most prominent and most striking in his meditation on Hegel and his designation of two types of negativity, two operations of death.

Thus, the analysis of the other night is predicated more on the distinction of the first night and the other night than on the distinction of the day and the night. However, the characterization of the first night requires some attention to the nature of the day. In a series of annex sections in which Blanchot adapts Heideggerian and Hegelian concepts to his analysis, he characterizes the day as the sector of illumination, cognition, and conceptual clarity (based on the dissimulation of Being), as well as the domain of productive endeavor, work, and activity (based on the negation of being and/or of beings), characteristics of Heidegger's *Welt.* Blanchot will assimilate Heideggerian dissimulation and Hegelian negation into the field of the day. In this way, he is able to account for the actual mechanics of the other night's occurrence and its necessity. Dissimulation, generally the dissimulation of Being, is interpreted in Hegelian terms as negation and power; it is integrated in the inexorable unfolding of history and work. Thus dissimulation dissimulates itself. In the world of the day, dissimulation is hidden, out of sight and out of mind. However, incomplete negation can occasion an incomplete dissimulation of dissimulation; when this happens, dissimulation will tend to appear. This appearance of dissimulation, of "all has disappeared" characterizes the other night. Blanchot expresses it as "il y a quelque chose" and cleverly calls it the "apparition" (indicating, as it does in English, the mode of appearance of both ghosts and saints).

> When concealment appears, concealment, having become appearance makes "everything disappear," but of this "everything has disappeared" it makes another appearance. It makes appearance from then on stem from "everything has disappeared." "Everything has disappeared" appears. This is exactly what we call an *apparition*. It is the "everything has disappeared" appearing in its turn. And the *apparition* says precisely that when everything has disappeared, there still is something: when everything lacks, lack makes the essence of being appear, and the essence of being is to be there still where it lacks, to be inasmuch as it is hidden. (SL, 253/EL, 344)

Levinas's *il y a* is palpably present in this thematization of the apparition formulated by means of Heideggerian dissimulation. Specifically, the persistence of something when all has disappeared and the generality of being, part of a configuration of no exit from being, reproduce the logic of the thought experiment that guides Levinas in the definition of the *il y a*, the characteristics that he attributes to it, and the consequences that he derives from it.

To the extent that the day is the domain of productive, "worlding" negation in which dissimulation is a form of negation, the first night or the night of the day belongs to the day and is appropriated by the day as an opposition or negation that permits the day's dialectical accomplishment (Libertson, *Proximity*, 97). Night and day are components of a totality that is day's higher accomplishment. "When we oppose night and day and the movements accomplished in each, it is still to the night of day that we allude" (SL, 167/EL, 222). It is the fragile, tentative nature of this arrangement, the fact that the harmony, stability, and security it implies are about to be dramatically revised by the horrifying encroachment and intrusiveness of the other night that accounts for the sarcasm and the hint of irony in Blanchot's acknowledgment of the efficacy of the dialectical relation of day and night: "Then day is the whole of the day and the night, the great promise of the dialectic" (SL, 167/EL, 222). Thus, the first night is a pause in the diurnal-nocturnal cycle. It is a suspension of productive activity that is effected in view of and as a condition of that productive activity.[16] It is silence, sleep, and rest. While it can be mysterious, it remains alluring and inviting; its mystery yields to the clarity of the day. Its essence is to be hospitable to the underlying demands and requirements of the day. Since its principle is negation, the first night is also the night in which one encounters death as limit and finitude, in the first of death's operations that Blanchot describes in "Literature and the Right to Death."

The characteristics of the other night that Blanchot defines in a general manner are opposed to the characteristics of the coupling of day and night. In these descriptions the similarity to Levinas is striking. In the other night, Blanchot writes, death is never dead enough (SL, 163/EL, 215). This image is one way that Levinas characterizes the "entretemps" in "Reality and Its Shadow": "It is as though death were never dead enough, as though parallel with the duration of the living ran the eternal duration of the interval — the meanwhile." (LR, 141/CPP, 11/RO, 786). The other night is also "outside"; it is, one could say using Levinas's aesthetic language, "exotic" or, borrowing Levinas's characterization of the *il y a*, it is an exteriority that cannot be correlated to an interiority (EE, 58/DEE, 95; SL, 164/EL, 216; EE, 52/DEE, 84). But

Blanchot's most dramatic characterizations of the "other" night are not theoretical or abstract but drawn from the stories of Tolstoy and Kafka, stories that recount the uncanny terror of the encounter of the other night.

Two Stories of the Other Night

The two stories to which Blanchot refers tell of reaching the limits of power. The first example is that of Brekhounov in Tolstoy's story, "Master and Man." The protagonist, a wealthy and successful merchant "decided and enterprising" (SL, 165, 166/EL, 219), becomes lost in the frozen night of the Russian winter with his servant Nikita. The story examines his reaction as it dawns on him that the trap of death is closing. Brekhounov's initial reaction is negation or denial. He still reasons in terms of power and obstacles; he abandons Nikita and his sled and goes off to find the way to safety. However, unbeknownst to him, he has entered that domain in which powerlessness replaces power as the operative principle of action, where, as Blanchot puts it, each step forward is also a step backward. The resolute march toward safety gradually turns into a circular wandering which leads Brekhounov back to his point of departure and to his dying servant Nikita. Still resolute, determined to confront the situation, Brekhouvov warms his freezing servant. At that point, however, he begins to crack. Interestingly, the expression that Blanchot uses to record the moment at which Brekhounov begins to falter, "But at that instant something happens [Mais à cet instant quelque chose se passe]" (SL, 166/EL, 219) is precisely the expression that Levinas uses, in a more general context, in order to describe the excess over nothingness of the *il y a*. He writes, "Let us imagine all beings, things and persons, reverting to nothingness. One cannot put this return to nothingness outside of all events. But what of this nothingness itself? Something would happen [Quelque chose se passe] if only night and the silence of nothingness. The indetermination of this 'something is happening' ['quelque chose se passe'] is not the indeterminateness of a subject and does not refer to a substantive" (DEE, 93/EE, 57). What "happens" to Brekhounov is neither fear nor anguish but the experience of weakness, of powerlessness, of a passivity that is not altogether unpleasant. Subsequently, Brekhounov's frozen body is found lying on top of his servant's (who survives) as if still trying to warm him. Blanchot then turns his attention to possible misreadings of this ending.

The obvious temptation is to draw moral conclusions from this ending. In such a scenario, Brekhounov would discover, in death, human solidarity. Blanchot even suggests and immediately discounts the possibility of an ironical Hegelian interpretation (such as that observed in the case of Ulysses): "To die is not to become a good master, or even one's own servant: it is not a moral advance" (SL, 166/EL, 220). Initially, Blanchot refuses to accord any meaning to Brekhounov's gesture. The gesture cannot be given positive moral meaning; it signifies nothing because it is a gesture that occurs outside the domain of Brekhounov's intention, initiative, and power. It is the involuntary, meaningless, and futile act of someone approaching death: "To lie down upon Nikita: this is the incomprehensible and necessary movement that death wrings from us" ["que nous arrache la mort"] (SL, 166/EL, 220). Yet once understood as a gesture beyond Brekhounov's power, it does have meaning, in the manner of a trace. The meaning, like that of the inscriptions in the cemetery or the various literary procedures and techniques that have been observed above, derives from what Brekhounov's gesture attempts to negate. The approach of the impersonal, anonymous, and indeterminate wrests from Brekhounov the gesture of one who is drowning, the desperate clinging to a form that is human.

Brekhounov's experience is an "expérience limite," the experience of a most radical otherness, an otherness that one does not survive. Here, the other night is encountered as part of the approach to death. However, Brekhounov's experience can be attributed to lack of judgment. He acted imprudently in wandering far from home into the night and the snow. He has, in a sense, approached the Sirens without taking the necessary precautions. So Blanchot turns his attention to the encounter experienced by one who has taken all of the necessary precautions, a character who has not only stayed home but whose energy, initiative, and action are devoted to securing his dwelling: the creature in Kafka's "The Burrow."[17]

In his *Poetics of Space*, Bachelard qualifies the animal's burrow as the preeminent image of coziness, security, safety, and intimate comfort (what we call colloquially "creature comfort") (91/93). While this may be so most of the time, Kafka's story records what happens in those rare moments when the burrow becomes the setting of the most disarming encounter. Making use once again (here and later) of the verb "livrer," Blanchot explains, "The more the burrow seems solidly closed to the outside, the greater the danger that you be closed in with the outside, delivered [livré] to the peril without any means of escape. And when every foreign threat seems shut out of this perfectly closed intimacy, then it is intimacy that becomes menacing foreignness. Then the essence of danger is at hand. There is always a moment when, in the night, the beast hears the other beast. This is the *other* night" (SL, 168/EL, 223). Like the apprehension of the *il y a*, described by Levinas as the sounds that one still hears in the silence of the night or the sound one hears in a sea shell (EI, 46–48/Ei, 48–50), the other creature's approach is experienced first as a faint, barely perceptible sound: "It is only a muffled whispering, a noise one can hardly distinguish from silence, the seeping sounds of silence. Not even that" (SL, 168/EL, 223). It is in the creature's waiting in vigilant attention to this noise that Kafka's story ends.

Once again, Blanchot identifies a telling misreading of Kafka's story. According to Blanchot, Kafka's editors have interpreted the story as incomplete. One editor speculates that the pages chronicling the "decisive" conflict of the two creatures and subsequent death of the protagonist are missing. Here, the editor commits a revealing gesture of negation in response to Kafka's accurate fictional portrayal of the temporality of the other night, a temporality in which such incompletion and incessance are integral components. The editor's gesture reveals the desire that the indeterminacy be determined, that the approach be followed and completed by presence, and that the waiting be resolved in confrontation and finitude, even in the form of death.

The encounter of Kafka's creature with the other night adds a complication to the story of Brekhounov demonstrating the relation of the other night's encounter with both any defensive strategy that one might devise in anticipation of it and with any evasive action that one might take in response to it.[18] Like Brekhounov's circular trajectory in the snow, defensive or evasive action only ensures the encounter that one is trying to avoid. One flees toward the threat, then realizes too late that one has twice misjudged and doubly miscalculated, taking the enemy for a friend and confidant, assuming security where threat was at its greatest.

Blanchot introduces a further dimension by associating the construction of the burrow with the activity of the day. Paradoxically, one can take the evasive action that guarantees the encounter prior to being aware of any threat. To secure the day through labor and activity is to annex the night to the purposes of the day. But since the night always contains the other night, *any* diurnal activity is already movement in the direction of the encounter with the other night: "But to labor for the day is to find, in the end, the night; it is thus to make night the job [l'oeuvre] of the day, to make night a task and an abode. It is to construct the burrow. And to construct the burrow is to open night to the *other* night. The risk of surrendering to [se livrer à] the inessential is itself essential. To flee it is to be pursued by it. It becomes the shadow which always follows you and always precedes you" (SL, 169/EL, 225). To be working for the day is to have embarked already on the path toward the night and thus to be exposed to the horrifying intrusion of the other night.

In marked contrast, therefore, to Brekhounov, whose encounter with the other night occurs under the most extreme circumstances and as a result of fatal imprudence, the story of Kafka's creature situates this encounter closer to home. It makes the encounter not only a common occurrence but an unavoidable one (Libertson, *Proximity*, 45). In his description of the essentially nocturnal character of the *il y a*, Levinas qualifies its apprehension as inevitable: "But this universal absence is in its turn, a presence, an absolutely unavoidable presence" (EE, 58/DEE, 94). Levinas emphasizes but does not account for this inevitability; Blanchot's reading of Kafka provides a model for the necessity of the encounter with the *il y a*, or with the other night.

Difference and the Other Night

The *il y a* is described by Blanchot as one of Levinas's "most fascinating propositions" (OCC, 49/NCC 86). It is also the site of perhaps the richest, longest, and most complicated encounter of the thought of Blanchot and Levinas. As noted in chapters 2 and 4 respectively, the *il y a* figures prominently and decisively in Blanchot's analyses of the problems of death and of the image. The concept, with its defining attributes of passivity, fascination, impersonality, nocturnality, indeterminacy, generality, and neutrality (opposed to the generosity and abundance, as Levinas puts it, of Heidegger's *es gibt*, and to the elevation of Hegel's formulations) is thematically rich. In addition, the *il y a* gives Blanchot a way to articulate life and death, being and nothingness, presence and absence, silence and sound, consciousness and unconsciousness within a relation of difference. This paradoxical relation or involvement is neither fusion nor dialectic and presents itself as prior to, and more basic than the distinction and opposition of these concepts. As both Levinas and Blanchot observe, these oppositions belong to the world, but prior to or beneath this world what is uncovered — in disarming and terrifying encounters or realizations — is an essential involvement, or belonging together. The *il y a*, like Blanchot's *neutre* (which expresses more explicitly this intermediary indeterminacy) is essentially a figure of a relation of difference.[19]

There are other features of the encounter in the other night which also articulate a relation of difference. As observed, the encounter with the other night in Blanchot is an encounter that takes place beyond the jurisdiction of a subject's power, manifested in the encounter's inevitability, specifically in the impossibility of avoiding or fleeing it. As both the stories of Brekhounov and Kafka's creature illustrate, the danger can neither be avoided nor countered because it has already invested the strategies of avoidance, opposition, and flight. Like prohibition in Bataille which makes transgression inevitable, action and decision are already involved with passivity with the latter as the basis of the former. Power's principle and context is its essential and prior involvement with powerlessness. Another reason that the encounter of the other night cannot be avoided is that it cannot be timed. The attempt to secure the temporal approach of the other night, to localize and identify a specific moment at which the first night passes into the other night runs into complication. This problem is evoked in the analogy of the spatial approach of the Sirens, the event of the encounter of the Sirens, and the origin of writing. It involves a "fissile present," an instant or moment which reveals itself to be composed of two events, each of which must precede the other. In this example, in which Blanchot borrows a formula from his analysis of Mallarmé's *Igitur* and in which, again, Blanchot's recourse to the verb "se livrer" is notable, the constitution of the present in terms of difference is particularly clear:

> Whoever senses the approach of the *other* night has the impression that he is approaching the heart of the night, the essential night which he seeks. And no doubt it is "at that moment" that he gives himself [se livre] up to the inessential and loses all possibility. Thus it is that moment which he must avoid, just as the traveler is advised to avoid the point where the desert becomes seductive mirage. But

such prudence is useless here. There is no exact moment at which one would pass from night to the *other* night, no limit at which to stop and come back in the other direction. Midnight never falls at midnight. Midnight falls when the dice are cast, but they cannot be cast till Midnight. (SL, 169; 116/EL, 224–25; 146)

Blanchot proposes that the approaching creature in "The Burrow" whose excavating noises are perceived is actually the self apprehended in a relation of disjunction or of noncoincidence with itself: "What the beast senses in the distance — the monstrous thing which eternally approaches it and works eternally at coming closer — is itself. And if the beast could ever come into this thing's presence, what it would encounter would be its own absence: itself, but itself become the other, which it would not recognize, which it would not meet" (SL, 169/EL, 224).

Thus at all levels of Blanchot's analyses of the other night — the characterization of the other night, the constitution of the subject, the thematization of the subject's action, initiative, and power, and the question of time — analysis evolves toward the various figures of relations of difference where figures of identity reveal prior involvement and figures of opposition or distinction indicate prior relatedness.

In his study of Blanchot and Levinas, Simon Critchley makes the provocative assertion that the *il y a* is "the secret of Blanchot's work" (*Very Little . . . Almost Nothing*, 63, 65).[20] Critchley's statement points to the problem of difference as a fundamental insight formulated and explored in virtually all of Blanchot's texts since the *il y a* is perhaps the most striking — and disturbing — thematic expression of difference.

Conclusion

Difference and Interpretation

In the course of the previous chapters, I have discerned certain threads and common principles in the texts of both Blanchot and Levinas. In novel and unusual configurations of subjectivity and intersubjectivity; in the theme of death; in the relation of art and otherness and the complex "phenomenology" of the image; in the problem of time; or in the general problem of the *il y a*, these texts present a common set of difficulties.

Paradox and oxymoron, aporetic formulations, contradictory, indeterminate, and ambiguous expressions form a common thematic feature of the works of both writers. I have also focused on Blanchot's tendency, both in his conceptual vocabulary and in the evolution of his analytic essays and stories, to progress toward ever greater abstraction, higher levels of logical difficulty and complexity. In following the often tortuous, circuitous paths of his studies and stories, one finds that rather than proceeding toward thematic or conceptual clarity, they tend to lead to what often resembles intractable hermeneutical complexity or interpretive impasse.

Many readers of both Blanchot and Levinas — and some of the most penetrating and discerning of these — have concluded that these texts hover on the very limits of sense and even cross its threshold; indeed, it has been proposed by some readers that these texts defy understanding and interpretation.[1] Such conclusions imply that the reader's role is to describe with accuracy the particular difficulties the texts present, to analyze the nature of this complexity, and to locate within the texts specific regions of particular interpretive resistance. While such tasks are both important and useful, it is also important to try to provide an account of the thematic necessity or justification of this complexity lest it be attributed to a penchant for obscurantism, and thus be ultimately an expression of stylistic idiosyncrasies, thematic eccentricities, poetic images and glib formulas intended to perplex, as readers have also suggested.[2]

For reasons intrinsic to their positions and arguments, both Blanchot and Levinas reject the intellectualizing, theorizing approach that integrates a multiplicity of diverse problems, varied texts, complex terms and images into a single principle, a common figure, or a unique method. As mathematician René Thom puts it, referring to the pioneering work of Emile Meyerson in the field of epistemology: "Theorizing is essentially the art of reducing to the principle of identity [réduire à l'identique]. On the basis of very diverse data, and often, at first glance, very different data, the scientific approach will manage to bring to light a single process, a single phenomenon [un seul processus, un phénomène unique]."[3] The rejection of this principle leads both Blanchot and Levinas to notoriously unstable conceptual vocabularies. A single metaphor, image, term or concept is invested with multiple and opposing meanings; common polarities are reversed; contradiction is essential rather than accidental; ambiguity is the condition, basis, and horizon of meaning rather than its temporary interruption or impediment. Both writers attend to the double-entendres, puns, ambiguities, and contradictions contained within the system of language.

In addition, both Blanchot and Levinas revisit, revise, rewrite, displace their own texts, each other's texts, and the texts of others. Both writers evince an uneasiness with systematic methodological practices and especially with the West's perennial theoretical bias in favor of unity, synthetic identification and totalization.[4] In particular, both thinkers reject the dialectical form of reasoning and argument as a form which both assumes and yields identity and unity. This stance poses other interpretive problems since their analyses will often either appear to adopt the dialectical form or will, in fact, adopt it but with the intention of undermining, subverting, or reversing its development. This leads to their relatively complicated intertextual systems of reference, involving creative appropriation, mimicry, parody, and subtle polemic, especially with respect to the texts of Hegel and, to a lesser degree, to those of Heidegger.[5] It has been one of this study's arguments that the principal vehicle of both thinkers' questioning of the dialectic has been their introduction, in its stead, of a relation of difference. The reverse dialectical pattern of their writing has consistently highlighted an oppositional relation in which the very identity, unicity, and totalization of the terms or concepts within the relation are at issue. The concept of difference describes this coherently although not without presenting other problems.

Whenever identity is put into question, there is a tendency to make a principle of incoherence, to postulate a conceptual vacuum and to thematize generalized indeterminacy and meaninglessness, a logical or illogical instability and formlessness. Yet the relation of difference does yield principles of coherence, as counterintuitive as they appear. As observed in chapter 1 and noted elsewhere, by questioning and establishing identity on the basis of prior relation, the principle of difference coherently thematizes two ideas which appear counterintuitive and which assume paradoxical or contradictory expressions: an instability, a mediation, or a relation within identity itself and a latent connectedness ("concealed solidarity") of separate, distinct, or opposite elements, terms, or concepts. When applied to basic thematic divisions, to such fundamental elements of our conceptual vocabulary as the problems of time, subjectivity and intersubjectivity, presence, Being and nothingness, and life and death, this principle yields striking, perplexing, and often disturbing images.

Among the configurations of time, there are: the concept of a "fissile" or "open" present, a moment of origin or encounter composed of prior elements preceding each other; the concept of a problematic *entretemps* formulating a latent relatedness of the present and of futurity; and the image of a problematic gap or interval in which characteristics of entities "separated" by this interval — present and future — meet, producing a temporality experienced as a distortion or an "absence" of time, as eternal duration, as "incessance," and "interminable" awaiting, the burden of perpetual patience and the suffering of impatience. A comparable configuration articulates the relation of the past and present in Levinas's trace, or in the constitution of the present in the manner of a recurrence or repetition, or in the thematization of an immemorial, forgotten past observed perhaps most dramatically in some of Levinas's definitions of the ethical subjectivity.

Striking interpretations of subjectivity follow from these formulas of difference. Blanchot's Thomas and his analysis of Kafka's burrow, as well as Levinas's economy of shadow and resemblance all highlight a disruption, a destabilizing, or an ungrounding of the subject. This study records complications in the relation of subject and object in the concept of the image, in Levinas's participation, and in Blanchot's solitude and fascination. Yet Levinas has used the principle of difference — of relation as the basis of unicity and identity — to reconfigure the subject in a novel interpretation of intersubjectivity as ethical *a priori*.

I have underscored how the economy of the image, Levinas's *il y a*, as well as Blanchot's versions of the other night can be interpreted in accordance with the concept of difference, specifically as a priority of the relation of Being and nothingness, of life and death, of presence and absence, over the separateness, distinctness, or opposition of these concepts. And I have ascertained the role of

Levinas's *il y a* in Blanchot's extrication from the reasoning and the intellectual horizon of Hegel's exemplary dialectic of life and death as the foundation of the life of Spirit.

It is not the purpose of this study to reproduce the theorizing reductiveness so pointedly criticized by Blanchot and Levinas and to thematize the extremely creative and varied formulations of these two authors in accordance with a single principle. Nor do I wish to suggest that all of the difficulties these texts present can be subsumed, accounted for, explained, or resolved by means of a single concept. Yet, even where the coherence of these texts resides in their challenges to conventional norms of coherence, where the basic posture of both thinkers involves a displacement of meaning and of the conditions of meaning, it is still the reader's role to seek to understand and express these issues in terms as straightforward and as conventional as possible (indeed, I have noted with disapproval the tendency of some readers of Blanchot and Levinas to employ as analytic tools the very images, metaphors, and concepts which need to be examined, clarified, or explained).[6] Thus the theorizing approach that has been adopted here has been used with an awareness of its necessity and the attempts to compensate for certain of its limitations through close attention to the texts themselves.

In the texts of Derrida and Heidegger, I considered some of the logical difficulties presciently anticipated and accurately described by Saussure in relation to his formula of "differences without positive terms." Some of the strikingly creative, original, and provocative formulations in the texts of both Levinas and Blanchot represent various thematic possibilities of the application of this principle.

From Art to the Ethical Subject

As readers of the *International Herald Tribune* may, perhaps, recollect, the venerable Swiss watchmaker Patek-Philippe touts its prestigious timepieces in terms of the degree of sophistication of their mechanical complications. That a complication can be an object of beauty and subject to an appreciation that is both intellectual and aesthetic, technical and artistic, is a premise of such marketing and invites comparison with Blanchot's and Levinas's approach to various themes and problems, including the problem of time. However, while the logical complexity in the works of Levinas and Blanchot makes an initial or even a lasting impression (Davis, *Levinas*, 91, 135, 140), many of the principles of these texts correspond to very simple, intuitive, and straightforward notions, as Levinas has emphasized in many interviews. Perplexing concepts like the *il y a* have been expressed through very accessible metaphors: the sound of the sea in a shell, the "sound of silence" when one is unable to sleep, or a child's nocturnal anguish (Bident, *Maurice Blanchot*, 46). Levinas's aesthetic investigations have as a common denominator the feeling of alienation experienced before a work of art. And some of his most complicated and laborious ethical formulas can, as he has repeatedly noted, be expressed in such simple and basic terms as the elementary courtesy of saying "after you, sir" or in the relation that one has with one's own child or with another's face.

Blanchot's typical analytic gesture and frequent articulation of difference are, essentially, a reminder that there are always two sides to every coin and to every issue, a dictum in which one hears echoes of F. Scott Fitzgerald and Laclos (quoted in the introduction to this study). Instead of poetical, paradoxical, or dialectical thematizations of this simple principle, the question of difference affords the possibility of not only confirming its validity but of understanding why it has validity. Because difference is one of the principles of identity, rivenness and internal tension are among identity's characteristics. Conversely, figures of distinction and opposition are characterized by latent involvement and complicity. These principles have been broadly generalized by the practitioners of deconstruction.

It has not generally been a concern of this study to situate

Blanchot and Levinas within a panorama of modern critical tendencies and practices, and it would prove unwieldy to initiate such a reflection here. However, the thought of Blanchot and Levinas significantly distinguishes itself from such a horizon in the analysis of the trace. In Blanchot's aesthetic analyses which relate to it (such as his analyses of Orpheus or Ulysses) and in virtually all of the major sectors of their investigations, Blanchot and Levinas have dissociated the notion of power from critical or aesthetic enquiry. This important distinction puts in perspective the assumptions of power latent or explicit in many modern critical approaches influenced by Marxism, Foucault, or involving questions of race, ethnicity, gender, and so on. From the critical analysis of strategies and tactics of "disempowerment" to the investigation of modes and methods of "re-empowerment," modern critical thought has remained "exhausted by the notion of power" (Libertson, *Proximity*, 1). Real and urgent questions of justice in the political, economic, and social realms of the modern world provide compelling reasons why power should be a central concern to all citizens, and Levinas in particular has addressed himself explicitly to such questions. But just as it would be naive to ignore the structures of power which influence art and inform criticism, it is important to recognize that the work of art often speaks from and to a sector of human experience for which power is neither an underlying principle nor a relevant concept. The aesthetic reflection of Levinas and Blanchot recalls the tragically unheeded warning issued by Tiresias to Pentheus in Euripedes' *The Bacchae*: "Mark my words, Pentheus. Do not be so certain that power is what matters in the life of man" (ll. 309–11). As Euripides' tragedy reveals, Tiresias's warning cannot be converted to positive form; no higher certainty derives from the certainty that it negates. Yet, in Levinas's challenge to ontology — a challenge for which the artwork has provided the primary and initial conceptual framework — Euripides' formula is succinctly taken one step further: "The human presents itself only in the case of a relation which is not one of power."[7]

As the previous example suggests, the aesthetic reflection of Blanchot and Levinas is elaborated in relation to a rich Western heritage of literature and philosophy, a heritage incorporating the Hellenic, Judaic, and Christian traditions.[8] There is at the same time, as Ciglia has put it, a pressing urgency to Levinas's ethical thinking, an "out of breathness,"[9] a conviction that the scope of the tragedies of twentieth century history evinces an ethical failing which may involve and reveal a structural flaw in the West's way of understanding the human subject. Such an intuition entails a need for new ethical solutions, for a new way of approaching the subject. If it remains the task and the responsibility of the writer to formulate original and creative ways of approaching old problems, both Blanchot and Levinas may be said to have done so through the relation of difference. The striking originality in the proposition of ethics as first philosophy and the attendant definition of the subject through a configuration of responsibility offer thought-provoking and creative avenues which nevertheless remain tied to and often expressed by a Biblical tradition and a relation to God. It is striking that an ethical reflection elaborated, in part at least, in response to historical tragedy on so vast a scale[10] can have as a guiding principle the extraordinary generosity of Levinas's ethical subject.

Notes

Notes to Introduction

1. Bernasconi and Critchley, eds., *Re-Reading Levinas*; Robert Bernasconi and David Wood eds., *The Provocation of Levinas: Rethinking the Other*; Bruns, *Maurice Blanchot*; Davis, *Levinas*; Hill, *Blanchot*; Lingis, Introduction to OB; Peperzak, *To the Other* and *Beyond*; Wyschogrod, *Emmanuel Levinas*.

2. See Joseph Libertson, *Proximity*, 207; Collin, *Maurice Blanchot*, 17–18, 21; Bruns, *Maurice Blanchot*, xxiv.

3. Lescourret, *Emmanuel Levinas*, xx; Leslie Hill, *Blanchot*, 10–11, and Introduction to Gill, *Maurice Blanchot*, 5. Bident, *Maurice Blanchot*, 43–44.

4. Bruns, *Maurice Blanchot*, xv. In characterizing Blanchot's relation to Hegel in "Literature and the Right to Death," P. Adams Sitney uses the expression "ironic aestheticization"; see his Afterword to GO, 175.

5. Moreover, Blanchot's rejection is predicated upon the concepts of the neuter and the *il y a* (OCC, 49/NCC, 85–86), as if seeking pointedly to invalidate Levinas's "break with the philosophy of the Neuter" announced at the end of *Totality and Infinity* (restated at the end of *Otherwise Than Being* [OB, 184/AE, 282]) and with which Levinas explicitly associates Blanchot's name (Ti, 298/TI, 332). For succinct formulations of this question, see also Bruns, *Maurice Blanchot*, 110–11 and "Blanchot/Levinas," 136, 140; Hill, Introduction to Gill, *Maurice Blanchot*, 15; *Blanchot*, 136–37; Shaviro, *Passion and Excess*, 157.

6. See below, chapter 1. See also Blanchot, NCC, 86/OCC, 49–50 and ED, 35–47/WD, 18–27. Consider also, for example, Libertson's account of Blanchot's misreading of Levinas in *The Infinite Conversation* (*Proximity*, 279–89).

7. Davis acknowledges the same back and forth conceptual movement in Levinas. For reasons which shall be explained subsequently, Davis is able to thematize this movement only in terms of paradox. See Davis, *Levinas*, 38, 72, 73, 127, 128, 136.

8. See, in particular, Libertson's introduction to *Proximity*, 1–8; see also Collin, *Maurice Blanchot*, 214; Peperzak, *To the Other*, 16; and Blegen, "Writing the Question," 13–17. Gregg, whose study is close to Libertson's in this respect, refers to this question when he speaks of "philosophers of difference," *Maurice Blanchot*, 26–27, 183–84.

9. Paradox, oxymoron, aporia, and ambiguity in the works of Levinas and Blanchot are far too consistent a feature of the criticism of both writers to warrant extensive documentation. However, some particularly forceful or useful formulations, including conclusions regarding the theoretical impasse that I have noted would include: Blegen, "Writing the Question," 14; Deguy, "Maurice Blanchot" 712–13; De Man, *Allegories of Reading*, 205, qtd. by Hill, *Blanchot*, 67; Gregg, *Maurice Blanchot*, 109; Hill, *Blanchot*, 61, 65–67; Laporte, *Maurice Blanchot*, 15, 40; Londyn, *Maurice Blanchot romancier*, 134; Shaviro, *Passion and Excess*, 143; qtd. by Mole, *Levinas, Blanchot, Jabès*, 120; Stamelman, *Lost Beyond Telling*, 35.

10. My translation of "souvent le paradoxe est le commencement d'une vérité" Laclos, *Oeuvres complètes*, 389. Diderot's Jacques makes a similar observation: "Paradoxical isn't necessarily the same as false [Un paradoxe n'est pas toujours une fausseté]" in *Jacques the Fatalist*, 46/*Jacques le fataliste*, 89.

11. Davis, *Levinas*, 25, 31, 35, 48. Davis concludes his monograph on Levinas and sums up Levinas's ethics with the theme of the encounter: "Levinas's ethics revolve around the possibility that I might encounter something that is radically other than myself. . . . The possibility of an encounter with the Other, in both ethical and hermeneutic senses, is the cornerstone of Levinas's thought" (142).

12. Blanchot, in fact, disparages this connection using Levinas's words against him and characterizing it as "an exigency that is beyond us (and frustrates us) [une exigence qui nous excède]" (OCC, 47/NCC, 84).

13. Levinas is fond of citing the pronouncement in Dostoevsky's *Brothers Karamazov* by the character Markel, the brother of Zosima: "we are all guilty towards others and I am the guiltiest of all" (347). See, for example, OB, 146/AE, 228; EN, 115, 117/en 105, 107; EI, 105, 108/Ei, 98, 101; II, 264; DDVI, 119, 134–35; TO, 108; DMT, 216/GDT, 187; Cohen, *Face to Face with Levinas*, 31; Petitdemange and Rolland, *Autrement que savoir*, 72; Malka, *Lire Levinas*, 112. In fact, Zosima's notion of unlimited answerability is remarkably consonant with Levinas's. Furthermore, Zosima's contention that the solution of the particular drama and pathos of the individual through the assumption of this unlimited responsibility is consonant with the most fundamental level of Levinas's ethics: "Rid yourselves of that despair, children. There is one way for you to overcome these obstacles: take firm hold of yourselves and make yourselves answerable for all men's sins. This is also the truth, friends! For as soon as a man sincerely accepts the idea that he is answerable for the sins of all men, he will realize that that is, indeed, the truth, that he is answerable for everybody and everything"

(387). See also Hand, Introduction to LR, 1; Robbins, *Altered Reading*, 147; Bernasconi and Critchley, *Cambridge Companion to Levinas*, 239.

Notes to Chapter One

1. See Bernasconi's excellent and detailed analysis of Derrida and Levinas, "The Trace of Levinas in Derrida," 13–29. See also Robbins, *Altered Reading*, 26–30.

2. For a broad and useful perspective on the various controversies provoked by Derrida's work in general see the introduction to Schultz and Fried, *Jacques Derrida*, xiii–li. A more focused analysis, while still a survey of various views about Derrida can be found in Richard Rorty, "Is Derrida a Transcendental Philosopher?," 235–46. This essay is also contained in Madison, ed. *Working through Derrida*, 137–46. In this collection, it is followed by a reply by John Caputo "On Not Circumventing the Quasi-Transcendental: The Case of Rorty and Derrida," 147–69. There are innumerable considerations of the concept of "différance." Among the more useful or focused are: Gasché, *Inventions of Difference*, especially chapter 3; Harvey, *Derrida and the Economy of Différance*, especially chapter 6; Allen, "Difference Unlimited" in Madison, ed., *Working Through Derrida*, 5–27 and Gutting, *French Philosophy*, 298–304. See also Wood and Bernasconi, eds., *Derrida and Différance*, especially Brogan, "The Original Difference: Différance," Bernasconi, "The Trace of Levinas in Derrida," 13–29 and Ormiston, "The Economy of Duplicity: Différance," 41–49.

3. John Searle, in his criticism of Derrida and of Culler's presentation of Derrida, does not concede this point. Hence, he challenges as a "false claim" and rejects as a "second thesis that does not follow from" Saussure's concept of difference, the constitution of meaning without positive entities, or, in Derrida's words, as a system of traces and referrals. On this particular point, I am not in agreement with Searle. See "The World Turned Upside Down" in Madison, ed., *Working through Derrida*, 176.

4. In *The Tain of the Mirror*, Rodolphe Gasché examines the concept of heterology in Derrida; see in particular 88–97.

5. Walter A. Brogan comments very clearly on Derrida's analysis of Heidegger's ontico-ontological difference in his essay "The Original Difference" in Wood and Bernasconi, eds., *Derrida and Différance*, 30–39.

6. In the discussion following the original reading of "La Différance" Brice Parain raises this question: "as you reached the main part of your discussion, I began to wonder what this *différance* might be since, in short, it is the source of everything. It is the source of everything and one cannot know it: it is the God of negative theology" (Wood and Bernasconi, eds., *Derrida and Différance*, 84). In answer to this question, Derrida repeats his argument that "différance" displaces

such concepts as those of source, origin, as well as any investigation in terms of being, thus différance "is not a source, it is not an origin . . ., it is not a being and is not God" (85). Parain's point is a good one; what he means to suggest, one suspects, is not that différance is God but that différance performs a function analogous to that of God. Derrida does not really address himself to that problem except obliquely by saying that the "infinite distance" of his paper with respect to negative theology is also an "infinitesimal distance."

7. In her introduction to the English edition of *Identity and Difference*, Joan Stambaugh notes that Heidegger "considered *Identity and Difference* to be the most important thing he has published since *Being and Time*" (7). Jean Greisch notes that Heidegger has almost never formulated in the same work the two fundamental axes of his thinking: the *Ereignis* and Difference. Greisch calls *Identity and Difference* "the most remarkable and the most unsettling case" of Heidegger's texts which articulates both of these questions ("Identité et différence," 95) According to Joseph Kockelmans: "In *Identity and Difference* (1957) we find the most comprehensive treatment of the ontological difference as such" (*On the Truth of Being*, 83).

8. Heidegger maps here with remarkable accuracy the misreading of difference committed by Roland Barthes in his *Elements of Semiology*. In this text, an attempt to systematize, generalize, and popularize Saussure's *Course in General Linguistics*, Barthes identifies, for rather obvious reasons, Saussure's metaphor of cutting with difference. This identification is incorrect, however, because it presupposes the anteriority of a unit which would then undergo or receive the operation of difference. In other words, this metaphor misconstrues, by reversing it, the unusual order of priority that Saussure, Derrida, and Heidegger are formulating. The possibility of this particular misunderstanding has also been anticipated by Derrida when he explains that the word "différance" is preferable to the word "differentiation" (MP, 14/mp, 13).

9. Compare with Heidegger's use of *Sprung* and *Ursprung* as well as with *Der Satz vom Grund*. On the latter work see: Daniel Panis *Il y a le il y a: L'enigme de Heidegger*. On the problem of the leap out of representational thinking, see Greisch: "*Der Satz* signifies at once the 'phrase' (or the proposition) and the 'leap.' Whence the apparently paradoxical exigency: the *Satz*- Proposition must become a *Satz*-Leap." Greisch also notes: "The transition to the *Ereignis* is not made in the mode of continuity [sous le signe de la continuité], but in the manner of a radical break which expresses itself in the metaphor of the 'Leap' (*Sprung*)" ("Identité et différence," 86, 77). See also Kockelmans, *The Truth of Being*, 90.

10. *Gestell* and especially *Ereignis* are central, complicated, and somewhat mysterious concepts in Heidegger's later work for which Greisch evokes, in order to discount them, the procedures of negative theology ("Identité et différence," 89, 91, 92). It is beyond the scope of this study to consider this extremely problematic concept in Heidegger's thought; however, two formulations of the *Ereignis* by Françoise Dastur and Greisch underscore the manner in which the relation

determines what is related; this is, according to Stambaugh, the primary conceptual difficulty of Heidegger's essay: "It is perhaps difficult for us to think of a relation as being more original than what is related, but this is what Heidegger requires of us. This relation is then no relation in the ordinary sense of that term" (Stambaugh, Introduction to Heidegger, *Identity and Difference*, 12). Noting how difficult it is to express the concept of *Ereignis* in language ("the *Ereignis* seems continually to escape the grasp of language"), Greisch characterizes it in the following manner: "To think identity as *Ereignis* corresponds to a completely new path of thought. One no longer starts with two co-present terms [deux termes en présence] but from the relation itself. This rapport or relation exists between two 'things' (*Sache*), thus Heidegger speaks of the relation as a *Sach-Verhalt*. The *Ereignis* is the *Sach-Verhalt* which is both fundamental and constitutive of thought. In this new perspective, the identity of Being and thought is no longer understood in the manner of a conjunction, since a conjunction is always secondary to its terms. The conjunction must become a 'belonging together' [une 'co-appartenance'] (*Zusammengehören*) where the belonging [l'appartenance] is primary" ("Identité et différence," 96, 90–91). Dastur fleshes out elements of this particular relation of man and Being: "Heidegger gives the name *Ereignis* to this belonging together, which is neither coincidence nor a dialectical intertwining but being-for-one-another, and constellation of man and Being (ID 25f). *Ereignis* is not one event among others, as the ordinary meaning of the word suggests, but is used by Heidegger as *singulare tantum* (ID 29) to name the happening of lighting. It is the happening of the disclosing of beings, i.e., the coming of beings to their own (*Eigen*), or proper manifestation. But this *Er-eigen*, this propriation, is not a process that takes place by itself but requires man's participation" ("Language and *Ereignis*" in Sallis, ed., *Reading Heidegger*, 364). See also Meschonnic, *Le Langage Heidegger*, 331.

11. In an analysis of Derrida, Barry Allen assimilates Saussure's and Heidegger's formulations of difference: "Heidegger and Saussure have something in common. While both introduce an idea of original difference, i.e. a difference which does not depend on prior entities but instead reverses the traditional priority, coming before and conditioning the identity of beings, both nevertheless limit this in a way that respects the traditional interpretation of being as presence" ("Difference Unlimited," in Madison, ed., *Working through Derrida*, 15).

12. Referring to Levinas's *En découvrant l'existence avec Husserl et Heidegger*, George Steiner puts Levinas "among the most qualified and sympathetic of Heidegger's readers" (*Heidegger*, 64).

13. Blanchot is very interested in both Heidegger's *Gestell* and *Ereignis*. He also relates Heidegger, Bataille, and Levinas by means of a complicated nexus of ideas of donation (*geben*) and *Ereignis* (WD, 108–10/ED, 168–69; see also WD, 97, 98, 101, 102/ED, 152, 153, 158, 159).

14. Levinas's formulation of the *il y a* in terms which explicitly reject Heidegger's *es gibt* suggests such an influence. See chapter 5, n. 5. Blanchot seems to

accord priority to Levinas in connection with this ("But what is there about what Levinas terms the *there is*, aside from all reference to Heidegger's *es gibt*, and even long before the latter had proposed a quite differently structured analysis of it?" [OCC, 49/NCC, 86]); however, commentators of Heidegger tend to emphasize its pervasiveness in Heidegger's writing from *Being and Time* on. Speaking of the *es gibt*, Greisch notes: "This expression, which appears already in *Being and Time*, traverses [parcourt] all of Heidegger's writings, up to the lecture *Zeit und Sein*. In the latter, it is the 'decisive term which supports the entire development' [le 'mot décisif qui porte tout le mouvement']. It therefore represents something wholly other than a simple pun. It contains the Heideggerian answer to the problem that has dogged his thought from the time of his reading of Franz Brentano (1907): what meaning is to be given to the word 'Being' that avoids making it into a being?" ("Identité et différence," 87).

15. There is, indeed, an emphasis on fluid metaphors in Levinas's description of the *il y a*: "The anonymous current of being invades, submerges every subject, person or thing" (EE, 58/DEE, 94); The "forms of things are dissolved in the night" (EE, 58/DEE, 94); "What we call the I is itself submerged by the night, invaded, depersonalized, stifled by it" (EE, 58/DEE, 95); "Things and beings strike us as though they no longer composed a world, and were swimming in the chaos of their existence" (EE, 59/DEE, 97); "The existence of one submerges the other, and there is thus no longer an existence of the one" (EE, 61/DEE, 99).

16. Pierre Yana, for example, characterizes *Thomas the Obscure* as "un traité de l'oxymore" ("Le Mal obscur," 211); Eva Tsuquiashi-Daddesio notes the numerous paradoxical and contradictory formulations in the story, "Plasticité graphique," (172–73, 180). Evelyne Londyn, in her reading of *Thomas the Obscure*, underscores Blanchot's "prédilection pour l'oxymoron" (*Maurice Blanchot romancier*, 134). Michel Deguy, commenting on Blanchot's *L'Attente l'oubli*, gives a particularly good account of what he calls Blanchot's nondialectical, antithetical formulas. Moreover, he comes very close to an articulation of this question in accordance with the principle of difference: "What these pages give us to ponder is also the following: paradox is not dialectics. The relation of life and death is not a 'dialectical' one. The coincidence of opposites [coappartenance des contraires] is deeper and more mysterious than the play of the two words, even a very skillful play, can suggest" ("Maurice Blanchot," 713). Deguy's particular choice of words here is striking; *coappartenance* translates *Zusammengehören*. See also Hill, *Blanchot*, 58, 59, 61, 65, 66; Shaviro, *Passion and Excess*, 142; Stamelman, *Lost Beyond Telling*, 35; Christophe Bident evokes the criticism of Blanchot's "metaphoric and oxymoric affectation [complaisance métaphorique et oxymorique]" (*Maurice Blanchot*, 139).

17. In particular, Strauss, *Descent and Return*, 251, 258; Tsuquiashi-Daddesio, "Plasticité graphique," 64; Londyn, "L'Orphique chez Blanchot," 261–68; Hartmann, "Maurice Blanchot," 107 n. 6; Hill, *Blanchot*, 60, 61; Stillers, *Maurice*

Blanchot, 180–84; Hillis-Miller "Death Mask," 191; Champagne, "A Mosaic View," 429; Michel, *Maurice Blanchot*, 27, 36.

18. Starobinski, "Thomas l'obscur," 498. In addition to Starobinski's study, there are several notable studies devoted to or devoting major segments to Blanchot's *Thomas the Obscure*, among them Derrida, "Pas" in *Parages*, 19–116; Londyn, *Maurice Blanchot Romancier*, 89–135; Tsuquiashi-Daddesio, "Plasticité graphique"; Giorgio Marcon, "Tra le rive del testo," 87–92; Nef, "Le Piège," 71–88; Ronchi "La Realtà," 77–104; Sato, "La comparaison," 135–49; Suárez, "Mundo y lenguaje," 49–66; Tommasi, "Per un'esperienza," 43–76; Ungar, "Night Moves," 124– 35; Yana, "Le Mal obscur," 201–18; Keller, "Maurice Blanchot," 182–97; Stillers, *Maurice Blanchot*; Gerald Bruns, *Maurice Blanchot*, 247–54. On the subject of Blanchot and Heraclitus, see in particular Steven Ungar, "Parts and Holes," 126–41; Bident, *Maurice Blanchot*, 139–47, 287–91.

19. Chapter 2 of the novel, especially the opening sequence of this chapter, examines and revises the volitional efficacy and transitivity of this relation to the self. It begins with three transitive, reflexive verbs: "He nevertheless decided [se décida] to turn his back to the sea and entered [s'engagea] a small woods where he lay down [s'étendit] after taking a few steps" (TtO, 13/TO, 14). It then records the transition from an action that is the result of a conscious decision, and that is the manifestation of a preliminary desire commanding power and initiative over personal movement, to actions whose principle is passivity and indecision: "when he began to walk, one might have thought that it was not his legs, but rather his desire not to walk which pushed him forward. . . . What dominated him was the sense of being pushed forward by his refusal to advance" (TtO, 13/TO, 15). For an analysis of this scene, see Libertson, *Proximity*, 68.

20. Yana's reading, in this regard, is very similar to Starobinski's: "Thomas's voyage thus corresponds to a trajectory from the same to the same [un parcours du même au même], which returns him, enriched, to his point of departure after having endured the test of the Foreign [l'épreuve de l'Etranger], and having encountered the Other" ("Le Mal obscur," 203). Tommasi, on the other hand, very skillfully notes the manner in which Thomas's trajectory resembles or mimics the movement of the Hegelian dialectic yet resists thematization in those terms: "Thomas's overcoming of the obstacles that gradually present themselves to him naturally suggests his capacity of becoming-other, of transforming himself and seems in effect to present some common features with Hegel's *Aufhebung*; but, on closer examination, such a movement does not imply the surpassing and the conservation of the preceding condition, rather, it suggests a slipping, a return to it, a forgetting. . . . Strictly speaking, it is not a matter of surpassing but of a regression. Thomas's transformations do not give rise to a progression but to a regressive movement that tends towards the simplest and most primitive forms" ("Per un'esperienza," 62).

21. Ungar, "Night Moves," 129. In "Pas," Derrida makes frequent references to Thomas's "drowning" (*Parages*, 40, 41, 67, 70, 88–89). Levinas, like Starobinski

(see below n. 33), notes that Thomas both drowns and does not drown ["se noya et ne se noya pas"] (SMB, 62).

22. For a fuller elaboration of the idea of "participation," see the next section "Levinas: Difference and the Ethical Relation" and chapter 5. See also Ronchi, "La Realtà," 83; Keller, "Maurice Blanchot," 183; Robbins, *Altered Reading*, 86–89.

23. Libertson, *Proximity*, 8, 136, 208–9. On the other hand, many readers of this scene consider it from the perspective of an "explosion" of the subject, for example Suarez: "The sea seems to represent at once, both a liberation and the experience of the self's disintegration" ("Mundo y lenguaje," 54). Tsuquiashi-Daddesio argues that the system of intertextuality challenges the notion of identity: "the textual unfolding of the title sets up . . . the beginning of a comparable process which pursues itself in the disseminating structuration of an intertextuality in which the notion of the identity of the subject no longer obtains" ("Plasticité graphique," 180). Keller speaks of a "fusion" in this scene ("Maurice Blanchot," 183).

24. Sato, "La comparaison," 142–43; Tsuquiashi-Daddesio, "Plasticité graphique," 56; Hill, *Blanchot*, 69; Bident, *Maurice Blanchot*, 141–42.

25. See Levinas's comments on the self and its shadow and on Blanchot's *Aminadab* in *Existence and Existents*, (EE, 88, 92, 96/DEE, 151, 158, 164). See also Londyn, *Maurice Blanchot romancier*, 125–26.

26. This problem is analyzed in *L'Entretien infini* in the essay "L'interruption" (EI, 106–12/Ei, 75–79).

27. Without fully explaining the relation involved here, Starobinski notes several of its consequences very succinctly: "What occurs is neither a struggle nor a drowning but a transformation which makes the struggle useless and the drowning impossible. The new resource discovered by Thomas involves entering into a mode of existence in which, through not only a modification of the self but through its radical metamorphosis, the asphyxiating depth of the water becomes habitable. An unforeseen ability [aptitude inattendue] allows him to survive in the deadly element, not by losing his identity, but by passing into another form, in a *being other* [dans un *être-autre*]" ("Thomas l'obscur," 507). See also Londyn, *Maurice Blanchot romancier*, 128–29.

28. In *Existence and Existents*, Levinas refers to the second chapter of this story and in particular to Thomas's relation with the night to illustrate the apprehension of the *il y a*. In a note, Levinas writes: "The presence of absence, the night, the dissolution of the subject in the night, the horror of being, the return of being to the heart of every negative moment, the reality of irreality are there admirably expressed" (EE, 63/DEE, 103) (chapters 2 and 4). Also SMB, 48; NP, 106–7; Marcon, "Tra le rive del testo," 87–88; Ronchi, "La Realtà"; Garth Gillian "Levinas on Blanchot," 50.

29. Jacques Madaule, *Une Tâche sérieuse?* 134–35. In connection with the figure of Lazarus and more generally, with the problem of death in Blanchot's narratives (chapter 2), see Gregg "Blanchot's Suicidal Artist," 47–58 and chapter 3 in *Maurice Blanchot*, 35–71.

30. Robinson states that the correct translation is actually "waters" (*Introduction to Early Greek Philosophy*, 91).

31. Consider the discussion about Heraclitus between Socrates and Theodorus in Plato's *Thaetetus*, 179d–180b (*Plato*, 884).

32. TO, 49/TA, 28; Ti, 60/TI, 53–54. See John Llewelyn, *Levinas*, 47. On the opposition of Heraclitus and Cratylus, see Meyerson *Identité et réalité*, 427; also Loy, *Nonduality*, 216, 321 n. 18, 19. See Blanchot's comments on Heraclitus and his thematization of Heraclitus's fragments in terms of difference (Ei, 82, 88/EI, 116, 124–25). See also Françoise Collin, *Maurice Blanchot*, 221 and Derrida's analysis of Heraclitus in "La Différance" MP, 23/mp, 22.

33. This is the type that Levinas criticizes in the scenario of Ulysses (chapter 3). As I have pointed out above (n. 20), Yana's reading, following Starobinski, is very much in accordance with Hegel's movement of the *oeuvre*. Hence, Yana argues in terms of a "great, formative journey" ("Le Mal obscur," 203) or that *"Thomas the Obscure* is, in its basic structure, the novel of the Subject arriving at self consciousness [parvenu à une conscience de soi]" (207). See also 204, 210; Keller, "Maurice Blanchot," 192. As noted (also in n. 20), Tommasi demonstrates very skillfully how Thomas appears to conform to this Hegelian formula but, in effect, reverses it ("Per un'esperienza," 61–63).

34. Adriaan Peperzak has some particularly insightful comments on Levinas's method, for example: "The idea of a completely transparent, completely self-conscious method and methodology is characteristic of ontology. The need for such a self-consciousness corresponds to the desire for a sure foundation on the basis of which one can master everything. The monopoly of this need deafens and blinds one to the enigmatic ambiguity of the Other that the philosophy of Levinas attempts to show" (*To the Other*, 233–34; also 220). In a footnote concerning his own method of approaching Levinas in general and *Totality and Infinity* in particular, Derrida characterizes the development of Levinas's method as follows: "the development of themes is, in *Totality and Infinity*, neither purely descriptive nor purely deductive. It unfolds with the infinite insistence of waves on a beach: a movement of return and repetition, always the same wave against the same shore, where, however, each time summing itself up, everything infinitely renews and enriches itself" ("*L'Ecriture et la différence*," 124 n. 1). See also Weber, in Münster, ed., *La Différence comme non-indifférence*, 74; Levinas, DDVI, 143; Conclusion, n. 4.

35. See in particular Levinas's essay "Lévy-Bruhl et la philosophie contemporaine," EN, 49–63/en, 39–51. In her study *Altered Reading*, Jill Robbins has an extensive analysis of the concept of "participation" in Levinas (86–89).

36. For particularly succinct early formulations of the subjectivity's "permeability" in Bataille, see Denis Hollier, ed. *Le Collège de sociologie*, 201, 221. In *Proximity*, Joseph Libertson has clearly outlined the various affinities of the thought of Levinas, Blanchot, and Bataille.

37. In Libertson's analysis, the former group of terms are grouped under the heading "proximity," the latter under the heading "récurrence" (*Proximity*, 146).

38. See Derrida, n. 34 above. See also Davis, *Levinas*, 35– 37.

39. See Derrida, *L'Ecriture et la différence,"* 203 et passim. For a particularly critical assessment of Derrida's reading of Levinas in this essay, see Libertson, *Proximity*, 284–87, and particularly the footnote on 285–86. For comments on the other as "hauteur" see Françoise Collin "La Peur," 339; Peperzak, *To the Other*, 20.

40. Peperzak, *To the Other*, 7, 212, 217, 231; Ciaramelli "Levinas's Ethical Discourse," in Bernasconi and Critchley, eds., *Re-Reading Levinas*, 86, 99, 105 n. 76; Davies, in Bernsasoni and Critchley, eds., *Re-Reading Levinas*, 215–16; Ciaramelli, *Transcendance et ethique*, 124–29.

41. en, 197/EN, 231–32. See also Lingis, Introduction to OB, xv–xvi.

42. See also DC, 353/EDE, 196; MT, 127–28; Rolland, Postface in Levinas, *La Mort et le temps*, 148.

43. HAH, 13, See also OB, 114, 142, 145–46, 149, 150, 152, 185/AE, 180– 81, 222, 226–29, 234, 238, 283; en, 228/EN, 241; Davies, in Bernasconi and Critchley, eds., *Re-Reading Levinas,"* 223; Davis, *Levinas*, 78–79.

44. MT, 127–28; Peperzak, 222; Lingis, Introduction to OB, xxx–xxxi; Davies in Bernasconi and Critchley, eds., *Re-Reading Levinas*, 215, 223. Jean Greisch observes an analogous grammatical analysis in Heidegger and relates it to Levinas (*La Parole heureuse*, 300).

45. The following long passage from *Otherwise Than Being* articulates and summarizes these various elements: "Subjectivity is being hostage. This notion reverses the position where the presence of the ego to itself appears as the beginning or as the conclusion of philosophy. This coinciding in the same, where I would be an origin or, through memory, a covering over [recouvrement, thus also recovery] of the origin, this presence, is, from the start, undone by the other. The subject resting on itself is confounded by wordless accusation. For in discourse it would have already lost its traumatic violence. The accusation is in this sense persecuting; the persecuted one can no longer answer it. More exactly, it is accusation which I cannot answer, but for which I cannot decline responsibility. Already the position of the subject is a deposition, not a *conatus essendi*. It is from the first a substitution by a hostage expiating for the violence of the persecution itself. We have to conceive in such terms the de-substantiation of the subject, its de-reification, its disinterestedness, its subjection, its subjectivity. It is a pure self, in the accusative, responsible before there is freedom" (OB, 127/AE, 202).

46. Peperzak, "Passages" in *Cahier de l'Herne*, 496. Davis, like Haar, ascertains a series of apparently irreducible paradoxes (*Levinas*, 72–73, 126–27, 136).

47. I cite from among Haar's questions in order to illustrate the considerable difficulty understanding Levinas's ethical principles without explicitly identifying the principle of difference, a relation more basic than the related elements: "How can a true ethical relation be founded on pure passivity, on pure suffering, on unilaterality, on non-reciprocity?" (in *Cahier de l'Herne*, 530); "How are we to understand that the Other be transcendentally at once the source of the greatest

evil (torture, death) and the greatest good (the ethical demand [l'exigence éthique]), both assigning subjectivity to its highest responsibility while delivering it to its persecutor? And, following the strange logic of the Other *within* the same, how can we allow [or understand] [comment admettre] that the one who is persecuted would derive his Identity from the persecutor that he would carry within himself or be himself!?" (530–31); "How can this I evicted from his home [expulsé de chez soi] be 'integral [indéchirable] and unique,' how can he, turned wholly inside out, like a glove, exposed to the point of having no basis, no ground on which to stand [exposé au point de n'avoir plus aucun fond qui se pose], uninstalled, 'an-archic' (an oft-repeated expression), yet be called 'responsible' [for the other]?" (535).

48. In a brief study which focuses on *Otherwise Than Being* as representative of "Levinas selon sa plus grande difficulté," Paul Ricoeur reproduces Haar's reading of this problem. Since Ricoeur does not recognize the logic of difference which informs Levinas's definitions, like Haar, he is unable to make sense of such figures as those of persecution, hostage, and substitution as principles of ethics. His definitions and his appraisal of the argument in terms of paradox demonstrate clearly that he has not observed in Levinas's text the priority of the relation over the elements of the relation, and thus its role in the constitution of its elements. Understood in this manner, it can make no sense to argue, for example, that "the Self occupies the place of the other without having chosen or desired it" since, according to Levinas's argument, a self exists as such only by virtue of this very "occupation." Ricoeur's assessment of this chapter recalls very explicitly Haar's various questions: "The paradox should be shocking, to state the ethical injunction on the basis of the condition of inhumanity. The non-ethical states the ethical by virtue of its sole excessive valence. If substitution is to signify something irreducible to a willingness to suffer in which the Self would recover jurisdiction over itself [l'empire sur lui-même] in the sovereign gesture of the offering and the oblation, it must remain an 'expulsion of the self from the self' . . .; the self emptying itself of itself (p. 175). In short, it must be by its 'very cruelty' [sa 'mechanceté même'] (p. 175) that the 'persecuting hatred' (ibid) *signifies* the 'enduring through others' ['subir par autrui'] of the injunction in accordance with the standard of the Good. I do not know if readers have properly assessed the enormity of the paradox in expressing through cruelty the degree of extreme passivity of the ethical condition" (*Autrement*, 24). As noted in connection with Haar, this interpretation is based on the error dramatized by Heidegger in the distinction he has drawn between *Zusammen*gehören and Zusammen*gehören*.

49. See also WD, 13, 21, 23–24, 25–25/ED, 28, 39, 43, 46. On Blanchot's comment on Levinas, see, among others, Davies, in Bernasconi and Critchley, eds., *Re-Reading Levinas*, 215–16; Ciaramelli, "Levinas's Ethical Discourse," in Bernasconi and Critchley, eds. *Re-Reading Levinas*, 105 n. 76; Libertson, *Proximity*, 288; Mole, *Levinas, Blanchot, Jabès*, 15–16; Gillian, "Levinas on Blanchot," 51–52.

50. Lingis, Introduction to OB, xiv; Ciaramelli, "Levinas's Ethical Discourse," in Bernasconi and Critchley, eds., *Re-Reading Levinas*, 86, 95, 98; Peperzak, "Passages" in *Cahier de l'Herne*, 495; Laporte, *Maurice Blanchot*, 38–40; Manning, *Interpreting Otherwise Than Heidegger*, 59–87.

51. In chapter 2, I will give more sustained consideration to the problem of death in Levinas. However, I should note here that there is an analogy — but not an equation — of the relation with death and the relation of the other. Thus to Simon Critchley's question *"must the face of the other always be a death mask?"* (*Very Little . . . Almost Nothing*, 74; also in "Il y a" in Gill ed., *The Demand of Writing*, 109) one must answer both "yes" and "no": yes, to the extent that the other's face is as unknowable as death or a "death mask"; no, because the other's face does not threaten in the manner that death does. On the other hand, and as I shall explore more fully below, the face of the other — the subject's responsibility for the other — places on the subject a demand which is absolute and limitless. But in this context, the apprehension about death implied in Critchley's question that generally inhabits his analysis is rendered irrelevant, as noted in the introduction. Francesco P. Ciglia accounts for this structure very clearly: "Indeed, the dual characteristic of the relation with death — dissymmetry of the terms and the powerlessness of the subject [impossibilité de pouvoir de la part de la subjectivité] — returns incessantly at all of the stages in the path followed by Levinas in his attempt to state philosophically the relation with the Other" ("Du Néant à l'autre" in *Les Cahiers de la nuit*, 160; also 161, 163).

52. "But how refer to an irreversible past, that is, a past which this very reference would not bring back, like memory which retrieves the past, like signs which recapture the signified? What would be needed would be an indication that would reveal the withdrawal of the indicated, instead of a reference that rejoins it. Such is the trace, in its emptiness and desolation. Its desolation is not made of evocations but of forgettings, forgettings in process, putting aside the past. The forgettings are surprised before this 'forgettingness' could reverse into a bond, reconnect this absolute past to the present, and become evocative. What is this original trace, this primordial desolation? It is the nakedness of a face that faces, expressing itself, interrupting order" (CPP, 65/EDE, 207–8; see also CPP, 67–68/EDE, 210).

53. In the French text, Levinas italicizes the adverb "anachroniquement." Some other references to this anachronistic or anarchic relation are OB, 10, 13, 88, 105, 109, 110, 111, 116, 117, 139, 145, 149, 150, 154, 166/AE, 24, 28, 141, 167, 173, 174, 176, 183, 184, 219, 227, 232, 235, 241, 259.

54. Peperzak, *To the Other*, 34, 222–23; Lingis, Introduction to OB, xiv; Ciaramelli, "Levinas's Ethical Discourse," in Bernasconi and Critchley, eds., *Re-Reading Levinas*, 86–87; Libertson, *Proximity*, 38–39.

Notes to Chapter Two

1. "One dies; there is not a single narrative by Blanchot in which someone does not die, not so much in violent or accidental circumstances, rather, in the peaceful eruption of the endlessly repeated [l'irruption paisible du ressassement]. Death is at the heart of Blanchot's writing and at the heart, for Blanchot, of all writing" (Collin, *Maurice Blanchot*, 49). "To approach the thought of Blanchot on the problem of death is to enter, at the outset, into the heart of his work" (Londyn, *Maurice Blanchot romancier*, 15).

2. Blanchot's short narrative is the object of a gloss and long commentary by Jacques Derrida in *Demeure: Maurice Blanchot*. On Blanchot's narrative, and Derrida's reading of it see De Vries "'Lapsus absolu.'" See also Bident, *Maurice Blanchot*, 581–83.

3. Derrida notes the association with Dostoevsky (*Demeure*, 64, 71, 97, 125–26).

4. Levinas summarizes this argument in several other essays on Heidegger which are essentially expositions of Heidegger's arguments in *Being and Time* (EDE, 85–86; 104). On Levinas as a reader of Heidegger, see Steiner, *Heidegger*, 64, 71. For an excellent discussion of Heidegger's "anticipation" of death see Lingis's Introduction to CPP, x, n. 7. See also, on this subject Llewelyn, *Emmanuel Levinas*, 22.

5. Regarding this formulation see MT, 77; Ti, 57/TI, 50; OB, 128/ AE, 204; SMB, 16. See also Critchley, *Very Little . . . Almost Nothing*, 66–68; Llewelyn, *Emmanuel Levinas*, 10, 22; Ciglia "Du Néant à l'autre," in *Les Cahiers de la nuit*, 158; IC, 54/EI, 78, SL, 240/EL, 326.

6. Levinas uses this expression very frequently. See, for example: TO, 74, 80, 82, 88, 90/TA 62, 71, 73, 82, 85; CPP, 55/EDE, 173; Ti, 84, 198/TI, 83, 215. See also Llewelyn, *Emmanuel Levinas*, 19–20; Ciglia, in *Les Cahiers de la nuit*, 159.

7. See especially the chapter of *The Space of Literature* entitled "Death as possibility" (SL, 87–107/EL, 101–31). On the question of suicide in Blanchot, see Gregg "Blanchot's Suicidal Artist" and chapter 3 of his *Maurice Blanchot*, 35–45.

8. Blanchot also uses this characterization of passivity, the specific expression of a "pouvoir de pouvoir" and the concept of "l'impossible" to comment on Bataille and, in particular, on transgression as a yielding of power (IC, 453 n. 3/ EI, 308 n. 1).

9. FP, 70. In *L'Entretien infini*, Blanchot returns to Camus and further develops this criticism (267–68), evoking Hölderlin's "La Mort d'Empédocle" which supplies him with the expression "ce droit à la mort" (IC, 179/EI, 268).

10. On this particular articulation of death as the impossibility of the present: "If you are, it is not; if it is, you are not" (TO, 71/TA, 59), see also Blanchot SL, 101/EL, 122; Ciglia, in *Les Cahiers de la Nuit*, 159.

11. Other references to the *entretemps* in Levinas, OB, 109/AE, 172; CPP, 68/EDE, 211; TI, 244/Ti, 221. Bruns, *Maurice Blanchot*, 68–69.

12. Blanchot employs the same phrase, "mort jamais assez mort" in *The Space of Literature* in order to characterize the "other night" (SL, 163/EL, 215).

13. EE, 61, 62, 63/DEE, 100, 102, 103. As noted in chapter 1, Levinas mentions the second chapter of *Thomas the Obscure* as a particularly salient illustration of the *il y a*. Blanchot refers to the pages describing the *il y a* in *Existence and Existents* in his essay "Literature and the Right to Death."

14. EE, 62/DEE, 102. Here too the use of the verb "livrer" in the passive voice is notable; see also TO, 70/TA, 57.

15. Ciglia states this point particularly clearly: "Levinas seeks to challenge, with regard to the problem of death, the traditional alternative of being and nothingness" (in *Les Cahiers de la nuit*, 157).

16. CPP, 11/LR, 140/RO, 786. See also TI, 258/Ti, 232–33; Ciglia, in *Les Cahiers de la nuit*, 157.

17. See also NP, 106–7; Laporte, *Maurice Blanchot*, 32.

18. Collin notes "But it is to Hegel that Blanchot himself refers most often, without, perhaps, having always been aware of what distinguishes his own thought of the negative from that of the German philosopher. The Hegel that Blanchot ponders is principally the author of *The Phenomenology of Spirit* introduced in France by Jean Wahl, translated and commented by Kojève, and by Hippolyte, and with whom the entire group of the journal *Critique* was struggling, and principally its founder, Georges Bataille, with whom Blanchot had close ties of friendship" (*Maurice Blanchot*, 22). There have been many readings "working through" or commenting specifically on the various arguments of "Literature and the Right to Death." Some notable studies are: Collin, "La Nuit — l'autre nuit: négativité et négatif"; Libertson, *Proximity*, 70–72; Gregg, *Maurice Blanchot*; Tommasi, "Per un'esperienza"; P. Adams Sitney, Afterword to GO, 175–80; Fynsk, "Crossing the Threshold" and Gasché, "The Felicities of Paradox" in Gill, ed., *Maurice Blanchot*; Blegen, "Writing the Question," 14; Critchley, *Very Little . . . Almost Nothing*, 49–66; Bruns, *Maurice Blanchot*, 38–55; Warminski, "Dreadful Reading," 267–75; Hill, *Blanchot*, 110–14; Schulte Nordholt, *Maurice Blanchot*, 31–57; Swenson, "Revolutionary Sentences," 11–29.

19. Following the leads of Collin and Libertson, Blegen, Tommasi, Fynsk, Gasché, and Warminski (see n. 18) have emphasized how Blanchot, in the first half of "Literature and the Right to Death" introduces complications, paradoxes, or aporias into the structure of the Hegelian dialectic with the intent of subverting, reversing, or arresting its functioning (Libertson, *Proximity*, 166–67). However, this occurs principally in the second half of "Literature and the Right to Death." I find, contrary to Fynsk and Gasché in particular, that Blanchot makes relatively minor adjustments to Hegel's arguments in the first half, especially in view of the wholesale appropriation of Hegelian concepts, vocabulary and structures of argument in this part of the essay. (It is true that this appropriation is even

more palpable in relation to Hippolyte's *Genèse et structure* than it is in relation to Hegel's *Phenomenology*.) In *Proximity*, Libertson notes very clearly the transition from the first half, inspired by Hegel, to the second half, inspired by Levinas: "this moment of transition from the first section of 'La Littérature et le droit à la mort,' with its Hegelian definitions, to the second section, which introduces the theme of the presence of absence within an entirely communicational logic, is a basic moment in Blanchot's career as a thinker" (243, also 153). Referring principally to the first half of the essay, Sitney remarks that Blanchot's analysis is an "ironic aestheticization," a "near-parody" of Hegel. He notes that Blanchot "veers toward self-parody" and that his writing "attains a degree of flippancy" in this analysis (Afterward to GO, 175–76). It is not entirely clear which view Critchley advocates. On the one hand, he seems to accredit both Sitney's and Libertson's views (Critchley uses the term "mimicry" to characterize Blanchot's relation to Hegel [Critchley *Very Little . . . Almost Nothing*, 51, and see Libertson, *Proximity*, 76]). On the other hand, by referring to Blanchot's "very Hegelian purpose in delineating . . . two slopes of literature" (61), he does not appear to recognize the "transition" to which Libertson, in the quote above, has referred. Bruns notes that "Literature and the Right to Death" is a "subversive gloss on Hegel's conception of the life of the spirit" (*Maurice Blanchot*, 55). Swenson emphasizes Blanchot's reading of Kojève's analysis of Hegel ("Revolutionary Sentences," 15–16; 21–24, 27). Following Libertson's lead, Hill gives a very thorough accounting of the importance of the *il y a* in Blanchot's reworking of Hegel; however, in another context, Hill mentions that the Hegelian dialectic is "left in place, if only partially or parodically, at the end of 'La Littérature et le droit à la mort'" (*Blanchot*, 117, 110–11).

20. Fynsk emphasizes that Blanchot's "subversive aim is to write Sade into the dialectic" (in Gill, ed., *Maurice Blanchot*, 71). Schulte Nordholt, *Maurice Blanchot*, 50; Bruns, *Maurice Blanchot*, 40–45.

21. The parallelism of the relation with death in the preface and in the master and slave dialectic with the analysis of freedom and the Terror is noted by Hippolyte (PEII, 137–39, in particular nn. 209, 214).

22. Here again, contrary to Tommasi, "Per un'esperienza" and Gasché and Fynsk in Gill, ed., *Maurice Blanchot* in particular, I am struck more by the tentativeness of Blanchot's critical gestures with regard to Hegel, at least at this juncture.

23. It is not entirely clear what Fynsk is referring to when he writes that "Blanchot's move is to substitute a figure of death where we expect life" (in Gill, ed., *Maurice Blanchot*, 74). Yet, his formulation appears to be very appropriate to this particular argument of "Literature and the Right to Death."

24. It is thus only at this point that I find myself in basic agreement with the readings by Gasché and Fynsk (in Gill, ed., *Maurice Blanchot*), Tommasi, "Per un'esperienza," and Shulte Nordholt, *Maurice Blanchot*. See also Bruns, *Maurice Blanchot*, 55.

25. Derrida, "Pas" in *Parages*, 98–99; Shaviro, *Passion and Excess*, 16–17.

26. Blanchot will not retain this structure of the image (see chapter 4).

27. Compare with Levinas's analysis of the materiality of words in *Existence and Existents* (EE, 53–54/DEE, 86–87).

28. More sustained attention will be given to these particular terms in chapter 5.

29. EE, 57–59/DEE, 93–96. Fynsk wonders whether this particular example does not involve a "kind of dialectical sleight of hand" or a "slippage" (in Gill ed., *Maurice Blanchot*, 79).

30. On the problem of ambiguity in Blanchot, see Collin, *Maurice Blanchot*, 45–46 and 92. The latter is also cited by Gasché in Gill, ed., *Maurice Blanchot*, 60 and n. 23. See also Bruns *Maurice Blanchot*, 54–55; Hill, *Blanchot*, 112–13, Critchley, *Very Little . . . Almost Nothing*, 49, 62, 66; Schulte Nordholt, *Maurice Blanchot*, 31, 45.

31. While the latter two formulations can be interpreted as representing independent alternative functions, Blanchot's subsequent phrasing associates them.

32. The structural analogy of this analysis with Bataille's analysis of prohibition, and especially of the relation of prohibition to negativity, is very striking, noted by Gregg in *Maurice Blanchot* after Libertson, *Proximity*. This comparison suggests a similar "working through" of Hegelian concepts, particularly negativity, and a comparable complication of negativity through difference. See Collin, *Maurice Blanchot*, 22 and Schulte Nordholt, *Maurice Blanchot*, 45, 350–51. On the subject of Bataille and Hegel, see Jacques Derrida "De l'Economie restreinte," in *L'Ecriture et la différence*, 369–407.

33. Hill observes that Blanchot's "delimitation" or "disabling" of the Hegelian dialectic is predicated upon Levinas's *il y a* (*Blanchot*, 117).

34. See above, n. 5.

35. Speaking of *Thomas the Obscure*, Bruns puts it this way: "The principal event in the story is Anne's death or, say, Thomas's exposure to her death" (*Maurice Blanchot*, 247). Shaviro, commenting on *Death Sentence*, notes, "The death of the Other is one of those overwhelming events which reverberate throughout *L'Arrêt de mort*, and indeed all of Blanchot's fiction" (*Passion and Excess*, 153).

36. Bruns relates the death of Anne to the naming analysis in "Literature and the Right to Death" (*Maurice Blanchot*, 250). See also Gasché, in Gill, ed., *Maurice Blanchot*, 68 n. 21.

37. Following Anne's death, the narrator observes, "For dying had been her ruse to deliver a body to nothingness [donner au néant un corps]" (TtO, 90/TO, 102); Hartman, *Beyond Formalism*, 96; Londyn, *Maurice Blanchot romancier*, 72, 132.

38. Both Madaule and Bruns observe such similarities and differences of *Thomas the Obscure* and *Death Sentence* (Madaule, *Une Tâche sérieuse?*, 79; Bruns, *Maurice Blanchot*, 250).

39. As Londyn observes: "speech bursts forth [jaillit] from the dying, as in the case of Henri Sorge at the end of *The Most High*" (*Maurice Blanchot romancier*,

15). For a particularly thorough and lucid reading of *The Most High*, see chapter 5 of Gregg, *Maurice Blanchot*, 72–126.

40. Shaviro gives extended consideration to this mode of perception (*Passion and Excess*, 119–22); Hillis-Miller, "Death Mask," 202; Derrida, *Parages*, 183–87; Hill, *Blanchot*, 155 n. 16.

41. In chapter 5, I will consider Blanchot's terminology of nocturnal and diurnal spheres, a terminology related to Levinas and to his analysis of the *il y a*.

42. These modes of language are explored more systematically in such fictional works as *Awaiting Oblivion* [*L'Attente l'oubli*] and *The One Who Was Standing Apart from Me* [*Celui qui ne m'accompagnait pas*] as well as in the essays "La Parole vaine" in *L'Amitié* 137–49 and "l'Interruption" (EI, 106–12/IC, 75–79).

43. As such, Bruns deems him a "figure of disaster" (*Maurice Blanchot*, 249); Champagne calls him a figure of the "wandering Jew" ("A Mosaic View," 428). Marcon refers to Derrida's analysis of the crypt ("Tra le rive del testo," 90 n. 8); Madaule, *Une Tâche sérieuse?* 134–35. In chapter 4, I will comment on the importance of the verb "arracher" in Levinas's analysis of exoticism.

44. This distinction is no doubt what Bruns refers to when he observes that Anne and Thomas occupy "different temporalities" (*Maurice Blanchot*, 248–49).

45. In *Existence and Existents*, Levinas analyzes the problem of fatigue as one of the modes of relation of the existent to existence. What is particularly pertinent to the scenario of Anne's death and to the case of her mother's fatigue is the analysis of fatigue as a temporal distortion or disjunction, a lag or delay: "fatigue marks a delay with respect to oneself and with respect to the present" (EE, 30–31/DEE, 42–44). See also Llewelyn's comments on fatigue, *Emmanuel Levinas*, 37–39.

46. This particular thematization of passivity, in all of its horror, is masterfully exploited by Zola in *Thérèse Raquin*. Madame Raquin, an invalid, but, unbeknownst to Thérèse and Laurent, still quite lucid, discovers the truth about their murder of Camille.

47. Hill, *Blanchot*, 59; Poulet qtd. by Keller, "Maurice Blanchot," 189 n. 7.

48. Stillers, *Maurice Blanchot*, 115–17. Although Lamberton's translation of "Le temps sortant de ses lacs" as "Time coming forth from its lakes" makes a very interesting thematic association of aquatic imagery with the problem of time (similar to the first chapter of *Thomas the Obscure*), the expression is properly translated: "Time breaking forth from its fetters."

49. TO, 71/TA, 59; Blanchot will refer to it in *The Space of Literature*, SL, 101/EL, 122.

50. Hill, *Blanchot*, 61; Laporte and Bruns read this scene in terms of the naming analysis in "Literature and the Right to Death" (Bruns, *Maurice Blanchot*, 250; Laporte, *Maurice Blanchot*, 29).

51. On the question of death in *Thomas the Obscure* in relation to Levinas's *il y a*, see Hill, *Blanchot*, 62–63 and Critchley, *Very Little . . . Almost Nothing*, 63–65. In this connection, recall Ciglia's very useful formulation of the *il y a* as a

thematization of death beyond, or independent of the alternatives of being and nothingness; see above, n. 15.

52. Levinas, TA, 61/TO, 73. This "viens" is the subject of a lengthy rumination by Derrida in "Pas"; Madaule, *Une Tâche sérieuse?*, 66–68; Hillis-Miller provocatively analyzes its performative character, "Death Mask," 191–93, 200–201; Shaviro, *Passion and Excess*, 124; Hill, *Blanchot*, 155, 157.

53. Noël situates these events with respect to Georges Bataille (Laporte and Noël, *Deux lectures de Maurice Blanchot*, 25); Hill does the same and notes and analyzes discrepancies with the dates in Blanchot's text (*Blanchot*, 146–49). See also Bident, *Maurice Blanchot*, 293–94.

54. Shaviro notes that both *Death Sentence* and *Au moment voulu* "do not seem to be appropriate subjects for interpretation," that "the seriousness of the labor of interpretation seems oddly beside the point," and that given the status of a work as "violent, impersonal affirmation," "there is simply no place for hermeneutical or rhetorical considerations" (qtd. by Mole, *Levinas, Blanchot, Jabès*, 120). Laporte shares Shaviro's assessment, *Maurice Blanchot*, 40; Hill, *Blanchot*, 144.

55. Laporte deems this sequence of events "so many challenges not only to plain, common sense, but to any intelligence that would consider itself penetrating" (*Maurice Blanchot*, 15).

56. Although he does not really provide a context in which to develop this insight, Shaviro likens specific narrative elements of Blanchot's stories to traces, in contradistinction to semiological "indices" (*Passion and Excess*, 139–40). Shaviro appears reluctant to exploit this promising insight fully as his observation above (n. 54) suggests.

57. In *Thomas the Obscure*, there are many references to breathing and suffocation (TtO, 37, 71/TO, 42, 78). See also *Death Sentence*, following J.'s death (DS, 33/AM, 57). In *Otherwise Than Being*, Levinas investigates the multiple meanings and relations of "expirer," "expiration," and "expiation" (AE, 277–79/ OB, 181–82). See Libertson's analysis of the "pneumatism" of proximity in Levinas, (*Proximity*, 145).

58. He has himself, apparently, a terminal illness (DS, 5/AM, 14); he has recommended suicide to J. (DS, 5/AM, 12–13); another female acquaintance who had tried to kill the narrator had subsequently committed suicide (DS, 6/AM, 15); and in the second half of the narrative, he manifests an involvement with death comparable to that of Thomas in *Thomas the Obscure*. In Bruns's words, the narrator is, like Thomas, a "figure of disaster" (See above, n. 43). This also recalls Hegel to whom the expression "*death* himself" is reputed to have been applied (Kaufmann, *Hegel*, 68).

59. Londyn, inappropriately in my view, considers the temporal problems in *Death Sentence* from the point of view of the fantastic (*Maurice Blanchot romancier*, 53). See also Laporte: "Blanchot's narratives disturb our representation of time to the point of introducing fearsome effects of unintelligibility [redoutables effets d'inintelligibilité]" (*Maurice Blanchot*, 17–18). I give more attention

to the problem of impatience in my analysis of Blanchot's interpretation of the myth of Orpheus in chapter 3.

60. In *Awaiting Oblivion* the concepts of waiting and forgetfulness as relations to death also figure prominently (AO, 55–56/ao, 27–28).

61. LR, 132/CPP, 3/RO, 773; EE, 80–83/DEE, 137–42; TO, 46– 47; 51–54/ TA, 25–26; 31–34.

62. Hill, *Blanchot*, 12; and Introduction to Gill, ed., *Maurice Blanchot*, 4–5; Critchley, *Very Little . . . Almost Nothing*, 26; Derrida, *Demeure*, 56, 136–38.

Notes to Chapter Three

1. As Gregg notes, Blanchot will also consider the stories of Jesus, Lazarus, and Oedipus. See in particular, chapter 4 of *Maurice Blanchot*.

2. Foucault, for example, revises the triumph of Ulysses and the failure of Orpheus: "But it could be that beneath the triumphant account of Ulysses [le récit triomphant d'Ulysse], there reigns the inaudible regret of not having listened longer or more attentively. of not having delved more deeply into the admirable voice in which the song would perhaps accomplish itself. And underneath the lamentations of Orpheus shines forth the glory [éclate la gloire] of having seen, though less than an instant, the inaccessible face, at the very moment when it turned away and faded into the night: a hymn to the clarity without name or place" ("La Pensée du dehors" in *Critique*, 538–39). See also Londyn, *Maurice Blanchot romancier*, 86. On this general opposition of Orpheus and Ulysses, see Tommasi, "Per un'esperienza," 75; Collin, *Maurice Blanchot*, 62–64; Libertson, *Proximity*, 139; Huffer, "Blanchot's Mother," 176–87.

3. "Orpheus's Gaze" is the second of three essays which form the central part of the book under the subtitle "Inspiration." In the preface of *The Space of Literature*, Blanchot writes: "A book, even a fragmentary one, has a center which attracts it. This center is not fixed, but is displaced by the pressure of the book and circumstances of its composition. Yet it is also a fixed center which, if it is genuine, displaces itself, while remaining the same and becoming always more central, more hidden, more uncertain and more imperious. He who writes the book writes it out of desire for this center and out of ignorance. The feeling of having touched it can very well be only the illusion of having reached it. When the book in question is one whose purpose is to elucidate, there is a kind of methodological good faith in stating toward what point it seems to be directed; here, toward the pages entitled "Orpheus' Gaze" (SL/EL, 5); see also Critchley, *Very Little . . . Almost Nothing*, 42.

4. Libertson states this particularly clearly. He notes that the dimension of art "has no power and dominates nothing. It is Blanchot's genius to refuse it the predication of a higher or other power" (*Proximity*, 141).

5. See, for example, *Awaiting Oblivion*: "Could it be that to forget death is

actually to remember it? Would forgetting be the only remembrance commensurate with death? — Impossible forgetting. Each time you forget, it is death that you recall in forgetting" (ao, 46/AO, 89).

6. See Bruns's reading which equates Eurydice and the work of art (*Maurice Blanchot*, 70–71).

7. Gregg, *Maurice Blanchot*, 50–53; Hill, *Blanchot*, 119–20; Libertson, *Proximity*, 139.

8. Bruns casts this temporal experience in terms of Levinas's *entretemps* (*Maurice Blanchot*, 70). See chapter 4.

9. Thus I am not in agreement with Stamelman who characterizes Blanchot's thought here as dialectical (*Lost Beyond Telling*, 44; Libertson, *Proximity*, 138, 140).

10. It is notable how unusual the use of the qualifier "vrai" in drawing distinctions of this type is in Blanchot's texts. He rejects the qualifier — and the qualifying opposition of truth and falsehood — quite explicitly in his definition of the "other night" which he notes "is not true night, it is night without truth, which does not lie however — which is not false" (SL, 164/EL, 216). I will consider the problem of the "other night" in chapter 5.

11. Hill mentions the "necessity of obliqueness and indirection" and the "law of indirection" (*Blanchot*, 119). These describe accurately Blanchot's reasoning but do not explain fully the paradox which is at issue here. Libertson describes this in the terms of *détour* and *errance* (*Proximity*, 138).

12. See Derrida's analysis of various Levinasian concepts, including the idea of the trace, in relation to the concept of difference (MP, 22–26/Mp, 21–23).

13. Libertson, *Proximity*, 136, 140. Both Gregg and Hill analyze the story of Orpheus principally in the Bataillian terms of prohibition and transgression (Gregg, *Maurice Blanchot*, 48–54; Hill, *Blanchot*, 118–19; Critchley, *Very Little . . . Almost Nothing*, 42). It is the relation of Bataillian prohibition and transgression usually formulated by Bataille as a relation of difference — though also occasionally as a dialectic — which affords Gregg the clearest articulation of difference, which he tends to express through such formulas as the "concealed solidarity" of opposite concepts.

14. In *Time and the Other*, Levinas relates and opposes death and eros as forms of otherness both of which involve a loss of power according to the expression "ne pas pouvoir pouvoir." Yet, in eros, the self survives the encounter (TA, 62–65, 82/TO, 71–77, 88–89; see also chapter 2).

15. Libertson articulates and relates these two (*Proximity*, 140–41). In an essay on Blanchot, Levinas articulates this very succinctly: "Writing would be, for its part, the unrealistic exercise [l'invraisemblable démarche] of a power which, at a point called inspiration 'veers off' into powerlessness ['vire' en non-pouvoir]" (SMB, 17).

16. EDE, 172, 196/CPP, 54, DC 353; TI, 56/Ti, 62; EI, 75– 76/IC, 53; MT, 133; Bruns, *Maurice Blanchot*, 135.

17. See also HAH 43, 44; for other references to Ulysses in Blanchot, see EI, 459/IC, 314; see also TI, 12, 248/Ti, 27, 225; AE, 127, 129/OB, 79–80, 81; DL, 23, 216, 330–31/DF, 10, 153, 236–37; Derrida, "Violence et métaphysique" in *L'Ecriture et la différence*, 138, 141, 228 n. 1; Llewelyn, *Emmanuel Levinas*, 3, 55, 114; Petitdemange "Emmanuel Levinas" in *Répondre d'autrui*, 78; Mole, *Levinas, Blanchot, Jabès*, 100–101; Peperzak, *To the Other*, 67, 68, 91 n. 11; Davis, *Levinas*, 33, 35. On Hegel's analysis of the figure of Abraham, see Hippolyte, *Genèse et structure*, 185. Libertson emphasizes Blanchot's deriding of the figure of Ulysses: "Ulysses is one of the very few cultural figures who elicit from Blanchot a note of true contempt" (*Proximity*, 150).

18. The pattern of progression toward ambiguity and the tendency to thematize this ambiguity by means of difference is also a structural characteristic of the essay "The Two Versions of the Imaginary" which I will consider in chapter 4.

19. I have already discussed in chapter 2 Levinas's analysis of the inadequacy of the concept of the present both to the event of death and to futurity in general in *Time and the Other*. In Bruns's analysis, Orpheus experiences the *entretemps* in his descent to recover Eurydice (*Maurice Blanchot*, 69–70). Orpheus experiences what Blanchot calls the "absence of time" which, could, in fact, be the same thing as the *entretemps*. However, Ulysses experiences the *entretemps* most explicitly.

20. Libertson analyzes this particularly clearly in his comment on the word *écart* which Blanchot uses to signify the present's noncoincidence: "This *écart* is not a negativity, but it is negativity's deferral and impossibility. It is the *écart* of difference itself" (*Proximity*, 156).

21. The expression "toujours encore à venir" can be read as "always still or yet to come" or "always to come again, return or recur."

22. Baudelaire's passerby also formulates the essential asymmetry of the interpersonal that Levinas describes in *Totality and Infinity* where the other's attitude with respect to the subject is one of "hauteur" (TI, 86, 237/Ti, 86–87, 215). The passerby, who is, incidently, doubtless a widow, is "majestueuse" and "graceful, noble, with a statue's form [agile et noble avec sa jambe de statue]." In relation to her, the poet's attitude is "trembling as a madman thrills [crispé comme un extravagant]" (*Oeuvres complètes*, 92/*Flowers of Evil*, 118).

23. EDE, 172, 196/CPP, 54, DC, 353; EI, 75–76/IC, 53; TI, 10, 12, 56/Ti, 25, 27, 62; DL, 410/DF, 294; Bruns, *Maurice Blanchot*, 135 (see n. 16).

Notes to Chapter Four

1. Heidegger, "The Origin of the work of Art" in *Poetry, Language, Thought*. In this summary of Heidegger's aesthetic analyses, I am referring also to other essays, principally "Poetically Man dwells" in *Poetry, Language, Thought* and "Hölderlin and the Essence of Poetry" in *Existence and Being*. As I will observe, Blanchot is particularly interested in these essays, especially those on Hölderlin.

2. I will give more attention to the Heideggerian terms of earth and world —
Erde and *Welt* — in my analysis of Levinas's *il y a* in chapter 5.

3. In his book on Blanchot, Levinas attributes a similar project to Blanchot.
For Blanchot, Levinas writes, the function of art is to uproot "the Heideggerian
universe" (SMB, 25). In this connection, Bruns considers Blanchot's analysis of
Orpheus as a "rewriting" of Heidegger's "The Origin of the Work of Art" (Bruns,
Maurice Blanchot, 62).

4. Anne-Lise Schulte Nordholt discusses the mutual influence of Blanchot
and Levinas on the subjects of the image and resemblance "It is clear that we
cannot say that Levinas precedes Blanchot in this new conception of the imaginary nor can we say that Blanchot 'goes beyond' Levinas's views in his essay of
The Space of Literature. In their common reflection on the imaginary and on
resemblance, Blanchot and Levinas inspire and complement one another" (*Maurice
Blanchot*, 205 n. 31). Notwithstanding Schulte Nordholt's assessment and recognizing the importance of the mutual influences, the pattern of Blanchot's "fitting"
certain analyses and arguments to aesthetic examples is clear here, as it is in the
case, for example, of "Literature and the Right to Death" (see chapter 2).

5. In *Matter and Memory*, Bergson defines the image in the following manner: "By 'image' we mean a certain existence which is more than that which the
idealist calls a *representation*, but less than that which the realist calls a *thing* —
an existence placed halfway between the 'thing' and the 'representation'" (9/
Matière et mémoire, 1). Bergson's book is criticized by Sartre: "We have wit-
nessed the failure of Bergson's attempt to provide a new solution to the problem
of images" (*Imagination*, 59/*L'Imaginaire*, 64–65). These studies provide the
general context for Levinas's, and subsequently Blanchot's analyses of the image. This concept, of obvious interest for phenomenology, has an equally obvious
correlate in the field of aesthetics. Indeed, Sartre's study ends with a section entitled "The Work of Art." Heidegger's influence on Sartre's works is notable and
clearly affirmed in Sartre's *What Is Literature?*

6. The editors even provide specific pages references to *What Is Literature?*
(RO, 770); Hand, LR, 129; Schulte Nordholt, *Maurice Blanchot*, 205; Robbins,
Altered Reading, 83; Malka, *Lire Levinas*, 32–33.

7. Levinas argues the view that art is essentially disengaged. Compare this
with the views of Sartre in *What Is Literature?*: "The word [la parole] is a certain
particular moment of action and has no meaning outside of it" (*What Is Literature?*, 35/*Qu'est-ce que la littérature?*, 71); or the following: "The 'committed'
writer knows that words are action. He knows that to reveal is to change and that
one can reveal only by planning to change" (*What Is Literature?*, 37/*Qu'est-ce
que la littérature?*, 73). Bruns, *Maurice Blanchot*, 17–18.

8. See chapter 1, "Difference and the Ethical Relation in Levinas"; EDE, 172/
CPP, 54; TI, 222, 309/Ti, 203, 276; Robbins, *Altered Reading*, 86–89. (Bataille
also mentions participation in *l'Erotisme*, 51.)

9. The notion of rhythm, in its broad ethnographic context, is initially seen as a relatively straightforward alternative to the totalizing intellectualism of the conceptual attitude — of the disclosure in light and truth — that Heidegger, for example, attributes to art. In one of his early challenges to Heidegger, "L'Ontologie est-elle fondamentale?" Levinas associates, tentatively to be sure, the notions of rhythm and the face: "Yet, we wonder whether rhythm's impersonal gait — fascinating, magic — is not art's substitute for sociality, the face, and speech" (En, 10/EN, 22/II, 133). However, in relation to the weightiness and seriousness of the ethical "accusation" Levinas develops in *Otherwise Than Being*, the aesthetic experience is deemed somewhat frivolous. Thus, in *Difficult Freedom*, for example, he notes that consciousness — understood a priori as ethical consciousness according to the logic observed in chapter 1 — is a "refusal of art's bewitching rhythms"; at this juncture, he refers to the essay "Reality and Its Shadow" (DF, 293/DL, 408). In a striking reversal of these uses of the term "rhythm," Levinas uses it to explain the *il y a* in *Existence and Existents*. In this example, however, rhythm indicates structure and form, qualities whose absence characterizes the *il y a*: "The *there is* lacks rhythm, as the points swarming [grouillants] in darkness lack perspective" (EE, 66/DEE, 111). Blanchot considers the concept of rhythm in ED, 172–75/WD, 112–13; Robbins, *Altered Reading*, 85.

10. Bruns calls this attitude "ecstasy" (Bruns, *Maurice Blanchot*, 18). Such a notion, however, needs to be reconciled with the *entretemps*. Ecstasy implies a beyond or an "au-delà" with respect to time; this is precisely what Levinas is trying to distinguish from an "en-deça": "Does to separate oneself from the world always mean to go *beyond*, toward the region of the Platonic ideas and toward the eternal that dominates the world? Can one not speak of a separation on the *other* side [dégagement *en deça*] and of an interruption of time by a movement that would tend toward the far side of time [mouvement allant en deça du temps], in its 'intervals' [dans ses 'interstices']?" (RO, 773/ LR, 131/CPP, 2–3) (Levinas's emphasis).

11. These distinctions recall the Heideggerian distinctions of readiness-to-hand, presence-at-hand, obtrusiveness, and conspicuousness (*Being and Time*, 102–4, 112–18), summarized by Levinas in "Martin Heidegger et l'Ontologie" (EDE, 63–64). Blanchot relates these structures to the artwork (SL, 222, 258– 59/ EL, 299, 352). See Libertson, *Proximity*, 250; Fynsk in Gill, ed., *Maurice Blanchot*, 81. Through the metaphor of the shadow, Levinas explores the doubling of the subject that has been observed in *Thomas the Obscure* in particular (EE, 88, 92/ DEE, 151, 158); in *Time and the Other*, it is related to one of Blanchot's narratives (TO, 56/TA, 37).

12. Etymologically, *allos* and *agorein:* to represent the other. In "Reality and its Shadow," Levinas writes, "An image, we can say, is an allegory of being" (LR, 135/CPP, 6/RO, 779). In "The Origin of the Work of Art," Heidegger makes the same point concerning this etymology (*Poetry, Language, Thought*, 19–20). In

this connection, one thinks of Baudelaire's "The Swan": "And the old suburbs drift off into allegory [tout pour moi devient allégorie]" (*Oeuvres complètes*, 86/ *Flowers of Evil*, 110).

13. Commenting on Bataille in *The Infinite Conversation*, Blanchot draws this distinction very clearly in terms of the relation of power and totalization (IC, 207/EI, 307–8).

14. It should be noted that, as models of the relation to the image, music and rhythm are characterized solely negatively as nonconceptual — they are not characterized in terms of difference; however, they serve to characterize this nonconceptual relation as a relation without power.

15. On Bataille, see Libertson, *Proximity*, 59–61; Collin, *Maurice Blanchot*, 211–12; Gregg, *Maurice Blanchot*, 10–17, 48–52; Bruns, *Maurice Blanchot*, 271 n. 15; Derrida, "De l'économie restreinte à l'économie générale" in *L'Ecriture et la différence*, 369–407.

16. The manner in which Levinas paraphrases "inter" here: "parmi" or among, illustrates further the notion of "participation." Note that there is a very different use of this etymology in *Otherwise Than Being*. In his critique of the concept of Being, Levinas uses the egoistic connotations of the word "interesse" to underscore the essential egoism in the concept of Being: "*Esse* is *interesse*" he writes. And "Being's interest takes dramatic form in egoisms struggling with one another, each against all, in the multiplicity of allergic egoisms which are at war with one another and are thus together. War is the deed or the drama of the essence's interest" (OB, 4/AE, 15/II, 137).

17. On the question of the *entretemps*, see chapter 3 and Bruns, *Maurice Blanchot*, 19, 69–70; Lingis, Introduction to CPP, xxv. (While the translation of the *entretemps* as "the meanwhile" successfully conveys the idea that such time is not the temporality of work or accomplishment but instead a temporality of waiting and anticipation, it loses the preposition "inter" which clearly alludes to the *inter esse* that Levinas uses to characterize the relation to the image. These terms, moreover, point clearly to the analysis's basic grounding not in being and time but instead in inter-being and inter-time.)

18. The economy of the image is expressed "as though something in a being delayed behind being" [comme si quelque chose dans l'être retardait sur l'être]" (LR, 137/RO, 779/CPP, 6–7). These two axes of time recall the temporality of Ulysses's encounter with the Sirens.

19. Zeno is a particularly appropriate reference under the circumstances since his analyses of motion assume a spatial interval that cannot be crossed. Collin notes Blanchot's interest in Zeno's Achilles paradox (*Maurice Blanchot*, 11). In *Matière et mémoire*, Bergson suggests that Zeno's four famous paradoxes concerning motion rest on an incorrect spatial representation of time (212–15). See also Loy, *Nonduality*, 220, 320, 322 n. 33.

20. In "Phenomenon and Enigma" Levinas gives sustained consideration to the temporal enigma of the other. He considers the time of the encounter as well

as the *entretemps*. In this analysis, he observes the structure of a "fissile present" whose very punctuality is a destructuring of itself as a unit (CPP, 68/EDE, 210). See also chapter 3.

21. See chapter 3 and consideration of Orpheus's impatience. The temporality of waiting is rightly associated with Beckett and Blanchot (*Awaiting Oblivion, The Writing of the Disaster*), yet one finds it formulated in strikingly similar terms by Baudelaire in "Dream of a Curious Person." In this poem, the experience of death is explicitly formulated in terms of a temporality of awaiting.

22. Artaud too employs metaphors of shadow and doubling to thematize an understanding of art based on difference. I have sketched out the pertinence of difference to some of Artaud's definitions in "Différence et communication chez Artaud."

23. Bruns's assessment that, at the end of the essay, Levinas "throws in with Sartre" or is "Hegel-like" (*Maurice Blanchot*, 19) is quite intriguing. The statement on which the first assessment is based is immediately contextualized by Levinas as one of the faces that art presents and for which a certain type of criticism appears designed to compensate (Sartre?). But it is neither this view of art nor this view of criticism that Levinas is espousing in his essay. Levinas goes on to show that such criticism is "still preliminary" and that it fails to consider "the artistic event as such" (LR, 142/CPP, 12–13/RO 788) which is an obscuring, an ambiguity, and an expression of the *entretemps*. Paradoxically, if Levinas can be said at this juncture to "throw in" with anyone, it would be with Heidegger, from whose theses about aesthetics Levinas is marking a certain distance. Yet, when Levinas writes that "philosophical exegesis will measure the distance that separates myth from real being" (ibid) he anticipates the reasoning and the principal metaphor (taking measure) of Heidegger's "Poetically man dwells," an essay which, incidentally, formulates the problem of the image (*Poetry, Language, Thought*, 225–26). Indeed, Levinas appears here to attribute to criticism the role of art in Heidegger's analysis. Jill Robbins expresses a view similar to Bruns's assessment. Robbins writes: "At the essay's end, Levinas specifies the approach to the work of art that a rehabilitated criticism would take: 'Criticism already detaches it [the artwork] from its irresponsibility by envisaging its technique. It treats the artist as a man at work . . . inquire[s] after the influences he undergoes.' He thereby seems in effect to endorse an extrinsic criticism, concerned with the relation of the work of art to features such as its author's biography, history, and social context" (*Altered Reading*, 84). Once again, however, following the sentences quoted by Robbins, Levinas discounts this view with the succinct judgment "critique encore préliminaire." He goes on to consider the relation of a "serious," intellectualizing, conceptual discourse of criticism and the frivolous, slightly mad discourse of art. He observes that modern art has amalgamated these two tendencies such that the creating and revealing functions normally attributed to God as well as analytic intellectualizing have been appropriated by the artist (contrary to the definition of art that has preceded). Finally, in a conclusion which once again

shows a tentative but genuine connection at this early juncture of aesthetics to the ethical, Levinas notes that philosophical exegesis would need to introduce the relation to others (*autrui*) since in an analogy — not an equivalence — with art, this relation also marks a qualitative limit to the discourse of the concept.

24. See chapter 2. This particular argument reproduces the form of Hegel's "thing-in-itself" (*Sache selbst*).

25. In *Existence and Existents*, Levinas begins by defining intentionality in the straightforward manner observed, only to demonstrate in subsequent chapters its collapse in, for example, the experience of the *il y a*. The organizing metaphor of intentionality in this section is that of taking, appropriating, and possessing. It is in this context that Levinas calls intentionality a "possession à distance" (EE, 46/DEE, 72). The frequency of Levinas's use of the words "possession," "prendre," and "posséder" presents a stark contrast with the incidence of the verb "arracher" in the section "Exoticism" and with that of the noun "horreur" in the section on the *il y a*.

26. This concept is shared by Bataille, Blanchot, and Levinas (Libertson, *Proximity*, 208).

27. Libertson, *Proximity*, 246–47. Gregg, *Maurice Blanchot*, 28–29; Fynsk, in Gill, ed., *Maurice Blanchot*, 83–84. Shaviro analyzes various modes of perception in terms of fascination in *Death Sentence*, *Aminadab*, and other of Blanchot's narratives (*Passion and Excess*, 119–20).

28. Sitney emphasizes the importance of Levinas's *il y a* and perhaps understates the importance of "Reality and Its Shadow" (Afterword of GO, 182–84). Hill relates very clearly Levinas's *il y a*, Blanchot's *neutre*, and Derrida's *différance* (*Blanchot*, 136).

29. I owe this particular metaphor of disappearance to Joseph Libertson.

30. This analysis of the image is parallel to the two types of death which Gregg distinguishes (following Libertson and Levinas) as "la mort" and "le mourir." The tendency of a suicide victim to take "one death for the other" suggests that this confusion is also parallel. See Gregg's excellent analysis of this problem in *Maurice Blanchot*, 35–45. Both of these distinctions recall the analysis of death in the second part of "Literature and the Right to Death." On the distinction in Levinas of "le mourir" and "la mort," see especially *Totality and Infinity*, 56–57/TI, 49–50. In *The Writing of the Disaster*, Blanchot frequently refers to this opposition (WD, 40, 47–48, 65/ED, 69–70, 81, 108); See also Critchley, *Very Little . . . Almost Nothing*, 32, 71; Schulte Nordholt, *Maurice Blanchot*, 51, 56.

31. Notice, for example, the use of the verb "fixer" by Sartre in *What Is Literature?*: "Thus by speaking, I reveal the situation by my very intention of changing it; I reveal it to myself and to others *in order* to change it. I strike at its very heart, I transfix it, and I display it in full view [je la fixe sous les regards]; at present I dispose of it" (*What Is Literature*, 37, see also 36, 49/*Qu'est-ce que la littérature?* 73, see also 72, 90).

32. Notice how Blanchot, commenting here on Nietzsche, states the ambiguity of art by playing repeatedly on the words "fond," "fondement," and "effondrement": "we have art in order that what makes us go all the way to the bottom not belong to the domain of truth. The very bottom, the bottomless abyss belongs to art. And art is that deep which is *sometimes* the absence of profundity, of the foundation, the pure void bereft of importance, and *sometimes* that upon which a foundation can be given, but it is also *always at the same time* one and the other, the intertwining of the Yes and the No, the ebb and flow of the essential ambiguity [nous avons l'art afin que ce qui nous fait toucher le fond n'appartienne pas au domaine de la vérité. Le fond, l'effondrement, appartient à l'art: ce fond qui est *tantôt* absence de fondement, le pur vide sans importance, *tantôt* ce à partir de quoi fondement peut être donné, — mais qui est aussi *toujours en même temps* l'un et l'autre, l'entrelacement du Oui et du Non, le flux et le reflux de l'ambiguïté essentielle]" (EL, 325/SL, 239).

33. Libertson and Gregg tend to express this particular relation by means of Bataille's terms which oppose a general and a restricted economy of being (Libertson, *Proximity*, 9–29; Gregg, *Maurice Blanchot*, 9–17).

34. Here again, Gregg's analysis of the two types of death is a useful point of comparison (*Maurice Blanchot*, 34–45 and n. 34).

35. The basic elements of this problem are examined by Heidegger in *Being and Time*, 282–83.

36. In the essay "The Original Experience," Blanchot develops this association of "errer" and "erreur": "Error is the risk which awaits the poet and which, behind him, awaits every man who writes dependent upon an essential work. Error means wandering [Erreur signifie le fait d'errer], the inability to abide and stay. For where the wanderer is, the conditions of a definitive here are lacking. In this absence of here and now what happens does not clearly come to pass as an event upon which something solid could be achieved" (SL, 238/EL, 323).

37. See above, note 30.

38. Levinas describes this function of ambiguity in *Existence and Existents* and sketches the broad outline of an argument which is extensively developed by Blanchot in "Literature and the Right to Death." Levinas indicates an essential duplicity in the word; he opposes the word's intelligibility to its materiality, an opacity and "thingly" quality which is also expressed by a word's multiplicity of meaning or ambiguity (EE, 54/DEE, 87). This analysis of an opaque materiality refractory to illumination is what leads Levinas to the formulation of the *il y a* (EE, 56–57/DEE, 91–92) (See chapters 2 and 5).

39. Blanchot evokes the "two possibilities for the image" (GO, 86/SL, 261/ EL, 355); Levinas, in "Reality and Its Shadow" speaks of "two contemporary possibilities of being" (LR, 136/CPP, 7/RO, 780).

40. In this connection, see Hill's judicious comment on Blanchot's "Our Clandestine Companion." Hill observes, in particular, Blanchot's tendency to speak "in the language of Levinas" yet with "both affectionate reserve and an awareness

of the complex differences of both emphasis and substance that separate them from each other" (*Blanchot*, 164). See also Bruns, "Blanchot-Levinas."

41. As indicated at the outset, the broad context of the problem of the image in terms of phenomenology is sketched by Bergson and Sartre.

Notes to Chapter Five

1. See, for example, the text, the preface and the book jacket of *De l'Existence à l'existant*. See also EI, 48–49/Ei, 49– 50.

2. Levinas does not, initially, read Blanchot's *The Space of Literature* through the *il y a* (although in *Ethics and Infinity*, he relates Blanchot's *neutre* and *dehors* and the *il y a* and he indicates the former as "the real subject of his novels and stories"). Yet, in describing the "other" night, or the "second" night as he puts it, the characteristics that he enumerates reproduce the images, the allusions, the very vocabulary of both "Reality and Its Shadow" and "Il y a" (SMB, 14–23); Critchley, *Very Little . . . Almost Nothing*, 63.

3. See Bruns's useful distinction of the anarchic and the archaic in terms of Heidegger's view of art and Blanchot's references to it (*Maurice Blanchot*, 12–13; Collin, *Maurice Blanchot*, 43; qtd. by Bruns, *Maurice Blanchot*, 268 n. 2). Considered in Freudian terms, such a view of the art object would invest all of art with an "uncanny" quality.

4. Reiner Schürmann examines the expression *il y a* in relation to Rimbaud and René Char and relates it to Heidegger's *es gibt* and to Hölderlin's poetry. Though not mentioning Levinas (Blanchot is mentioned as a critic of René Char), Schürmann's essay examines many propositions that are pertinent to Levinas's use of the expression *il y a* ("Situating René Char" in Spanos ed., *Martin Heidegger*).

5. Levinas repeatedly seeks to distinguish the *il y a* from Heidegger's *es gibt*. See, in particular *Ethics and Infinity* and the preface of *Existence and Existents*. The difference he draws appears to be more one of content than of form or structure such that Bruns, for example, will characterize the *il y a* as "the surreal equivalent of Heidegger's *es gibt*" (*Maurice Blanchot*, 58–59; Critchley, *Very Little . . . Almost Nothing*, 57). While a list of primary and secondary references to the concept of *il y a* could prove useful, it would be impractically voluminous. Some particularly useful or notable analyses of this problem include, Ciglia in *Les Cahiers de la nuit*, 152–58; Libertson, *Proximity*, 41, 204–8, 294; Collin, "La peur" in *Cahier de l'Herne*, 336–39; Llewelyn, *Emmanuel Levinas*, 28, 45, 48, 64; Critchley, *Very Little . . . Almost Nothing*, 31–32, 35, 55–56, 77–78; Davies in *Re-Reading Levinas*, 214; Hill advances the provocative idea that in *Thomas the Obscure*, Blanchot effects a transition from the Heideggerian *es gibt* to the Levinasian *il y a* (*Blanchot*, 62–63; see also 110–12; 115–16; 239 n. 7 and 235 n. 12). Lingis, Introduction to CPP, xxvii; Mole, *Levinas, Blanchot, Jabès*, 30–33;

Davies, "A Linear narrative?" in Wood, ed., *Philosophers' Poets*, 42; Robbins, *Altered Reading*, 91–97.

6. *La Bible: Ancien testament*, vol. 1:3 n. 2; Chalier, *Levinas*, 42; Mole refers to Chalier but, in an obvious editorial error, refers to the "chaos following creation in Gen. 1:2" *Levinas, Blanchot, Jabès*, 31, *sic*.

7. In *Totality and Infinity*, Levinas opposes the night of the *il y a* and the night of eros (Ti, 258–59/TI 289). In general, see the section "Phenomenology of Eros" (Ti, 256–66/TI, 286–99). See also TO, 84–90/TA, 77–84; Lingis, Introduction to CPP, xv–xvii.

8. Critchley gives an intriguing commentary of Maupassant's story "Le Horla" in terms of Levinas's *il y a*. This is a particularly interesting connection authorized by Levinas's text. However, Critchley's analysis is not tenable on several important points; in particular, it is not correct to equate the "il" that describes the Horla and the "il" of *il y a* (*Very Little . . . Almost Nothing*, 80). The former is neither neutral, nor impersonal, nor neuter. A more fruitful association would be that of Kafka's "The Burrow" as read by Blanchot and Maupassant's "Le Horla."

9. Levinas's very different use of rhythm to characterize the *il y a* (EE, 66/ DEE, 111) has been observed previously (chapter 4, n. 9).

10. Strictly speaking, Bruns is no doubt correct to emphazise that the *il y a* "has no temporal modality" (*Maurice Blanchot*, 59). However, the very striking parallels in the derivations and articulations of the *entretemps* and the *il y a* suggest the association of these concepts. Bruns appears to recognize this implicitly since he characterizes the temporality of disaster as that of the *il y a* (*Maurice Blanchot*, 209).

11. The use of the verb "livrer" to express the passivity of subjectivity in relation to the *il y a* is relatively common in *De l'Existence à l'existant* (96, 102). Note also its use in *Thomas l'obscur*, 53.

12. The emphasis on shadow and the economy of resemblance is, indeed, very marked in this passage. Note how, in the subsequent characterization of the persecutive or involuntary prehension, the principles of power and mastery are essentially undermined by the economy of resemblance through the metaphor of shadow: "The writer seems to be master of his pen, he can become capable of great mastery over words, over what he wants to make them express. But this mastery only manages to put him in contact, keep him in contact, with a fundamental passivity in which the word, no longer anything beyond its own appearance, the *shadow* of a word, can never be mastered or even grasped; it remains impossible to grasp, impossible to relinquish, the unsettled moment of fascination. The writer's mastery does not lie in the hand that writes, the 'sick' hand that never lets go of the pencil, that cannot let it go because it does not really hold what it is holding; what it holds belongs to *shadow*, and the hand itself is a *shadow*" (GO, 67/SL, 25/EL, 15, my emphasis).

13. Hill reconciles these two vocabularies so that, as in the case of "Literature

and the Right to Death," it is Levinas who tempers, corrects, or limits the function of Hegelian negation (*Blanchot*, 115–16).

14. Blanchot will reject the notion of an emergence from or break with the *il y a*. Blanchot and Levinas have famously disagreed on this question. See the end of *Totality and Infinity;* OCC, 48–49/NCC, 85–86; ED, 43, 45–46/WD, 23–24, 25–26; Critchley, *Very Little . . . Almost Nothing*, 55–56; Hill, *Blanchot*, 136–37; Bruns, *Maurice Blanchot*, 110–11 and "Blanchot-Levinas" in *Research in Phenomenology*, 136, 140. I have alluded briefly to this moment in Blanchot's and Levinas's relations in the introduction and in chapter 1.

15. Ciglia states this particularly forcefully: "But the break with the density of Being [rupture de la compacité de l'être], effected by the very event of subjectivity is not assured of longevity and the *il y a* returns, knocking on the door, and threatening to close off the path opened by the self. . . . It is interesting to observe that Levinas's principal efforts, at all of the fundamental stages of his thought, are focused on this attempt to identify and unmask the constantly differing and changing forms taken by this incessant and destructive return of the *il y a*" (in *Les Cahiers de la nuit*, 155). Critchley argues along similar lines: "why does the *il y a* keep on returning like the proverbial repressed, relentlessly disturbing the linearity of the exposition?" (*Very Little . . . Almost Nothing*, 77). "Is not the *il y a* like a shadow or ghost that haunts Levinas's work, a revenant that returns it again and again to the moment of nonsense, neutrality, and ambiguity" (*Very Little . . . Almost Nothing*, 78). Notwithstanding the drama inherent in Critchley's formulations, this manner of applying Levinas's own images to his analysis is not particularly helpful here. In chapter 1, I have described how the thematization of subjectivity in *Otherwise Than Being* as unconditionally responsible for the other, as a hostage willing to substitute itself for the other, and owing its identity and unicity only to this responsibility represents a configuration of subjectivity which departs significantly from the concept of essence which remains haunted by the *il y a*. In other words, it is only in as much as the subject remains rooted in the concept of essence that the *il y a* returns to threaten it. In the last chapter of *Otherwise Than Being*, Levinas writes: "This work interprets the subject as a hostage and the subjectivity of the subject as a substitution breaking with the essence of Being" (OB, 184/AE, 282). On the other hand, as I have observed, it is precisely this departure that Blanchot refuses to concede. See ED, 35/WD, 18; OCC, 49–50/NCC, 85–86, and chapter 1.

16. See Blanchot's analysis of night and sleep — an analysis explicitly informed by Levinas's analysis in *Existence and Existents* — in the appendix section of *The Space of Literature* (SL, 266/EL, 364).

17. Libertson puts it this way: "The basic irony which structures the bulk of Kafka's *The Burrow* is that every underground dwelling designed as a refuge from other animals must have an entrance at the surface" (*Proximity*, 96).

18. It is in this respect that the analogies with Maupassant's *Le Horla* are most striking; indeed, the narrator continually finds that his defensive strategies have been preempted by the haunting figure he calls the Horla.

19. Hill, *Blanchot*, 136–37. Davis describes these characteristics of the *il y a*. However, since he is not attentive to the principle of difference which informs the *il y a*, Davis ultimately is led to enumerate the logical difficulties which the *il y a* presents. According to Davis, it "invalidates the available tools of philosophical analysis"; it poses "immense difficulties"; Levinas's exposition of the *il y a* evokes "the figure of giving with one hand and taking with the other"; his text "hovers on the edge of nonsense," and "for readers the sense that we have grasped the point is perhaps more misleading than the recognition that we have not" (*Levinas*, 130–31).

20. Critchley refers to Levinas's statement in *Ethics and Infinity* to the effect that the *neutre* is "the real subject of [Blanchot's] novels and stories" (*Very Little . . . Almost Nothing*, 63; Ei, 50/EI, 48), see n. 2 above.

Notes to Conclusion

1. For example, Hill speaks of the "radical uninterpretability" of Blanchot's fiction (*Blanchot*, 65). As I observed in chapter 2, Shaviro wonders whether Blanchot's narratives are "appropriate subjects for interpretation" (*Passion and Excess*, 142). Of Levinas, Michel Haar writes, "Yet, in wishing to hover above the waters of philosophy, one risks losing all probing force. In wishing to dispense with the Same, one risks yielding to the vertiginous magic of the Dissimilar" ("L'Obsession de l'autre" in *Cahier de l'Herne*, 536). As noted in the previous chapter, Davis essentially echoes Haar's assessment: "reading Levinas entails in constantly recognizing and rediscovering those parts of his writing which make sense to us, whilst passing over those parts which remain rebarbative. Understanding as much as we do may be at the cost of a necessary blindness towards what continues to elude us. Commentary becomes an art of paraphrase in which fundamental questions are more or less skillfully evaded. The problems involved in understanding the *il y a* and the face are characteristic of difficulties posed throughout Levinas's writing. Other key notions employ the same fraught combination of ordinary language with paradox which places them right at the edge, or perhaps just beyond the edge of intelligibility" (*Levinas*, 135–36).

2. Christophe Bident, who extensively chronicles the reception of Blanchot's narratives, cites a judgment of Blanchot as "an alchemist who will no doubt someday recognize that the best way to obtain water is to turn on the kitchen faucet. And to say 'it's a nice day' the best way to go about it is still to say: 'it's a nice day'" (*Maurice Blanchot*, 297 n. 3).

3. It is notable that Thom considerably simplifies Meyerson's argument which formulates the "epistemological paradox" of the reduction to principles of the same and the respect for the otherness of the other (Thom, Interview).

4. In an interview, Levinas notes, "I do not believe that there is a transparency possible in matters of method, nor do I believe that philosophy is possible as transparency. Those who have spent their lives on problems of method have written

many books in place of the more interesting books which they might have written. It is a shame for that dream of a journey under a sun which casts no shadows that philosophy might be" (DDVI, 143). Also cited by Weber "Anamnèse de l'immémorial" in Münster, ed., *La Différence comme non-indifférence*, 74.

5. Libertson puts this particularly clearly: "The opacity of Blanchot's theoretical text, in 1955 as in 1980, is its mimicry of phenomenological procedures and existential themes, and its description of a reality which is as incomprehensible to phenomenology as it is to the formalisms which succeeded phenomenology" (*Proximity*, 76). Hill also notes this tendency in Blanchot's relation to Heidegger: "Blanchot proceeds indirectly. He writes largely alongside Heidegger, that is to say, with Heidegger, but also, simultaneously, against him. This is a common strategy in Blanchot, who in all his writing, rather than endorsing or opposing a philosophical argument, tends instead to accompany it through its various twists and turns in order to prise it apart by confronting it with the limits of its own possibility" (*Blanchot*, 82).

6. This tendency is noted in Critchley's analysis of Levinas's *il y a* for example (chapter 5, n. 15).

7. "L'humain ne s'offre qu'à une relation qui n'est pas un pouvoir" (EN, 22/II, 133/en, 11). Levinas's transition from aesthetics to ethics is particularly interesting in this essay, notably in the very explicit association of the work of art and the face: "Isn't art an activity that gives things a face?" (en, 10/EN, 22/II, 133; also EN, 68/en, 57).

8. See Peperzak's thoughtful assessment of Derrida's use of Joyce's "Jewgreek" and "Greekjew" to characterize Levinas (*To the Other*, 8–12); Derrida, "Violence et métaphysique" in *L'Ecriture et la différence*, 228; ED, 45/WD, 148–49; Mole, *Levinas, Blanchot, Jabès*, 16.

9. "A breathless, almost out of breath meditation" (Ciglia, in *Les Cahiers de la nuit*, 154). See also Davis: "The restlessness and rawness of Levinas's enquiry derive from the urgency of his topic" (*Levinas*, 143).

10. In "Our Clandestine Companion" and *The Writing of the Disaster*, Blanchot comments on the dedication of Levinas's *Otherwise Than Being* to the victims of the Holocaust, among whom were, as most readers know, almost all of the members of Levinas's immediate family (OCC, 50/NCC, 86–87; ED, 129–34/WD, 81–84).

Bibliography

Works by Blanchot

Aminadab. Paris: Gallimard, 1942.

L'amitié. Paris: Gallimard, 1971.

Après-coup, précédé par le ressassement éternel. Paris: Editions de Minuit, 1983.

L'arrêt de mort. Paris: Gallimard, 1948. Translated by Lydia Davis. *Death Sentence* (Barrytown: Station Hill, 1978).

L'attente l'oubli. Paris: Gallimard, 1962. Translated by John Gregg. *Awaiting Oblivion* (Lincoln: University of Nebraska Press, 1997).

Au moment voulu. Paris: Gallimard, 1979. Translated by Lydia Davis. *When the Time Comes* (Barrytown: Station Hill, 1977).

Celui qui ne m'accompagnait pas. Paris: Gallimard, 1953. Translated by Lydia Davis. *The One Who Was Standing Apart from Me*. (Barrytown: Station Hill, 1993).

Le dernier homme. Paris: Gallimard. 1957. Translated by Lydia Davis. *The Last Man* (New York: Columbia University Press, 1987).

L'entretien infini. Paris: Gallimard, 1969. Translated by Susan Hanson. *The Infinite Conversation* (Minneapolis: University of Minnesota Press, 1993).

L'écriture du désastre. Paris: Gallimard, 1980. Translated by Ann Smock. *The Writing of the Disaster* (Lincoln: University of Nebraska Press, 1986).

L'espace littéraire. Paris: Gallimard, 1955. Translated by Ann Smock. *The Space of Literature*. (Lincoln: University of Nebraska Press, 1982).

Faux pas. Paris: Gallimard, 1971.

La folie du jour. Montpellier: Fata Morgana, 1973. Translated by Lydia Davis. *The Madness of the Day*. (Barrytown: Station Hill, 1985).

The Gaze of Orpheus, ed. P. Adams Sitney and trans. Lydia Davis. Barrytown: Station Hill, 1981.

L'instant de ma mort. Montpellier: Fata Morgana, 1994. Translated by Elizabeth Rottenberg. *The Instant of My Death/Demeure: Fiction and Testimony* by Maurice Blanchot and Jacques Derrida. (Stanford: Stanford University Press, 2000).

Lautréamont et Sade. Paris: Editions de Minuit, 1963.

"La littérature et le droit à la mort" in *Critique* 20 (January 1948): 30–47.

Le livre à venir. Paris: Gallimard, 1959.

La part du feu. Paris: Gallimard, 1949. Translated by Charlotte Mandell. *The Work of Fire* (Stanford: Stanford University Press, 1995).

Le pas au-delà. Paris: Gallimard, 1973. Translated by Lycette Nelson. *The Step Not Beyond* (Albany: State University of New York Press, 1992).

"Le règne animal de l'esprit" in *Critique* 18 (November 1947): 387–405.

The Sirens' Song, trans. Sacha Rabinovitch. Bloomington: Indiana University Press, 1982.

The Station Hill Blanchot Reader: Fiction and Literary Essays, ed. George Quasha and trans. Lydia Davis, Paul Auster, and Richard Lamberton. Barrytown: Station Hill Press, 1999.

Thomas l'obscur nouvelle version. Paris: Gallimard, 1950. Translated by Richard Lamberton. *Thomas the Obscure* (Barrytown: Station Hill, 1973).

Le très haut. Paris: Gallimard, 1975. Translated by Alan Stoekel. *The Most High* (Lincoln: University of Nebraska Press, 1996).

Works by Levinas

A l'heure des nations. Paris: Editions de Minuit. 1988.

Autrement qu'être au au-delà de l'essence. Paris: Librairie générale française, 1974. Translated by Alphonso Lingis *Otherwise Than Being* (Dordrecht: Martinus Nijhoff, 1981).

Collected Philosophical Papers, Trans. Alphonso Lingis. (Dordrecht, Martinus Nijhoff, 1987).

De Dieu qui vient à l'idée. Paris: Vrin, 1982.

De l'évasion. Montpellier: Fata Morgana, 1982.

De l'existence à l'existant. Paris: Vrin, 1981. Translated by Alphonso Lingis *Existence and Existents* (Dordrecht: Martinus Nijhoff, 1978).

Dieu la mort et le temps. Paris: Grasset, 1993. Translated by Bettina Bergo *God, Death, and Time* Stanford: Stanford University Press, 2000.

Difficile liberté: essais sur le judaïsme. Paris: Albin Michel, 1976. Translated by Seán Hand *Difficult Freedom: Essays on Judaism* (Baltimore: Johns Hopkins University Press, 1990).

En découvrant l'existence avec Husserl et Heidegger. Paris: Vrin, 1974 Translated and edited by Richard A. Cohen and Michael B. Smith *Discovering Existence with Husserl* (Evanston: Northwestern University Press, 1998).

Entre nous: essais sur le penser-à-l'autre. Paris: Grasset, 1991 Translated by Michael B. Smith and Barbara Harshav *Entre Nous: On Thinking-of-the-Other* (New York: Columbia University Press, 1998).

Ethique et infini. Paris: Fayard, 1982. Translated by Richard A. Cohen *Ethics and Infinity*. (Pittsburgh: Duquesne University Press, 1995).

Humanisme de l'autre homme. Montpellier: Fata Morgana, 1972.

L'intrigue de l'infini. Ed. Marie-Anne Lescourret. Paris: Flammarion, 1994.

The Levinas Reader. Ed. Seán Hand. Oxford: Blackwell, 1989.

La mort et le temps. Paris: L'Herne, 1991.

Noms propres. Montpellier: Fata Morgana, 1976. Translated by Michael B. Smith *Proper Names* (Stanford: Stanford University Press, 1996).

Quatre lectures talmudiques. Paris: Editions de Minuit, 1968.

Sur Maurice Blanchot. Montpellier: Fata Morgana, 1975. Translated by Michael B. Smith *Proper Names* (Stanford: Stanford University Press, 1996).

"La réalité et son ombre." *Les temps modernes* 38 (November 1948): 769–89.

Le temps et l'autre. Paris: Presses Universitaires de France, 1983. Translated by Richard A. Cohen *Time and the Other* (Pittsburgh: Duquesne University Press, 1987).

Théorie de l'intuition dans la phénoménologie de Husserl. Paris: Vrin, 1970.

Totalité et infini: essai sur l'extériorité. The Hague: Martinus Nijhoff, 1971. Translated by Alphonso Lingis *Totality and Infinity: An Essay on Exteriority* (Pittsburgh: Duquesne Unniversity Press, 1969).

"The Trace of the Other," trans. Alphonso Lingis. In *Deconstruction in Context*, ed. Mark C. Taylor, 345–59. Chicago: University of Chicago Press, 1986.

Collective Works on Blanchot and Contributors

Critique 229 (1966). (René Char, Georges Poulet, Jean Starobinski, Emmanuel Levinas, Michel Foucault, Paul de Man, Françoise Collin, Jean Pfeiffer, Roger Laporte)

L'Esprit créateur, vol. 24, no. 3 (fall 1984). (Ann Smock, Monique Canto, Kristin Ross, Tony Corn, Jefferson Humphries, Alexandre Leupin, Andrew Bush)

Gramma: Ecriture et lecture 3/4 (1976). (Patrick Rousseau, Mike Holland, Frédéric Nef, Alain Coulange, Jacques Derrida, Georges Bataille)

Gramma: Ecriture et lecture 5 (1976–1977). (Mike Holland, Patrick Rousseau, Christian Limousin, Françoise Collin, Alain Coulange)

Nuova corrente 32 (1985). (Alberto Castoldi, Wanda Tommasi, Rocco Ronchi, Santino Mele, Augusto Ponzio, Rainer Stillers, Ulisse Jacomuzzi, Giorgio Patrizi)

Substance 14 (1976). (Mike Holland, Walter A. Strauss, Garth Gillian, Emmanuel Levinas, Roger Laporte, Denis Hollier, Tom Conley, Gerald Prince, Ann Smock, Jean-Louis Schefer)

Yale French Studies: The Place of Maurice Blanchot 93 (1998) (Thomas Pepper, James Swenson, Hent de Vries, Jean-Pol Madou, Dominique Rabaté, Michel Syrotinski, Denis Hollier, Simon Critchley, Ann Banfield, Lynne Huffer, David R. Ellison, Thomas Schestag, Hans-Jost Frey)

Collective Works on Levinas and Contributors

Cahier de l'Herne: Emmanuel Levinas. Ed. Catherine Chalier and Miguel Abensour. Paris: Editions de l'Herne, 1991. (Alphonso Lingis, Ludwig Wenzler, Elisabeth de Fontenay, Alain David, Marc Richir, Jean-Louis Chrétien, Jacques Taminiaux, Pierre Trotignon, Guy Petitdemange,

François Marty, Françoise Collin, Robert Bernasconi, Richard Cohen, Gilles Bernheim, Emmanuel Levinas, Annette Aronowicz, Charles Mopsik, Catherine Chalier, David Banon, Marc Faessler, Adriaan Peperzak, Monique Schneider, Michel Haar, Elisabeth Weber, Alain Finkielkraut, Miguel Abensour, Françoise Armengaud)

Les Cahiers de la nuit surveillée. Ed. Jacques Rolland. Paris: Verdier Cerf, 1984. (Jacques Rolland, Jacques Colette, Guy Petitdemange, Jean-Louis Schlegel, Francis Wybrands, Catherine Chalier, David Banon, Marc Faessler, Francesco Paolo Ciglia, Harita Valavanidis-Wybrands, Silvano Petrosino, Jean Greisch, Jean-Luc Marion, Alain David, Olivier Mongin, Adolfo Fernandez-Zoila, Emmanuel Levinas)

Emmanuel Levinas: L'ethique comme philosophie première. Ed. Jean Greisch and Jacques Rolland. Paris: Editions du Cerf, 1993. (Jean Greisch, Jean-Luc Marion, Catherine Chalier, Stéphane Mosès, Silvano Petrosino, Monique Schneider, Pierre-Philippe Jandin, Edvard Kovac, Tadao Hisashige, David Banon, Bernard Dupuy, Marc Faessler, Bernhard Casper, Alain David, Olivier Mongin, Guy Petitdemange, Richard Kearney, Harita Valvanidis-Wybrands, Thomas Weimer, François Aubay, Jacques Rolland, Emmanuel Levinas)

Etudes phénoménologiques 6, no. 12 (1990). (Etienne Feron, Jean-Luc Lannoy, Fabio Ciaramelli, Francis Jacques)

Répondre d'autrui. Ed. Jean-Christophe Aeschlimann. Neuchâtel: La Baconnière. 1989. (Emmanuel Levinas, Paul Ricoeur, Stéphane Mosès, Catherine Chalier, Guy Petitdemange, Marc Faessler)

Textes pour Emmanuel Levinas. Ed. François Laruelle. Paris: Jean-Michel Place, 1980. (Maurice Blanchot, Jeanne Delhomme, Jacques Derrida, Mikel Dufrenne, Jean Halperin, Edmond Jabès, François Laruelle, Jean-François Lyotard, André Neher, Adriaan Peperzak, Paul Ricoeur, Edith Wyschogrod)

Selected Bibliography

Bachelard, Gaston. *La poétique de l'espace.* Paris: Presses Universitaires de France, 1974. Translated by Maria Jolas *The Poetics of Space* (New York: Orion Press, 1964).

———. *L'eau et les rêves: essai sur l'imagination de la matière.* Paris: Librairie José Corti, 1973.

Bailhache, Gérard. *Le Sujet chez Emmanuel Levinas*. Paris: Presses Universitaires de France, 1994.

Barthes, Roland. *Elements of Semiology*. Trans. Annette Lavers and Colin Smith. New York: Hill and Wang, 1991.

———. *Oeuvres complètes: tome 1 1942–1965*. Ed. Eric Marty. Paris: Editions du Seuil, 1993.

Bataille, Georges. *L'érotisme*. Paris: Editions de Minuit, 1957.

———. *L'expérience intérieure*. Paris: Gallimard, 1954.

Batlay, Jenny H. "Analyse littéraire versus fiction romanesque: réflexions sur *Le livre à venir* de Maurice Blanchot." *L'Esprit créateur* 14 no. 3 (1974): 247–54.

Baudelaire, Charles. *Oeuvres complètes*. Ed. Claude Pichois. Paris: Gallimard, Bibliothèque de la Pléiade, Tome I, 1975.

———. *The Flowers of Evil*. Ed. Marthiel and Jackson Mathews. New York: New Directions, 1989.

———. *The Parisian Prowler: le spleen de Paris, petits poèmes en prose*. Trans. Edward K. Kaplan. Athens: University of Georgia Press, 1989.

Bergson, Henri. *Essai sur les données immédiates de la conscience*. Paris: Presses Universitaires de France, 1958.

———. *Matière et mémoire*. Paris: Presses Universitaires de France, 1949.

———. *Matter and Memory*. Translated by Nancy Margaret Paul and W. Scott Palmer. New York: Zone Books, 1988.

Bernardi, Marina. "Sur *L'arrêt de mort* de Maurice Blanchot: le chant des sirènes ou les ruses du récit." *Francofonia* 9, no. 17 (1989): 103–11.

Bernasconi, Robert and Simon Critchley, eds. *The Cambridge Companion to Levinas*. Cambridge: Cambridge University Press, 2002.

———. *Re-Reading Levinas*. Bloomington: Indiana University Press, 1991.

Bident, Christophe. *Maurice Blanchot: partenaire invisible*. Seyssel: Champ Vallon, 1998.

Blegen. John. Review of *Maurice Blanchot et la question de l'écriture*, by Françoise Collin. *Modern Language Notes* 86, no. 6 (December, 1971): 952–54.

———. "Writing the Question: About Maurice Blanchot." *Diacritics* (summer 1972): 13–17.

Boyer, Philippe. "Le point de la question." *Change* 22 (March 1975): 41–72.

Bruns, Gerald. *Heidegger's Estrangements: Language, Truth, and Poetry in the Later Writings*. New Haven: Yale University Press, 1989.

———. *Maurice Blanchot: The Refusal of Philosophy*. Baltimore and London: Johns Hopkins University Press, 1997.

———. "Blanchot/Levinas: Interruption (On the Conflict of Alterities)." *Research in Phenomenology* 26 (1996): 132–54.

Burggraeve, Roger. *Emmanuel Levinas: une bibliographie primaire et secondaire (1929–1985)*. Leuven: Peeters, 1986.

Camus, Albert. *Essais*. Paris: Gallimard, Bibliothèque de la Pléiade, 1965.

Chalier, Catherine. *Levinas: l'utopie de l'humain*. Paris: Albin Michel, 1993.

Champagne, Roland A. "A Mosaic View: The Poetics of Maurice Blanchot." *Literary Review* 21 (1978): 425–35.

Ciaramelli, Fabio. *Transcendance et ethique: essai sur Levinas*. Brussels: Editions Ousia S.C., 1989.

Clark, Timothy. *Derrida, Heidegger, Blanchot: Sources of Derrida's Notion and Practice of Literature*. Cambridge: Cambridge University Press, 1992.

Cohen, Richard A., ed. *Face to Face with Levinas*. Albany: State University of New York Press, 1986.

Collin, Françoise. *Maurice Blanchot et la question de l'écriture*. Paris: Gallimard, 1971.

———. "Ecriture et matérialité." *Critique* 179–80 (1970): 747– 58.

———. "La nuit, l'autre nuit: (négativité et négatif)." *L'éphémère* 13 (1970): 97–107.

Critchely, Simon. *Very Little . . . Almost Nothing: Death, Philosophy, Literature*. London and New York: Routledge, 1997.

Cronel, Hervé. "Maurice Blanchot: l'impossible silence." *La nouvelle revue française* (April 1973): 103–7.

Culler, Jonathan. *Ferdinand de Saussure*. Ithaca, N.Y.: Cornell University Press, 1986.

————. *On Deconstruction: Theory and Criticism after Structuralism.* London: Routledge, 1982.

————. Review of *Maurice Blanchot et la question de l'écriture,* by Françoise Collin. *French Studies* 27 no. 2 (April 1973): 231–32.

————. *Roland Barthes.* New York: Oxford University Press, 1983.

Davis, Colin. *Levinas: An Introduction.* Notre Dame: University of Notre Dame Press, 1996.

Deguy, Michel. "Maurice Blanchot: *L'attente l'oubli.*" *La nouvelle revue française* (October 1962): 710–14.

Deleuze, Gilles. *Différence et répétition.* Paris: Presses Universitaires de France, 1976.

De Man, Paul. *Allegories of Reading: Figural Language in Rousseau, Nietzsche, Rilke, and Proust.* New Haven: Yale University Press, 1979.

De Quincey, Thomas. *Confessions of an English Opium-Eater and Other Writings.* Oxford: Oxford University Press, 1985.

Derrida, Jacques. *Adieu to Emmanuel Levinas.* Trans. Pascale-Anne Brault and Michael Nass. Stanford: Stanford University Press, 1999.

————. *De la grammatologie.* Paris: Editions de Minuit, 1967.

————. *Demeure: Maurice Blanchot.* Paris: Editions Galilée, 1998.

————. *La dissémination.* Paris: Editions du Seuil, 1972.

————. *L'ecriture et la différence.* Paris: Editions du Seuil, 1967.

————. *Marges de la philosophie.* Paris: Editions de Minuit, 1972.

————. *Margins of Philosophy.* Trans. Alan Bass. Chicago: University of Chicago Press, 1982.

————. *Parages.* Paris: Editions Galilée, 1986.

————. *Positions.* Paris: Editions de Minuit, 1972.

————. *La voix et le phénomène.* Paris: Presses Universitaries de France, 1972.

Descartes, René. *Oeuvres et lettres.* Paris: Gallimard, Bibliothèque de la Pléiade, 1953.

Descaunes, Luc. Review of *L'arrêt de mort,* by Maurice Blanchot. *Cahiers du sud* 291 (1948): 377–78.

Diderot, Denis. *Jacques le fataliste.* Paris: Garnier-Flammarion, 1997.

————. *Jacques the Fatalist.* Trans. David Coward. Oxford: Oxford University Press, 1999.

Dostoevsky, Fyodor. *The Brothers Karamazov*. Trans. Andrew H. Mac-Andrew. New York and London: Bantam Books, 1981.

———. *The Idiot*. Trans. Henry and Olga Carlisle. New York: Signet Classics, 1969.

Douglas, Kenneth. "Blanchot and Sartre." *Yale French Studies* 2 (1949): 85–95.

Euripides. *The Bacchae*. Trans. William Arrowsmith. *Greek Tragedies*. Eds. David Grene and Richard Lattimore. Chicago: University of Chicago Press, 1960.

Fleiger, Jerry Aline. "Blanchot and Beckett: *En attendant Godot* as a 'Discontinuous' Play." *French Forum* 5 (1980): 156–67.

Feron, Etienne. *De L'idée de transcendance à la question du langage: l'itinéraire philosophique d'Emmanuel Levinas*. Grenoble: Jérôme Millon, 1992.

———. "Respiration et action chez Levinas." *Etudes phénoménologiques* 3, nos. 5–6 (1987): 193–213.

Fitzgerald, Francis-Scott. *The Crack-Up*. New York: New Directions, 1945.

Foucault, Michel. "La pensée du dehors." *Critique* 229 (1966): 523–46.

Gans, Eric. "Différences." *Modern Language Notes* 96, no. 4 (1981): 792–808.

Gasché, Rodolphe. *Inventions of Difference: On Jacques Derrida*. Cambridge and London: Harvard University Press, 1994.

———. *The Tain of the Mirror: Derrida and the Philosophy of Reflection*. Cambridge: Harvard University Press, 1986.

Gill, Carolyn Bailey. *Maurice Blanchot: The Demand of Writing*. London: Routledge, 1996.

Gillian, Garth. "Levinas on Blanchot: Commentary." *Substance* 14 (1976): 50–53.

Gregg, John. *Maurice Blanchot: The Literature of Transgression*. Princeton: Princeton University Press, 1994.

———. "Blanchot's Suicidal Artist: Writing and the (Im)Possibility of Death." *Substance* 55 (1988): 47–58.

Greisch, Jean. *La parole heureuse: Martin Heidegger entre les choses et les mots*. Paris: Beauchesne, 1987.

———. "Identité et différence dans la pensée de Martin Heidegger: Le chemin de l'*Ereignis*" *Revue des sciences philosophiques et théologiques* 57 (1973): 71–112.

Greisch, Jean, and Jacques Rolland. *Emmanuel Levinas: L'ethique comme philosophie première*. Paris: Editions du Cerf, 1993.

Guibal, Francis. *Et combien de dieux nouveaux II: Levinas*. Paris: Aubier-Montaigne, 1980.

Gutting, Gary. *French Philosophy in the Twentieth Century*. Cambridge: Cambridge University Press, 2001.

Hamilton, Edith and Huntington Cairns, eds. *Plato: The Collected Dialogues*. Princeton: Princeton University Press, 1978.

Hartman, Geoffrey. "Maurice Blanchot: Philosopher-Novelist." *Beyond Formalism: Literary Essays 1958–1970*, 93–110. New Haven: Yale University Press, 1970.

———. Introduction. "Death Sentence." Trans. Lydia Davis. *The Georgia Review* 30, no. 2 (1976): 379–81.

Harvey, Irene E. *Derrida and the Economy of Différance*. Bloomington: Indiana University Press, 1986.

———. "Contemporary French Thought and the Art of Rhetoric." *Philosophy and Rhetoric* 18 (1985): 199–215.

Hegel, G. W. F. *La phenomenologie de l'esprit*. Trans. Jean Hippolyte. Paris: Aubier Montaigne, 1941.

———. *The Phenomenology of Spirit*. Trans. A. V. Miller. Oxford: Oxford University Press, 1979.

Heidegger, Martin. *Being and Time*. Trans. John Macquarrie and Edward Robinson. New York: Harper and Row, 1962.

———. *Identity and Difference*. Trans. Joan Stambaugh. New York. Harper and Row, 1969.

———. *Poetry, Language, Thought*. Trans. Albert Hofstadter. New York: Harper and Row, 1971.

———. *Existence and Being*. Trans. Werner Brock. Chicago: Henry Regnery, 1949.

Hell, Henri. "A propos des romans de Maurice Blanchot." *La table ronde* (December 1948): 2051–56.

Hill, Leslie. *Blanchot: Extreme Contemporary*. London: Routledge, 1997.

Hillis-Miller. J. "Death Mask: Blanchot's *L'Arrêt de mort.*" *Versions of Pygmalion*. Cambridge: Harvard University Press, 1990.

Hippolyte, Jean. *Genèse et structure de la phénoménologie de l'esprit de Hegel*. Paris: Aubier Montaigne, 1946. Translated by Samuel Cherniak and John Heckman, *Genesis and Structure of Hegel's Phenomenology of Spirit* (Evanston: Northwestern University Press, 1974).

Hollier, Denis, ed. *Le collège de sociologie*. Paris: Gallimard, 1979.

Huffer, Lynne. "Blanchot's Mother." *Yale French Studies*, ed. Thomas Pepper, 93 (1998): 175–95.

Kaufmann, Walter A. *Hegel: A Reinterpretation*. Notre Dame: University of Notre Dame Press, 1978.

Kéchichian, Patrick. "La mort à la lettre." Review of *L'instant de ma mort*, by Maurice Blanchot. *Le Monde* 25 November 1994.

Keller, Luzius. "Maurice Blanchot: *Thomas l'obscur.*" In *der moderne französische Roman: Interpretationen*, 182–97. Berlin: Erich Schmidt Verlag, 1968.

Kockelmans, Joseph J. *Heidegger on Art and Art Works*. Dordrecht: Martinus Nijhoff, 1985.

———. *On the Truth of Being: Reflections on Heidegger's Later Philosophy*. Bloomington: Indiana University Press, 1984.

Krysinski, Vladimir. "La narration clivée: une lecture de *L'arrêt de mort* de Blanchot." *Revue des lettres modernes* (1981): 605–10.

La Bible: ancien testament. Ed. Edouard Dhourme. Paris: Gallimard, Bibliothèque de la Pléiade, 1956.

Lacan, Jacques. "Le stade du miroir comme formateur de la fonction du je telle qu'elle nous est révelée dans l'expérience psychanalytique." In *Ecrits*, 93–100. Paris: Editions du Seuil, 1966.

Laclos, Pierre Choderlos de. *Oeuvres complètes*. Paris: Gallimard, Bibliothèque de la Pléiade, 1979.

Lamont, Michele. "How to Become a Dominant French Philosopher: The Case of Jacques Derrida." *American Journal of Sociology* 93 no. 3 (1987): 584–622.

Laporte, Roger. *Maurice Blanchot: L'ancien, l'effroyablement ancien*. Montpellier: Fata Morgana, 1987.

Laporte, Roger and Bernard Noël. *Deux lectures de Maurice Blanchot*. Montpellier: Fata Morgana, 1973.

Lescourret, Marie-Anne. *Emmanuel Levinas*. Paris: Flammarion, 1994.

Libertson, Joseph. *Proximity: Levinas, Blanchot, Bataille and Communication*. The Hague: Martinus Nijhoff, 1982.

Llewelyn, John. *Emmanuel Levinas: The Genealogy of Ethics*. New York: Routledge, 1995.

———. *Derrida: On the Threshold of Sense*. New York: St. Martin's Press, 1985.

Londyn, Evelyne. *Maurice Blanchot romancier*. Paris: Nizet, 1976.

———. "L'Orphique chez Blanchot: voir et dire." *French Forum* 5 (1980): 261–68.

Loy, David. *Nonduality: A Study in Comparative Philosophy*. New Haven: Yale University Press, 1988.

Madaule, Jacques. *Une tâche sérieuse?* Paris: Gallimard, 1973.

Madison, Gary B., ed. *Working through Derrida*. Evanston: Northwestern University Press, 1993.

Malka, Salomon. *Lire Levinas*. Paris: Editions du Cerf, 1984.

Manning, Robert J. S. *Interpreting Otherwise than Heidegger: Emmanuel Levinas's Ethics as First Philosophy*. Pittsburgh: Duquesne University Press, 1993.

Marcon, Giorgio. "Tra le rive del testo: gli enigmi di *Thomas l'obscur.*" *Il lettore di provincia* 21 (1989): 87–92.

Mehlman, Jeffrey. "Blanchot at *Combat*: Of Literature and Terror." *Modern Language Notes* 95, no. 4 (May 1980): 808–29.

———. "Orphée scripteur: Blanchot, Rilke, Derrida." *Poétique* 20 (1974): 458–82.

Meschonnic, Henri. *Le langage Heidegger*. Paris: Presses Universitaires de France, 1990.

Mesnard, Philippe. "Maurice Blanchot, le sujet et l'engagement." *Infini* 48 (1994): 103–28.

Meyerson, Emile. *Identité et réalité*. Paris: Félix Alcan, 1908.

Michel, Chantal. *Maurice Blanchot et le déplacement d'Orphée*. Saint-Genouph: Nizet, 1997.

Mole, Gary D. *Levinas, Blanchot, Jabès: Figures of Estrangement*. Gainesville: University Press of Florida, 1997.

Münster, Arno, ed. *La différence comme non-indifférence: ethique et altérité chez Emmanuel Levinas*. Paris: Editions Kimé, 1995.

Nef, Frédéric. "Le piège: sur un fragment de *Thomas l'obscur*." *Gramma* 3/4 (1976): 71–88.

Norris, Christopher. *Derrida*. Cambridge and London: Harvard University Press, 1987.

Oster, Daniel. "D'un statut d'évangéliste." *Littérature* 33 (1979): 11–128.

Oxenhandler, Neal. "Paradox and Negation in the Criticism of Maurice Blanchot." *Symposium* 16, no. 1 (spring 1962): 36–44.

Panis, Daniel. *Il y a le il y a: l'énigme de Heidegger*. Bruxelles: Ousia, 1993.

Peperzak, Adriaan Theodor. *Beyond: The Philosophy of Emmanuel Levinas*. Evanston, Ill.: Northwestern University Press, 1997.

———. *To the Other: An Introduction to the Philosophy of Emmanuel Levinas*. West Lafayette, Ind.: Purdue University Press, 1993.

Peperzak, Adriaan Theodor, ed. *Ethics as First Philosophy: The Significance of Emmanuel Levinas for Philosophy, Literature, and Religion*. New York: Routledge, 1995.

Petitdemange, Guy and Jacques Rolland. *Autrement que savoir: Emmanuel Levinas*. Paris: Editions Osiris, 1988.

Petrosino, Silviano and Jacques Rolland. *La vérité nomade: introduction à Emmanuel Levinas*. Paris: La Découverte, 1984.

Picon, Gaëton. "L'oeuvre critique de Maurice Blanchot." Part 1, *Critique* 111–12 (1956): 673–94. Part 2, *Critique* 113 (1956): 836–54.

Poirié, François. *Emmanuel Levinas: qui êtes-vous?* Lyons: La Manufacture, 1987.

Pouget, Pierre-Marie. *Heidegger ou le retour à la voix silencieuse*. Lausanne: L'Age d'Homme, 1975.

Poulet, Georges. "Maurice Blanchot as Novelist." *Yale French Studies* 8 (1951): 77–81.

Ricoeur, Paul. *Autrement: lecture d'Autrement qu'être ou au-delà de l'essence d'Emmanuel Levinas*. Paris: Presses Universitaires de France, 1997.

Robbins, Jill. *Altered Reading: Levinas and Literature*. Chicago: University of Chicago Press, 1999.

Robinson, John Mansley. *An Introduction to Early Greek Philosophy*. New York: Houghton Mifflin Company, 1968.

Rolland, Jacques. *Emmanuel Levinas*. Lagrasse: Editions Verdier, 1984.

Ronchi, Rocco. "La realtà e la sua ombra." *Nuova corrente* 32 (1985): 77–104.

Ropars-Wuilleumier, Marie-Claire. "La prise de la parole." *Littérature* (December 1986): 3–12.

Roudiez, Léon S. "Maurice Blanchot." *French Fiction Today: A New Direction*. New Brunswick, N.J.: Rutgers University Press, 1972.

Sallis, John, ed. *Reading Heidegger: Commemorations*. Bloomington: Indiana University Press, 1993.

Sartre, Jean-Paul. "Aminadab: ou du fantastique considéré comme un langage." *Situations I*, 122–88. Paris: Gallimard, 1943.

———. *L'imaginaire*. Paris: Gallimard, 1940.

———. *Imagination: A Psychological Critique*. Trans. Forrest Williams. Ann Arbor: University of Michigan Press, 1972. Originally published as *L'Imagination* (Paris: Presses Universitaires de France, 1965).

———. *What Is Literature?* Trans. Bernard Frechtman. Cambridge: Harvard University Press, 1988. Originally published as *Situations II: qu'est-ce que la littérature?* (Paris: Gallimard, 1948).

Sass, Hans-Martin. *Martin Heidegger: Bibliograhy and Glossary*. Bowling Green, Ohio: Philosophy Documentation Center, Bowling Green State University, 1982.

Sato, Wataru. "La comparaison entre les première et nouvelle versions de *Thomas l'obscur* de Maurice Blanchot." *Etudes de langue et littérature françaises* 32 (1978): 135–49.

Saussure, Ferdinand de. *Cours de linguistique générale*. Ed. Tullio de Mauro. Paris: Payothèque, 1972. Translated by Wade Baskin *Course in General Linguistics* (New York: McGraw Hill Book Company, 1966).

Schulte-Nordholt, Anne-Lise. *Maurice Blanchot: l'écriture comme expérience du dehors*. Geneva: Droz, 1995.

Schultz, William R., and Lewis L. B. Fried. *Jacques Derrida: An Annotated Primary and Secondary Bibliography*. New York: Garland Publishing, 1992.

Shaviro, Steven. *Passion and Excess: Blanchot, Bataille, and Literary Theory*. Tallahassee: The Florida State University Press, 1990.

Spanos, William V., ed. *Martin Heidegger and the Question of Literature: Toward a Postmodern Literary Hermeneutics*. Bloomington: Indiana University Press, 1979.

Stamelman, Richard. *Lost Beyond Telling: Representations of Death and Absence in Modern French Poetry*. Ithaca, N.Y.: Cornell University Press, 1990.

Starobinski, Jean. "*Thomas l'obscur*: chapitre premier." *Critique* 229 (1966): 498–513.

Steiner, George. *Heidegger*. London: Fontana Press, 1992.

Stillers, Rainer. *Maurice Blanchot: Thomas l'obscur: erst-und-zweifassung als Paradigmen des Gesamtwerks*. Frankfurt am Main: Verlag Peter Lang, 1979.

Strauss, Walter A. *Descent and Return: The Orphic Theme in Modern Literature*. Cambridge: Harvard University Press, 1971.

Suárez, Ramón. "Mundo y lenguaje en los relatos de Maurice Blanchot." *Revista chilena de litteratura* (April–November 1986): 49–66.

Swenson, James. "Revolutionary Sentences." *Yale French Studies*, ed. Thomas Pepper 93 (1998): 11–29.

Thom, René, Interview by Roger Pol Droit. *Le Monde* 22–23 (January 1995): 14.

Tommasi, Wanda. "Per un'esperienza non dialettica della parola: la presenza di Hegel nel primo Blanchot." *Nuova corrente* 32 (1985): 43–76.

Toumayan, Alain. "Différence et communication chez Artaud." *Romanic Review* 76 (1985): 55–64.

Tsuquiashi-Daddesio, Eva. "Plasticité graphique et métamorphose dans l'écriture de Maurice Blanchot: une lecture de *Thomas l'obscur*." *DA* L89/90 (1988): 457A. University of Minnesota.

Ungar, Steven. "Night Moves: Spatial Perception and the Place of Blanchot's Early Fictions." *Yale French Studies* 57 (1979): 124–35.

———. "Parts and Holes: Heraclitus/Nietzsche/Blanchot." *Substance* 14 (1976): 126–41.

———. *Roland Barthes: The Professor of Desire*. Lincoln: University of Nebraska Press, 1983.

————. "Waiting for Blanchot." *Diacritics* 5, no. 2 (1975): 32–36.

Van Tonteren, Paul, Paul Sars, Chris Bremmers and Koen Boey, eds. *Eros and Eris: Contributions to a Hermeneutical Phenomenology. Liber Amicorum for Adriaan Peperzak*. Dordrecht: Kluwer, 1992.

Vries, Hent de. "'Lapsus Absolu": Notes on Maurice Blanchot's *The Instant of My Death*." *Yale French Studies* 93 (1998): 30–59.

Wahl, Jean. *Introduction à la pensée de Heidegger*. Paris: Librairie Générale Française, 1998.

Wall, Thomas Carl. *Radical Passivity*. Albany: State University of New York Press, 1999.

Warminski, Andrzej. "Dreadful Reading: Blanchot on Hegel." *Yale French Studies* 69 (1985): 267–75.

Wilhelm, Daniel. "Hors de prix." *Critique* 329 (1974): 875–90.

Wood, David, ed. *Derrida: A Critical Reader*. Oxford: Blackwell, 1992.

————. *Philosophers' Poets*. London: Routledge, 1990.

Wood, David and Robert Bernasconi, eds. *Derrida and Différance*. Evanston, Ill.: Northwestern University Press, 1998.

Wybrands, F., ed. *Exercices de la patience*. Paris: Obsidiane, 1980.

Wyschogrod, Edith. *Emmanuel Levinas: The Problem of Ethical Metaphysics*. New York: Fordham University Press, 2000.

Yana, Pierre. "Le mal obscur." *Revue des sciences humaines* (April–June 1985): 201–18.

Ziarek, Krzysztof. *Inflected Language: Toward a Hermeneutics of Nearness: Heidegger, Levinas, Stevens, Celan*. Albany: State University of New York Press, 1994.

Zola, Emile. *Thérèse Raquin*. Paris: Garnier-Flammarion, 1970.

Index

Abraham, 101, 105, 112

absence, 71, 83, 90, 129, 155–56, 159, 168. *See also* presence and absence

abstract, the, 55–56, 79–80

absurd, the, 47–48

accusation, 32, 34, 36

action, 98–99, 122, 167

aesthetics, 115, 124, 142, 145, 154, 198 n. 5, 201–2 n. 23, 208 n. 7; Levinas and, 4, 149

ambiguity, 62–64, 87, 108–9, 118, 128, 159, 203 nn. 32, 38; in Blanchot and Levinas, 20, 170, 178 n. 9; and difference, 197 n. 19; and duplicity, 139–42; of the present, 109–13

anonymity, 138, 148, 155–56

aquatic imagery, 20, 23–25, 27, 29, 68–69, 72–73, 75, 193 n. 48

art, 116–19, 149, 153–57, 175, 195 n. 4, 199 n. 9; ambiguity of, 203 n. 32; classical, 136–38; and inspiration, 86, 99; and Levinas, 58, 63, 198 n. 3; origin of, 51–52, 96–99, 110, 116; plastic, 71, 82, 121–22. *See also* artwork; work of art

Artaud, Antonin, 86, 123, 201 n. 22

artwork, 1–2, 85, 93, 114, 116, 146–48, 156, 199 n. 11; and the image, 136–39; narrated, 121, 123. *See also* art; work of art

assignation, 32, 34–35

"au-delà," the, 101, 120–21. *See also* "en-deça," the

autonomy, 31, 34, 43

Bachelard, Gaston, 20, 22, 28, 164

Bataille, Georges, 31, 63, 167, 192 n. 32, 196 n. 13, 203 n. 33; Blanchot and, 96, 181 n. 13, 190 n. 18; *L'Erotisme*, 97, 120, 133–34

Baudelaire, Charles, 100, 111–12, 197 n. 22, 201 n. 21; "The Artist's *Confiteor*," 96; "Correspondances," 77; "To a Passerby," 111

Being, 12, 49, 57, 68, 116, 152, 160, 181 n. 10, 200 n. 16; density of, 206 n. 15; Heidegger and, 14–19, 38, 181–82 n. 14; man and, 15, 17–18; and nothingness, 1, 172

being, 49, 115–17, 119, 145, 153, 160, 184 n. 27, 203 n. 33; and the image, 143–44; materiality of,